AN **AMERICAN** STORY

AN **AMERICAN** STORY

THE SPEECHES OF **BARACK OBAMA**

A Primer by DAVID OLIVE

ECW Press

Published by ECW Press
2120 Queen Street East, Suite 200
Toronto, Ontario, Canada M4E 1E2
416.694.3348 / info@ecwpress.com

LIBRARY AND ARCHIVES CANADA CATALOGUING IN PUBLICATION

Olive, David, 1957–
An American story : the speeches of Barack Obama : a primer / David Olive.

Includes text of 21 speeches by Barack Obama.
ISBN 978-1-55022-864-9

1. Obama, Barack. 2. Speeches, addresses, etc., American. 3. Obama, Barack—Oratory. 4. United States—Politics and government—2001-. I. Obama, Barack II. Title.

E901.1.O23O45 2008 328.73092 C2008-904943-8

Cover and Text Design: Tania Craan
Cover photo: © Michael Maloney/San Francisco Chronicle/Corbis
Typesetting: Gail Nina
Second printing: Webcom

The publication of *An American Story* has been generously supported by the OMDC Book Fund, an initiative of the Ontario Media Development Corporation, and by the Government of Canada through the Book Publishing Industry Development Program (BPIDP).

Canada

PRINTED AND BOUND IN CANADA

For Allison Nowlan

"Through the night with a light from above."

– Irving Berlin, "God Bless America"

"We look forward to a world founded upon four essential human freedoms.

The first is freedom of speech and expression — everywhere in the world.

The second is freedom of every person to worship God in his own way — everywhere in the world.

The third is freedom from want — which, translated into world terms, means economic understandings which will secure to every nation a healthy peacetime life for its inhabitants — everywhere in the world.

The fourth is freedom from fear — which, translated into world terms, means a worldwide reduction of armaments to such a point and in such a thorough fashion that no nation will be in a position to commit an act of physical aggression against any neighbor — anywhere in the world."

– Franklin Delano Roosevelt,
"The Four Freedoms," address to the U.S. Congress, January 6, 1941

Table of Contents

Acknowledgments

I'm grateful to Jack David of ECW Press, who conceived the project, for his patience and diligence and that of his superb team at ECW. I'd also like to thank J. Fred Kuntz and Joe Hall, former editor-in-chief and managing editor, respectively, of the *Toronto Star*, for their encouragement and support.

I owe a considerable debt to librarians at several news organizations and to campaign staff of Barack Obama, John McCain, and Hillary Clinton for their assistance. They have helped make this "rough working draft of history" as accurate as possible.

Introduction

"The country needs and, unless I mistake its temper, the country demands bold, persistent experimentation. It is common sense to take a method and try it. If it fails, admit it frankly and try another. But above all, try something."

— U.S. President **Franklin Delano Roosevelt**, commencement address at Oglethorpe University, Atlanta, Georgia, May 23, 1932

"I have long believed there was a divine plan that placed this land here to be found by people of a special kind, that we have a rendezvous with destiny. Yes, there is a spirit moving in this land and a hunger in the people for a spiritual revival. If the task I seek should be given to me, I would pray only that I could perform it in a way that would serve God."

— Future U.S. President **Ronald Wilson Reagan**, 1976 campaign letter

"There is nothing wrong with America that cannot be cured by what is right with America."

— U.S. President **William Jefferson Clinton**, inaugural address, January 20, 1993

I was sitting cross-legged on the double bed in my nineteenth-floor aerie in Boston's historic Custom House, now a Marriott but still a reminder of the city's maritime tradition, when Barack Obama said the words that propelled him onto the national stage in 2004. I was hunched over a laptop, struggling to meet a newspaper deadline. The young man on the TV had been describing one of the most unlikely backgrounds of any major U.S. political figure, and now he had my undivided attention as he described an "us and them" mentality that had poisoned U.S. politics for much too long.

"The pundits like to slice-and-dice our country into Red States and Blue States; Red States for Republicans, Blue States for Democrats," Obama told the crowd at the Fleet Center a few blocks from where I sat. "But I've got news for them, too. We worship an awesome God in the Blue States, and we don't like federal agents poking around our libraries in the Red States. We coach Little League in the Blue States and have gay friends in the Red States. There are patriots who opposed the war in Iraq and patriots who supported it. We are one people, all of us pledging allegiance to the stars and stripes, all of us defending the United States of America."

Who *was* this rail-thin Midwesterner, by way of Honolulu, Jakarta, Los Angeles, Manhattan, and Cambridge, Massachusetts, now poised to become only the third African-American elected to the U.S. Senate in the history of the republic?

Whoever he was, the keynote speaker at the 2004 Democratic National Convention that nominated John Kerry as its presidential candidate was an unusually compelling orator and, more importantly, was describing the America for which I had so much affection. It was America before it fell hostage to the take-no-prisoners "culture wars" calculated to splinter the country into distinct voting blocs that could be wooed or ignored as the mood of policy strategists in Washington dictated. The media reflected these divisions, catered to and nurtured them — though only at the national level. Pigeonholing politicians and think-tank experts as liberal or conservative, rural or urban, powerful or on the outs was habitual with *Meet the Press* and the other Washington-based Sunday morning political talk shows. There wasn't much room for nuance, for delving into the complexities of issues.

That wasn't so much the case with the local NBC affiliate in Savannah, where the newscasts continued to be dominated by local heroes — the churches and their homeless shelters, the food-bank drives, the families that took in Sri Lankan refugees, and the citizens who put a full-court press on city hall, or even the state legislature, to finance an overpass at the level crossing where two young boys had been killed in the past three years. Where these real Americans fit into the tired Washington battles over feminism, tax cuts, abortion, racial profiling — or if they did at all — just didn't matter to them. In Sacramento and St. Louis, everyday folks were eager to be drawn into a larger cause by a larger leader, someone who would win their nodding approval four years' hence in observing that "our can't-do, won't-do, won't-even-try" politics had "grown small."

As a sometime speechwriter and observer at three of these conventions, I wondered how this young statesman had so ably captured the America that I've always thought America wants to be and usually is — if you go out and look for it. That is a privilege denied, apparently, to the Washington-based pundits, who need to get out more.

Obama was describing my self-reliant relatives in a Buffalo suburb and in Southern California and my colleagues in New York, Pennsylvania, and Indiana. The communal spirit of New York City in the aftermath of 9/11 was no surprise to anyone who'd spent time there, as I had on my honeymoon, taking in the harbor from atop the World Trade Center. But a sense of unity and open-heartedness has defined every part of this country, which I've traveled for over forty years. There are the town folks in Hershey, Pennsylvania, for instance, whom I watched as they collectively, and successfully, thwarted a takeover of their iconic namesake industrial enterprise by a carpetbagger candy-maker from Chicago. Or the proud Long Beach, California, homeowner who explained to me that his Mission-style house was of distinctly American design, no less so than the white-clapboard chapels of Manchester, New Hampshire — the Spanish influence in architecture so enraptured Southern Californians that they embraced it as their own. Or the African-American pastor who patiently explained to me in the lobby bar at the Chicago Hilton & Towers why, contrary to my impression, Bill Clinton and not his wife was the more capable politician: "He likes people, and they like him. As a preacher you learn quickly that if your flock thinks you're aloof they won't follow you." Or my tutorial in local politics from a Tuscaloosa game warden over dinner at the world's greatest rib joint, Dreamland, a tar-paper shack tucked into the forest a few miles east of town, where the menu is ribs, half ribs, bread, and Bud.

Of *course*, it's the *United* States of America, one of the few nations whose inhabitants don't rise from bed wondering what part of their country is threatening to separate, where the likes of Scottish nationalists, rebellious Chechens, and Quebec separatists are thin on the ground. Favored nations sometimes need to be reminded of their good fortune, especially in times of stress.

Americans were promised "a uniter, not a divider" in the White House eight years ago. But George W. Bush and his chief political strategist, Karl Rove, seem to have not only widened existing divides at home but also hived the U.S. off from a world it once saved from fascism on two faraway fronts. The politics of "us and them," which should have died with the anti-immigrant Know-Nothings' extinction in 1860, was back with a vengeance. Post–September 11, 2001, Islamic-Americans were added to the list of folks we don't quite trust, along with the liberals, neo-cons, Hispanics, lesbians, Mormons, farmers (ripping us off with all that subsidy money), urbanites (decadent secularists, all of them), and everyone else that didn't look and act like you or live nearby. At this rate, with hate-radio rousing you from bed, you were exhorted to wish certain neighbors would seek exile — and good riddance.

Appealing to base instincts had worked so well for office-seekers for so long that one had to listen to this young Illinoisan simply to be reminded of America's founding ideals: one united people whose conception of liberty, widespread prosperity, and communal goodwill would give rise to the greatest nation in history. A republic that had overcome crises without fear or hesitation and with an ingenuity that occasionally surprised even itself.

Four years after Obama's star turn in Boston, the crises have piled up. An energy crisis manifesting itself in four-dollar-a-gallon pump prices, and forty-seven million Americans without health-care coverage in a dysfunctional medical system that ranks first among industrialized nations only in cost (15 percent of GDP). It's an America suffering some of the lowest rates of literacy and numeracy among affluent countries, ill-equipped to meet the new competitive challenges posed by the rising economic superpowers China and India. Hindered by an inexpert grasp of how to combat a global war on terrorism, the U.S. also faces the grim prospect of a terrorist group getting its hands on even one "dirty bomb" from among the unguarded stockpiles of nuclear material strewn across the former Soviet Union. There's also a lack of consensus on solutions to the threat posed by climate change and the economic devastation of America's manufacturing sector that is hollowing out the economies of the Midwest and Northeast. Add to that a housing crisis that erased eight trillion dollars worth of homeowners' value in 2007–08, causing hundreds of thousands of Americans to lose their homes, with an additional million American homeowners facing the possibility of foreclosure. Then consider a proud military led by delusional civilian leaders into an Iraqi quagmire from which it will take the U.S. Armed Forces a decade to rebuild, and an America with reliable major allies it could now count on the fingers of one hand. "What a burden the next president is going to confront," acclaimed U.S. historian Robert Dallek, biographer of presidents John F. Kennedy and Lyndon B. Johnson, said in July 2008. "It'll be like Franklin Roosevelt coming in, in 1932."

The conventional wisdom until the U.S. economy went into a slump last year, and people began losing their homes, was that the 2008 presidential contest would be historic in featuring the first viable woman and African-American candidates and that, for the first time since JFK, a U.S. senator would be taking the oath of office in January. But what's at stake is far greater. For the first time in modern history, America goes to the polls at a time of both economic distress and an unpopular war. An economic malaise cost George H.W. Bush his job in 1992; the conflict in Southeast Asia ended LBJ's career in 1968. America has been in a bad place for some time now — crumbling schools, a widening gap between rich and poor, an estimated $350-billion "infrastructure deficit" of century-old bridges and hospitals in need of replacement, a national debt that has almost doubled since 2000, to nine trillion dollars, triggering a collapse in the greenback. So much to repair, restore, revive.

Thus when Obama, having created the biggest grassroots movement in U.S. political history, invokes Dr. King's warning about "the fierce urgency of *now*," it's difficult to disagree. The labels begin to fall away because the folks who wore their ideology on their sleeves failed the nation these past two decades. There was a chance during the booming nineties to end poverty and the class divisions and violence that go with it. There was a chance after 9/11 to unite the world against a common enemy, which would later strike in Bali, Madrid, and London. The squandering of those epic opportunities makes the need of this hour all the more pressing. And the complacency of Washington in contrast to the can-do spirit in everyday America makes it all the more unacceptable.

FDR, Reagan, and Clinton knew how to tap into the youthful vigor of the nation. As politicians, they connected with everyday Americans, who would have to do the hard work of making things right again. No claim is made here that Barack Obama has that quality of leadership that moves mountains — or rather, gets thousands of fellow Americans to move one. But he has shown the potential to do so, rekindling a sense of America's hopeful possibilities, and none too soon.

I wondered in 2004 if Obama had a history-making future beyond his closing lines: "This country will reclaim its promise. And out of this long political darkness a brighter day will come. Thank you and God bless you." And I kept wondering, long after Obama won his U.S. Senate seat later that year in a 70 percent landslide, carrying African-American and white counties across one of the nation's biggest states.

Fate plays such an inordinate role in history that it's a fool's mission to attempt conclusive answers to such questions. How many Americans are still convinced Barack Hussein Obama, a name chosen to honor his father of the same name, is a Muslim and not a devout Christian? How many, 135 years after the Emancipation Proclamation, will reject him on his color alone? Will he be found to be inexperienced, though Obama boasts more exposure to the legislative rough-and-tumble than Lincoln, FDR, or Reagan at the time they were sworn into the highest office in the land? Will he be deemed "soft" on national security — pretty much the GOP's only remaining high card — even though his record suggests Obama is as much or more of a hardliner than most of the men and women who've sought the presidency? Will those who mock his Churchillian respect for the value of talking with adversaries ("To jaw-jaw is always better than to war-war," Winnie famously counseled) recall that President George H.W. Bush managed to topple Panamanian strongman Manuel Noriega without calling in the Marines but simply by playing execrable rock music at concert volume outside his villa?

About the only thing one feels certain about is that a combination of urgency and a curiosity about fresh ideas for solving problems is an acceptable rationale for seeking the toughest job in the world — and bending quickly to the task of restoring America's leadership in it.

And that in the matchup between Obama and John McCain, the media wouldn't disgrace itself again by framing the contest in terms of which potential leader of the free world voters would rather have a beer with.

On November 4, 2008, just four years after first introducing himself to a national audience, Obama was elected forty-fourth president of the United States. Americans, betrayed by a political and Wall Street establishment that had brought the nation to the brink of economic ruin, embraced the promise of a new kind of inclusive politics and national unity in facing economic crisis at home and U.S. forces fighting two wars abroad.

"No drama Obama," the nickname given by his campaign staffers, equally calm in moments of triumph and setbacks, accepted the voters' unusually strong mandate with humility but also resolve, putting the policies by which he would govern in place long before his inauguration almost three months' hence. Believing America's best days to be ahead, Obama lost no time pursuing his ideals with a hope contrasting sharply with the difficult challenges he inherited.

The Politics of HOPE & **REALITY**

Among the most devout Christians to seek the presidency, Barack Obama has a near-religious faith in the power of America to restore and reinvent itself in the midst of tough times. He has history on his side. While the Obama candidacy has raised expectations very high, such is Obama's understanding of everyday Americans that he knows their grit and ingenuity can be tapped again to solve not only America's problems, but the world's.

Who is Barack Obama? Arguably, the right man pursuing the right job at precisely the right time. Physically, he exudes an avuncularity that is both calming and suggestive of a wisdom based not on ideology but the facts on the ground. Assaying his second book, *The Audacity of Hope*, reviewer Michael Tomasky in the *New York Review of Books* may have done the best job so far of capturing the effect of Obama's appearance: "His eyes and face project ease and warmth and sincerity; nothing about them is hard or inscrutable."

And what drives him? A keen interest in problems and how to solve them, not an uncommon trait among the ablest statesmen; an ambition to restore the American spirit after too many years of setbacks and doubt; and a goal — grandiose or imperative, history will decide — to transform the civic and political culture of the world's oldest major democracy and rid it of the rancor, partisanship, and elitism that have characterized it for long stretches of time, such as this one, for more than two centuries. To replace that tired model with a genuine citizen's democracy in which Americans don't have their say only at the ballot box but every day. A nation where ideas and solutions flow up from the commonwealth of everyday people and aren't imposed by fiat after mysterious decision-making in the halls of power where only the privileged tread. A democracy of unprecedented transparency, where any citizen with access to a television or the Internet is as well informed as presidents and city councilors, and has a stake in the issues and a motive to have things turn out a certain way.

It would be — and has been — enough for seekers of the highest office in the free world to promise a tax cut here, an education reform there, to vow that there will be enough gasoline at reasonable prices, and that the terrorists will not strike the homeland again. Which is fine as far as it goes. But America, the nation that led the world in thinking big and will do so again someday, deserves better.

In almost every election there is the option of selecting a caretaker; sometimes only caretakers are on the ballot. In 2008, America and the world were offered something bigger: a candidate with an expansive mind for whom strengthening every fiber of American muscle is but a prerequisite for the larger task at hand, which is to guide Americans in reinventing their country as a fundamentally better place for its own citizens and the billions of people with whom they share the planet. A tall order, but deteriorating conditions demanded it. America has been increasingly defined at home by a cabal of highly placed, misguided ideologues and abroad by manufacturers of hatred for America. "When I am president," Obama has said, "we will author our own story." He believes himself ready to lead the U.S. into a second American Century. "My attitude is that you don't want to just be president," Obama says. "You want to change the country. You want to be a *great* president."

Not long after Bill Clinton secured his party's presidential nomination at the conclusion of the primaries season in the late spring of 1992, his advisers were alarmed to discover from polling data that the vast majority of Americans knew almost nothing about the Arkansas governor. Who was he? What did he stand for? How would he change America?

Sixteen years later, Barack Obama clinched his party's presidential nomination in June 2008 only to discover that he, too, was a virtual unknown to most Americans. Who was he exactly, other than a man whose confidence when speaking reminded some of John F. Kennedy and others of Ronald Reagan? Where did he stand on stem cell research, illegal immigrants, and *Roe v. Wade?* What would he do about soaring prices at the gas pump and America's energy security? How would he protect the country from future terrorist attacks? What is his plan for dealing with the Iraqi quagmire? Would he help the estimated million Americans facing foreclosure keep their homes? And was he a covert Muslim, as rumors on the Internet and assertions at the coffee shop and farm-supplies depot would have it?

The professional political consultants who dominate campaigns in the major leagues — everything from gubernatorial and U.S. Senate races up — would have recommended a nationwide TV marketing campaign to blanket the country with slick advertisements about their candidate's recent descent from heaven to make the country's woes disappear. For good measure there would be attack ads — relatively gentle ones from the candidate's campaign and less gentle broadsides from shady third parties — to tear down the candidate's opponent.

What Barack Obama, forty-seven, decided to do instead was to go back to where he started. Except rather than talking to fellow Democrats in their living rooms, town halls, and church basements, Obama would traverse every part of the nation and introduce himself and his wife, Michelle — and if it wasn't past their bedtime, his children, Malia, ten, and Sasha, seven — to Republicans, independents, Democrats who'd voted for someone else in the primaries, and the vast majority of Americans who hadn't yet tuned into the presidential contest. The emphasis this time would be on town squares, shopping centers, factory gates, and school auditoriums, rather than the spectacular Obama rallies of the primary season — including one in Portland, Oregon, that drew a record 74,000 people to see the first viable African-American candidate for president of the United States. The Pacific Northwest city held the attendance record briefly: in July more than 200,000 U.S. flag-waving Germans turned out for an Obama speech in Berlin, one of many European capitals where public appearances by George W. Bush drew only protestors.

Obama would tell his story: the Harvard-trained civil-rights lawyer and community organizer, who opposed the Iraq war as an Illinois state senator and passed hundreds of laws in Springfield, Illinois, and the U.S. Senate to help veterans, farmers, undernourished kids, teachers in failing schools, seniors with eroding benefits, single moms (as his own mother had been), and other folks who were getting a raw deal.

And he would tell his version of the American story. It's a story about a resourceful people who have been a little short on hope these past few years and need to be reminded of how their past triumphs proved they have it in them to build an even more prosperous, caring, and globally respected nation than their predecessors had so remarkably forged. And if the planets lined up for this improbable candidate, who spoke by turns of individual responsibility and collective compassion, America would never be the same again.

It would reclaim its once unquestioned leadership in diplomacy, through which it had reshaped the post-1945 world and won the Cold War; in entrepreneurship, which made Coca-Cola, Whirlpool, and Microsoft household names from Budapest to São Paulo; and in humanitarianism, with initiatives such as the Marshall Plan and the Peace Corps, by which America earned its reputation as the most benevolent empire in history.

Having lived abroad in the world's most populous Muslim nation, Indonesia, majored in international relations at Columbia University, and traveled extensively in Europe, the Middle East, and Africa, Obama grasps that America's power remains an awesome thing, frightening to many of the world's six billion inhabitants but not if used intelligently. During one of his official foreign trips to the Middle East as a U.S. senator, Obama looked up at a passing U.S. helicopter and wondered, as those around him did, if it was going to drop food or fire rockets. What, Obama wondered, if the sound of approaching U.S. aircraft always meant relief from suffering? If the usually well-meaning foreign-policy establishment in Washington, where Obama was a relatively recent arrival, could suspend its hesitancy about limited possibilities and imagine "the world as it should be, not as it is" how much greater would be the scope for American culture to take hold in friendly and hostile regions alike, and for the U.S., in turn, to absorb the best practices of others? (The Dutch prowess, of necessity, for engineering the world's best levees, for instance.)

Those who called Obama unrealistic, a dreamer, had a valid concern. Many of his boldest ideas had not been tried. And it had been a long time since big ideas were in fashion. Too many people had forgotten how successful Franklin Roosevelt had been in tapping into the American core value of intolerance for complacency, famously conveyed in an FDR campaign speech in 1932: "The country needs and, unless I mistake its temper, the country demands bold, persistent experimentation. It is common sense to take a method and try it. If it fails, admit it frankly and try another. But above all, try something."

America's political leadership has been trapped in "the world as it is" for so long that it has lost touch with what the American people are capable of individually and as a nation. The Revolutionary War, the Emancipation Proclamation, women's suffrage, the eradication of fascism in Europe and the Pacific, and even the triumphs of the Apollo missions are such faded memories that they might as well have been someone else's story. "At every turn in our history," Obama said, referring to the introduction in the 1930s of Social Security, denounced by critics at the time as communistic, "there's been somebody who said we can't. . . . I'm here to tell you, yes we can." Obama was impatient, he said, with the "can't-do, won't-do, won't-even-try" mentality in Washington that kills so many promising ideas.

Enough Americans were hungry for a new vision of America that on its strength alone Obama built the biggest grassroots political movement in U.S. history in 2007–08, with 1.5 million volunteers knocking on doors in every state and U.S. territory, asking Americans if they were satisfied with a lethargy that, in Obama's words, has "caused our politics to become small and timid, calculating and cautious." Record numbers of young voters, dismissed as chronically alienated, plus African-Americans, Hispanics, Asian-Americans, women, seniors, and veterans registered to vote in the Democratic primaries, some for the first time, some for the first time in decades.

His campaign, Obama so often said, was not about him. "I'm just a blank slate that people project their ideas on," he has said. The Obama insurgency that toppled Hillary Clinton, the prohibitive favorite to capture the Democratic nomination as recently as Obama's startling upset victory January 3, 2008, in the lead-off contest in Iowa, "is about you," Obama told shivering crowds unable to find a seat in packed auditoriums to whom he came outdoors to speak.

But what does that mean? And don't all politicians say that? The answer was in an earlier Iowa speech, the previous

December, in which Obama bemoaned the squandered opportunity of the tragedy of September 11, 2001, when every American and hundreds of millions of people around the world waited for the call to serve, to defeat terrorism at its roots, to sacrifice on the home front to pay for the military mission, and to send Americans into the world to understand the hostile forces at work. "We were ready to answer a new call for our country," Obama said. "But the call never came. Instead, we were asked to go shopping, and to prove our patriotism by supporting a war in Iraq that should never have been authorized, and never been waged." And to accept tax cuts for the first time in wartime, a windfall for the country's wealthiest income earners who neither needed nor asked for it. The tax cuts helped transform the unprecedented federal surpluses of the late 1990s into record triple-digit deficits in the Bush years, resulting in a doubling of the national debt, to more than one trillion dollars, and the emergence of the Peoples' Republic of China, holders of about one trillion, two hundred billion dollars of that debt, into America's largest creditor.

The Obama campaign was not about him because the real goal was to unleash the American spirit of hard work and ingenuity onto noble causes. "I have no doubt that in the face of impossible odds people who love their country can change it," Obama said. "Americans have shown they want to step up. I see it everywhere I go: the brave young men and women who have signed up to defend our country; the volunteers fighting poverty in rural America and to rebuild New Orleans; students getting their colleges to divest to stop the genocide in Darfur; the thousands of young Americans who have flooded the applicant pool for Teach for America; retirees who are devoting their time to serve.

"I won't just ask for your vote as a candidate; I will ask for your service and your active citizenship when I am President of the United States," Obama said, before outlining a series of initiatives ranging from cleaning up inner-city neighborhoods to volunteering at VA hospitals and nursing homes to offering four thousand dollars a year in federal college tuition in exchange for one hundred hours of service — or two hours a week — in expanded AmeriCorps and Youth Corps programs to lead seniors in therapeutic dance routines or help troubled youth with their homework. "This will not be a call issued in one speech or program; this will be a cause of my presidency."

As much as editors at national media organizations might attach great importance to the Republican and Democratic primaries and caucuses that take place in the first few months of each fourth year, these are family affairs whose drama is of little or no interest to everyday Americans: Great Plains ranchers coping with skyrocketing feed costs amid a global food crisis; working-class families struggling with the loss of jobs with decent pay and benefits while food-price inflation is at a seventeen-year high; hundreds of thousands of Americans who've lost their homes in the collapse of the "housing bubble" and homeowners everywhere who've suffered an estimated eight-trillion-dollar plunge in the value of their properties; the melee of injured and chronically sick people waiting for relief in the local hospital's emergency room, many of whom are among the forty-seven million uninsured Americans for whom the ER is the only source of medical care; the grieving families and friends of the more than four thousand Americans who have perished in Iraq and Afghanistan, while relatives of the about 150,000 armed-services personnel still in Iraq worry about the coping skills of young men and women — trained professionals though they might be — who are on their third, fourth, or fifth rotation; and everyday citizens who have come to realize that their local Iraq-depleted National Guard unit cannot be relied upon as before to help put out fires, build levees against floods, and pull drowning children from the river.

Recalling his time in the 1980s as a community organizer in Chicago, Obama once remarked that one of the virtues of that profession is that "politicians have a map of the country, but an organizer knows what's actually happening in the streets" — at the beauty salon, the savings and loan, the recreation center, the church and bingo halls, the shopping malls, the school board, the farm-equipment dealer, the used-car lots. Obama is still young enough to know what he doesn't know and that some of what he does know is wrong. The necessary corrective to that is to talk with fellow citizens who are experts on grain prices and rates of violent crime; to sit at the back of a classroom and watch how students and teachers relate to each other; to hear citizens' arguments pro and con for the municipal application to build a new Wal-Mart; and to catch the all-important hospital triage nurse on his or her break and ask about the types of injuries and ailments that are showing up in the ER. Is drug overdose subsiding? What about complications from youth obesity? Any fewer cases of angina and stroke since the new storefront preventive-medicine clinic opened a year ago?

For all the excited talk, especially in U.S. business magazines and foreign-policy journals, about the rise of the economic superpowers China and India, a resurgent Russia, and a unified Europe, America remains a singularly amazing place, ranking third among all nations in both population and land mass. It still boasts by far the world's biggest economy. And unlike the aforementioned nations and regions, it is bereft of separatist enclaves and united behind a single language, which happens to be the global language of commerce, science, and the Internet. A visit to the U.S. Patent Office is a reminder that the U.S. continues to lead the world in inventiveness. A check with the Pentagon shows an annual military budget — the conflicts in Iraq and Afghanistan excluded — that is equal to all other global military spending combined.

America is a nation where people from all walks of life were erecting sand-bag barriers against a rising Mississippi

River in Iowa and other states in 2008 without anyone asking them to, and whose navy was moored in the Andaman Sea within sight of the former Myanmar capital of Yangon (formerly Rangoon) ready to deliver medicine, food, clothing, and tents to cyclone victims earlier this year if only that country's thuggish military "government" would suspend its paranoia about outsiders long enough to save millions. Obama said this year, referring to global crises of terrorism, energy shortages, climate change, and the proliferation of "loose nukes" in the territories of the former Soviet Union, that "America cannot meet this century's challenges alone; but the world cannot meet them without America."

The truth of that is evident from the stalled progress of resolving the dispute between Israel and the Palestinian territories during the last five years, during which the current U.S. administration was almost wholly focused on Iraq, and in the growing threat to energy security as that same administration clung to depleting world supplies of fossil fuels rather than investing to develop new technologies and create high-paying jobs in the emerging industry of U.S.-sourced alternative fuels. It is also evident in the lack of cooperation from former Soviet republics, including Russia, in tracking down unaccounted-for nuclear materials that could be made into a so-called dirty bomb in whose hands a terrorist group could kill half a million Americans; and in the lives "lost" in a dysfunctional domestic education system of failing schools, where teachers are forced to spend more time calculating test scores than helping their students discover the world.

There is a Hemingway line about a man whose life went into decline gradually and then suddenly. That is how it tends to be with crises, whether "yellowjack" (malaria) in the U.S. South in the nineteenth century or global warming in this century. Or, to pick a recent case, the subprime-mortgage crisis, in which Wall Street investment banks and Main Street subprime-mortgage vendors, insufficiently regulated by Washington and state governments, were skating closer and closer to triggering a global financial-system meltdown between 2005 and 2007 then suddenly slid over the edge. By then, there was no time for the system and its participants to do anything other than take the most drastic actions imaginable to prevent a classic "run" on all the world's banks. Noting this historic tendency of ignoring problems until it's too late — from the increasingly belligerent language of the future combatants in the First World War, a conflict no one wanted, to the gradual cost-cutting at NASA that culminated in the 1985 *Challenger* tragedy — Obama chose from the beginning of his bid for the 2008 Democratic nomination to quote a less familiar but arguably more important line from Martin Luther King's landmark 1963 speech on the Washington Mall. To tell the Americans who flocked to his rallies that he was there to talk about "the fierce urgency of *now*."

In its entirety, Dr. King's call to action is a brilliant rhetorical formulation. It is both a warning — a prophetic one, as it happened, with America's major cities going up in flames during race riots later in the decade — but also an assertion of hope. Not false hope, but the very real triumphs of the assembly line, rural electrification, Salk's polio vaccine, crop-yield management that created the world's most bountiful harvests, the silicon chip, the personal computer, and the Internet. "We have also come to this hallowed spot to remind America of the fierce urgency of *now*," Dr. King said 45 years ago in the nation's capital. "Now is the time to make real the promises of democracy. *Now* is the time to rise from the dark and desolate valley of segregation to the sunlit path of racial justice."

And now is the time to redress the injustice of the one hundred thousand U.S. military veterans who are homeless. To protect the millions of Americans who if hit with a catastrophic illness will have to choose between payments for treating it or keeping their home. Time to pioneer in stem cell research rather than forfeit the chance to keep loved ones alive and improve the quality of life for the living. To lead the global solution to climate change or witness the gradual and then sudden change in character of that crisis, from polar bears stranded on Arctic ice floes to the destruction of more than half of America's great cities by flooding as ocean levels rise. Check a map for the number of U.S. cities of a million or more inhabitants that are not located on an ocean or other large body of water including the Great Lakes. There are about half a dozen, and New York, Boston, San Francisco, Chicago, Seattle, Miami, New Orleans, and San Diego are not among them.

Barack Obama has the kind of life story that, once you've heard it, you never forget. That might be a liability, since Obama couldn't know if he was chosen forty-fourth president of the republic because Americans wanted to prove themselves ready to elect the first African-American chief executive in their 232-year history or because of his values, ideas, approach to problem-solving, and ability to make Americans believe again — to believe that the 21st century, like the one before it, can also be an American Century, and that he has the gifts to set that process in motion.

Certainly Obama harbors few doubts that he can inspire Americans to fight for a better future, or he wouldn't be seeking the top office in the land. "I think that there's the possibility — not the certainty, but the possibility — that I can't just win an election," Obama said in March 2007, a month after he formally declared his presidential candidacy, "but can also transform the country in the process, that the language and the approach I take to politics is sufficiently different that I could bring diverse parts of this country together in a way that hasn't been done in some time, and that bridging those divisions is a critical element in solving problems like health care or energy or education."

Much already has been said about how Obama was, at least in certain regards, a most improbable candidate for the presidency. He is the first African-American head of state not only of America, but of any Western nation. He became the fifth-youngest president on taking the oath of office in January 2009. Obama is the first U.S. president with a background as a community organizer, which may be the most important distinction, since his approach to governance is more influenced by motivating ordinary people than by striking deals with fellow power brokers — although the record shows he's good at that, too, regardless of the political affiliation of his negotiating partner. "What Washington does is cause everybody to concentrate on where they disagree as opposed to where they agree," says Tom Coburn, the hard-right Republican U.S. senator from Oklahoma who has cosponsored legislation with Obama. "But leadership changes that. And Barack's got the capability, I believe — and the pizzazz and the charisma — to be a leader of America, not a leader of Democrats."

What Americans are most likely to know of Obama is that he is the mixed-race son of a white Kansas mother and a Kenyan father who in his youth was a goat-herder. In his teens, Obama decided to self-identify as black and put aside the name his mother gave him to make his path easier in a racially charged nation, Barry, in favor of Barack Hussein Obama Jr., in honor of his father. Obama is the first president born and raised in Hawaii, the country's most multicultural state, where racial bigotry effectively does not exist. (Obama did not encounter racism until he relocated to the mainland in his late teens.)

Obama was abandoned by his father at age two, and his globetrotting mother was sufficiently peripatetic that he did not see too much of her, either, although her impact on him was considerable. It was his mother, Stanley Ann Dunham, who imparted to Barry his moral code that drives him to help the disadvantaged. She also gave him a world religion course of sorts: while not devout herself, Dunham was fascinated with religious rituals and took her son to prayer services at every church and mosque within a few miles of where they happened to be living — in Hawaii, for the most part, and for five years in Jakarta, where Obama attended both Christian and Muslim schools between grades six and ten. In Indonesia, the homeland of Dunham's second husband, Obama encountered Muslim traditions of food, dress, and religious practice. He also saw violent political repression and grinding poverty in the slums of the country's capital city. Eventually, he moved back to Honolulu to live with his maternal grandparents.

Obama has been a high-achieving student, a businessman, an athlete, a community organizer, a civil-rights lawyer, a best-selling author, and a legislator. On the strengths of a winning personality and his athletic prowess, especially in basketball and football, Obama made friends easily. He left Hawaii for Occidental College, a liberal arts school in Los Angeles, then moved to New York, where he graduated from Columbia in international relations. Determined to do social work, Obama passed up many opportunities in New York and, always in search of a new city, finally accepted a community-organizing job funded by black churches in Chicago. For three years he helped guide residents of run-down municipal housing projects to get asbestos removed from their homes, set up youth programs, and successfully pressure city hall to provide more police and other city services in the neglected neighborhood. He faced negativity everywhere he turned during this time, from residents who had already tried and failed to improve their living conditions, from municipal councillors who cared little about the concerns of folks who lived between a shuttered steel plant and one of the Windy City's larger garbage dumps, and from rival black ministers and local political leaders — a fractious lot characterized by rivalry and mutual mistrust — who regarded Obama as an interloper and insufficiently "black."

That Obama was able to achieve anything owed in part to his voracious reading at Columbia, the one sojourn in his life marked by relative solitude. He incessantly patronized New York's bounty of second-hand bookstores and read the collected works of Aristotle, Thackeray, Churchill, Malcolm X, and pretty much every other published author he could cram into an eighteen-hour day (which may account for his distinction in the 2008 race of being the only candidate to quote Socrates on the campaign trail).

The author most relevant to Obama's vocation in community organizing is Saul Alinsky, the legendary U.S. labor organizer. Alinsky's methods were later to have a great influence on the civil-rights movement. The overriding rule for Alinsky was to listen. In 2007, there was a revealing video clip of Obama — for ten years a professor of constitutional law at the University of Chicago, one of the world's top schools — his head resting on his fists, perched on a chair he'd swung around to get the local news from three farmers in a diner in largely white downstate Illinois. They talked about how rising gasoline prices to run their machinery were wiping out their windfall from the sudden jump in corn prices, their concern about soil depletion as they tried to keep up with rising demand, and their fear of losing Washington subsidies that kept their operations viable during bad times — and until recently, most years had been bad. Obama sat silently, asking the occasional question before making his own, sympathetic, observations. Then, without losing eye contact with each man he addressed, Obama asked in a casual tone if anyone in the district was experimenting with price hedging. He talked about different models of fuel-efficient cultivation methods and harvesting equipment on the market. Were the costs of such upgrading beyond the reach of most farmers in the area? In a roundabout way, without dictating solutions or putting any of the three men on the spot, he got them talking about half a dozen things they could do to improve their efficiency and drive down costs. It's a style of discussion too seldom used, one in which no one is "the smartest man in the room," no one is embarrassed (perhaps one of the men doesn't grasp the math of hedging but sees now he might be well advised to find someone who does), and people bond around an idea. It's a style of problem-solving, or organizing, that can be summed up in three words: listen, motivate, act.

The three major influences Obama cites are Lincoln, Gandhi, and Martin Luther King Jr. — all liberators. But while Dr. King figures in many of Obama's speeches — partly for his doctrine of social justice and partly for a cadence that works with Obama's oratorical style — it's Franklin Roosevelt whom Obama most frequently draws upon.

FDR is hardly an unalloyed hero in the history of black America, although it was FDR who brought African-Americans into his governing coalition, and as a community blacks came to feel he best represented their interests. Those feelings arose chiefly from Social Security and other New Deal elements of FDR's social safety net that protected Americans regardless of race. Among FDR's faults was a stubborn refusal, despite Eleanor Roosevelt's constant protestations, to deal with a segregationist Democratic South whose support he needed in Congress.

Yet Obama embraces FDR, even while having said of Lincoln that "I cannot swallow whole the view of Lincoln as the Great Emancipator." Fair enough. Lincoln was primarily concerned with keeping the country together. As for the former slaves, Lincoln, like many abolitionists, doubted the possibilities of racial cohabitation and thought it best to return the African-Americans to Africa — failing to grasp or acknowledge that American blacks of several generations standing in the North American colonies were, in fact, Americans. They fought in the Revolutionary War and every war since. (Liberia, with its capital Monrovia named for U.S. President James Monroe, is the, some might argue, failed experiment that arose from that misguided idea.)

Obama recognizes in the "patrician of the Hudson" perhaps the best example of America's can-do spirit: the ability to galvanize a people using the bully pulpit of the presidency to do giant things of which they did not know they were capable. FDR was purposeful, of course — he loved being president and meant to exercise the powers of the Oval Office to the fullest and occasionally beyond (as with his humbling in failing to pack the Supreme Court). While academics argue about how effective he was in reviving a Depression economy, Roosevelt kept his nation from succumbing to fascism, and he was perhaps the most effective civilian war strategist in the republic's history. FDR was genial as all get out, but he dispensed with even his highest-ranking subordinates with alacrity the moment it was clear they were over their heads.

FDR thrived on adversity and was open to unfamiliar ideas. He signed off on the Manhattan Project — the costliest and most daunting engineering challenge in U.S. history to that point — after a cursory briefing from Albert Einstein, of whom he had heard but had never met. FDR was prescient and did not let a war get in the way of planning for peace, one manifestation of which was his idea for a United Nations and another his articulation, in 1941, of his "Four Freedoms," one of the world's greatest doctrines. Obama is the first major contemporary politician to recite the Freedoms often. They are noble and still unmet goals: freedom of speech, freedom of worship, freedom from want, freedom from fear — in each case, at FDR's insistence, "everywhere in the world." Could there be a doctrine more worth fighting for? A cause more just?

Obama's speeches and legislative work dating back to his years in the Illinois Senate all circle back to variations of those Four Freedoms, a doctrine of social justice first articulated by one of the richest men in the country. For Obama, the fierce urgency of the moment is to return to the path toward social justice "everywhere in the world" that the lengthy Cold War, more than anything, caused America to stray from.

In one of his first speeches as a U.S. senator, at the National Press Club in Washington in 2005, Obama gave an extensive tribute to the living legacy of FDR. "He understood that the freedom to pursue our individual dreams is made possible by the promise that if fate causes us to stumble or fall," Obama said, "our larger American family will be there to lift us up. That if we're willing to share even a small amount of life's risks and rewards with each other, then we'll all have the chance to make the most of our God-given potential.

"And because Franklin Roosevelt had the courage to act on this idea, individual Americans were able to get back on their feet and build a shared prosperity that is still the envy of the world."

While hardly an iconoclast, Obama is something of an inconvenient candidate for the Democrats. Not at odds with his party as often as John McCain has been — before this election year in which the Arizona Republican has oddly cleaved to the failed policies of the incumbent president — Obama has often bucked the establishment of his party and of conventional Washington wisdom. His Secret Service detail was onto something in giving Obama the code name "Renegade."

Risking support among his own party's key constituencies, Obama has broken with orthodoxy on religion, war, race, free trade, and health care. At odds with the realpolitik of careerists in the U.S. State Department, Obama was met with ridicule from both Hillary Clinton and John McCain for asserting his determination to pursue Osama bin Laden and his confederates into a sovereign Pakistan, with or without the consent of Washington's unreliable allies in Islamabad. Yet within weeks of that supposed diplomatic gaucherie, U.S. armed forces began striking inside Pakistan, taking out one of al Qaeda's top strategists.

In his 2004 U.S. Senate bid, Obama stepped into an Illinois union hall and declared, "There's nobody in this room who doesn't believe in free trade." The AFL-CIO leaders, longtime Democratic organizers and demonizers of free trade, looked at each other in disbelief. But, as Obama later told writer William Finnegan, "Look, those guys are all wearing Nike shoes and buying Pioneer stereos. They don't want the borders closed. They just don't want their communities destroyed" by unrestrained outsourcing.

Risking the ire of African-Americans, another bulwark of Democratic support, Obama said in a 2006 speech that blacks suffered from "our long-held grudges and petty disputes, our frantic diversions and tribal allegiances." And from Martin Luther King Jr.'s own Atlanta pulpit in January 2008, Obama told the black congregants: "We must admit that none of our hands is entirely clean. . . . We have scorned our gay brothers and sisters instead of embracing them. The scourge of anti-Semitism has, at times, revealed itself in our community. For too long, some of us have seen immigrants as competitors for jobs instead of companions in the fight for opportunity."

Crossing swords with another traditional Democratic constituency, Obama complained to Jewish leaders in Cleveland in February 2008 that, "There is a strain within the pro-Israel community that says unless you adopt an unwavering pro-Likud approach to Israel that you're anti-Israel. And that can't be the measure of our friendship with Israel."

Obama shed the flag lapel pin he'd been wearing since September 11, 2001, several years later, when it began to strike him as a cheap substitute for patriotism. He was fighting for increased benefits for military service personnel on the U.S. Senate Committee on Veterans' Affairs, and it seemed almost everyone standing in his way, eager to slash benefits, including President Bush, was wearing a flag pin. Obama didn't give up this silent protest until June 2008, after many months in which supporters gave him pins until his suit pockets were bulging with them. One particular woman supporter, her blouse bedecked with several "Obama for President" buttons, told him quietly that "It means so much to people [that you wear one]. And would it really cost you that much?" This was the voice of reason, Obama knew; he was hurting a great many people who had no part in his private grudge. He now is rarely seen without a U.S. flag pin in his lapel.

Noting that about three-quarters of Americans believe in angels, Obama in a 2006 speech widely circulated on the Internet faulted Democrats for their patronizing secularism. For decades, Democrats have objected to displays of the Ten Commandments in government buildings and picked other pointless fights in which they have come off looking like heathens. Obama reminded his party of the social-justice causes advanced by the church, from the civil-rights movement to churches providing refuge in Topeka, Memphis, Cincinnati, and elsewhere in the American heartland for Vietnamese boat people.

Obama explained his views on religion in a keynote address at a religious renewal conference in Washington: "When we ignore the debate about what it means to be a good Christian or Muslim or Jew; when we discuss religion only in the negative sense of where and how it should not be practiced, rather than in the positive sense of what it tells us about our obligations toward one another . . . others will fill the vacuum, those with the most insular views of faith, or those who cynically use religion to justify partisan ends."

On issues even closer to home, probably no aspiring first couple has been so obsessed with parenting as Michelle and Barack Obama. In speech after speech, Obama admonishes parents to "get our kids to turn off the TV sets and put away the video games and hit the books — even if that means, for black children, that they might be accused of 'acting white.'" The "misogyny" common in contemporary music also troubles Obama. So does the pride some adolescents take in merely staying out of jail. "It's like the Chris Rock line," Obama said in his Father's Day address this year. "You're not *supposed* to be in jail. That's not something to brag about." So much does Obama dwell on healthy child rearing he appeared at times to be running for Father-in-Chief.

Political progressives have a weakness for lost causes and for accentuating the negative. Obama, by contrast, is a self-described "hope mongerer." Yet his pragmatism has disappointed supporters when he has declined to expend political capital on unwinnable causes. "He is idealistic," Chicago poverty activist John Bouman told Obama biographer David Mendell. But, he added, "for Barack, it's not a constant flow of glorious defeats."

Better to accumulate a record of getting things done. In his last two years in the Illinois Senate, Obama secured passage of more than 280 bills. The inspiration for many of them, including bigger tax breaks for the working poor and expanded child-education programs, was a desire to correct a social imbalance tilted against the poor and people of color.

Obama has been conventional at times. He has been largely AWOL from the poverty and race issues arising from Hurricane Katrina. And as the primary in layoff-devastated Ohio approached, free traders Obama and Hillary Clinton pandered to Ohioans by scapegoating the North American Free Trade Agreement (NAFTA) for a crisis both knew is rooted in cheap Chinese imports being snapped up by patriotic American shoppers at Wal-Mart and Home Depot, and not Mexican labor and environmental standards (lax though they are).

Arguably more worrisome is that Obama knows he's hot stuff. His victory in the lead-off Iowa caucuses January 3, 2008, was front-page news in more than 300 European newspapers. In April, Britain's august *Financial Times* headlined a lead editorial, "Democrats must choose Obama." Yes, there is a stubbornly virulent Internet campaign among the deeply misinformed to warn Americans that Obama is Muslim, a Manchurian Candidate poised to replace Gideon Bibles at Motel 6 with the Koran. The racial bigots are having their say, as well. One of them came up with a button that read, "If Obama is President . . . will we still call it the White House?"

But the die was cast when prominent conservatives, of all people, threw in their lot with Obama. Long disgusted with the mendacity, incompetence, and lack of frugality of fellow Republican George W. Bush's administration and uninspired by the eleven candidates for the 2008 GOP presidential nomination, they recognized in Obama a moderate progressive and began to propel his candidacy. Even among Republicans, wrote Peggy Noonan, the *Wall Street Journal* columnist and former Reagan speechwriter, "there is a quiet pining" for an Obama presidency. Conservative columnist David Brooks of the *New York Times*, in a column headed "Run, Obama, Run," asserted the junior U.S. senator for Illinois was the only genuine agent of change among the twenty-one candidates from both parties seeking the presidency. And for every racial slur in the blogosphere, there were twenty glowing Obama magazine cover stories like *US Weekly*'s "Barack Obama: Is He Really Just Like Us? (The Answer: He Really Is!)." In *Atlantic Monthly*, recovering Iraq-war cheerleader Andrew Sullivan argued that Obama's face alone would restore America's standing in the world. "Obama," said former George W. Bush Deputy Assistant Peter Wehner, "is among the most impressive political talents of our lifetime." Bush himself, reflecting on "Obamania," called him "the Pope."

When the media gush became more than some could bear, the online newsmagazine *Slate* launched a "Messiah Watch" to report sightings of Obama turning water into wine and strolling the length of Lake Michigan. *Time*'s politics columnist, Joe Klein, a generally positive commentator on Obama, wrote "there's something just a wee bit creepy about the mass messianism" of an Obama event. Obama himself was a bit creeped out during a July European tour when the German tabloid *Bild* published a tell-all account by a stealth reporter who monitored his daily gym ritual. "I'm getting hot, and not from the workout," she wrote. "What a man." "Did she describe what my T-shirt smelled like?" Obama asked with some astonishment when informed of the detailed report. (Yes. Fabric softener with spring scent.) An urban legend flourished that supporters at an Obama rally had applauded him when he sneezed. It was true that at a Dallas event Obama excused himself mid-speech to blow his nose and the crowd cheered. "When people go wild watching you blow your nose," *Al Jazeera* observed in February, "you know you've caught lightning in a bottle."

Frank Rich, the *New York Times* columnist who has been one of Obama's most enthusiastic chroniclers, made note in an otherwise flattering June 2008 column of Obama's "cockiness. His own tendency to preen and coast could be encouraged by recent events rocking [McCain's] Straight Talk Express: McCain so far is proving an exceptionally clumsy candidate prone to accentuating everything that's out-of-touch about his American vision."

"I can't help it if I give a good speech," Obama said during the 2008 primary season when accused by Clinton of offering voters little more than ear candy. Usually given to an attractive self-deprecation, Obama does hold his head high in the manner of a Roman emperor, applauds his own speeches at their conclusion (actually a device for rousing his audiences, but easily mistaken for self-congratulation), and has a professorial aloofness that doesn't lend itself to rope-line empathy in the manner of a Bill Clinton. "I love you!" someone invariably screams at Obama during his events, leaving the candidate not much choice but to pause in his speeches to say, "I love you back!"

Yet there's a stubborn streak in Obama that overrides

expediency at critical moments when he might be better advised to act more safely. It seemed that he might denounce his long-time pastor Jeremiah Wright Jr. — due to retire shortly, after having built Chicago's Trinity United into one of America's largest churches, with about eight thousand parishioners — when a selective culling of Wright's more intemperate remarks flooded the Internet in the spring of 2008. As it happens, nothing Wright said in faulting U.S. foreign policy, for instance, matched Dr. King's 1967 fulmination against the Vietnam War: "God didn't call America to engage in a senseless, unjust war," King said. "And we are criminals in that war. We have committed more war crimes almost than any nation in the world."

In the only historic speech in the 2008 campaign, on March 18, Obama repudiated Wright's more egregious sermonizing but refused to "disown" him. Obama then opened the Pandora's box of racial grievances during an election cycle that everyone, especially Obama, was hoping would not be about race. While the continued anger of many African-Americans and other minorities is counterproductive, Obama allowed, "the anger is real; it is powerful; and to simply wish it away, to condemn it without understanding its roots, only serves to widen the chasm of misunderstanding that exists between the races."

Over the next few months, Obama showed a political cunning FDR would have admired. Reverend Wright, failing to realize his good fortune in not being disowned entirely, popped up at the National Press Club to deliver an updated fiery condemnation of most things American, exhibiting the traits not of an angry truth-teller but a nut. Obama promptly disowned him after all. For good measure, he dumped Wright's Trinity United church — Obama's place of worship for two decades — within twenty-four hours of an unflattering pantomime of Hillary Clinton at the Chicago church by a visiting white pastor.

In a single week in June, Obama supported a compromise

bill on warrantless wiretaps loathed by left-wing liberals. He reacted to one Supreme Court decision that struck down Louisiana's practice of condemning sex offenders to death row by reasserting his support of capital punishment when the crime is particularly "heinous." In lauding another Supreme Court decision striking down the District of Columbia's ban on handguns, he allied himself with the National Rifle Association, agreeing the measure violated Americans' Second Amendment rights.

As a frontrunner not eager to give the underdog free time on the airwaves, Obama rejected McCain's offer of a series of televised town-hall debates. And he opted out of the public campaign-financing system to which McCain had committed himself — and the spending restrictions that go with it. McCain cried foul over Obama's earlier and purposely vague suggestion that he, too, would restrict himself to public funds if his opponent did so. What changed in the meantime was Obama's unprecedented ability to generate donations from small-dollar contributors among his burgeoning population of Internet-based supporters, to whom he could return time and again before they hit their federally mandated donation ceilings. As a result, Obama would go into the general election with the same daunting financial advantage he had wielded over Hillary Clinton in the primaries, outspending her in some states by a three-to-one margin.

All this left David Brooks, house conservative columnist at the *New York Times*, breathless with disgust and admiration. "On the one hand," Brooks wrote, "Obama did sell out the primary cause of his professional life, all for a tiny political advantage. If he'll sell that out, what won't he sell out? On the other hand, global affairs ain't beanbag. If we're going to have a president who is going to go toe to toe with the likes of Vladimir Putin, maybe it is better that he should have a ruthlessly opportunistic Fast Eddie Obama lurking inside.

"All I know for sure is that this guy is no liberal goo-goo. Republicans keep calling him naive. But naive is the last word I'd use to describe Barack Obama. He's the most effectively political creature we've seen in decades."

On securing the Democratic presidential nomination, Obama did not run to the political center in pursuit of moderate and independent voters to embellish the base of the left-of-center grassroots supporters he had created. He didn't do so because, while Obama is a progressive as defined by concern for social justice, he already is a centrist and in no way antiwar, anticapitalism, or antiestablishment.

However, all this didn't stop Reverend Jesse Jackson, twice a U.S. presidential candidate in the 1980s, from complaining in July that Obama's admonition to black audiences to brush up on their parenting skills was "not useful." As a reminder of why the strident Jackson had not been electable, the ordained minister, in an off-air moment during a *Fox News* interview, complained that Obama was "talking down to black people — I want to cut his nuts off," for which he promptly apologized, obscuring whatever point he might have had. Obama was nonplussed, telling *Meet the Press* in July that Jackson had campaigned on the same issues of black responsibilities in his own presidential bids. "And today, when fathers are absent from half of African-American households, that's a problem you can't be silent about," Obama said.

Tom Hayden joined that backlash among self-identified pure progressives, detecting loopholes in Obama's vow to end U.S. military involvement in Iraq. Hayden, whose promising career as a 1960s antiwar activist peaked with a stint as a California state legislator, parsed this July Obama statement on Iraq: "I've always said that the pace of our withdrawal would be dictated by the safety and security of our troops and the need to maintain stability" — two conditions, Hayden argued, that could justify leaving American troops in combat indefinitely. "And when I go to Iraq and have a chance to talk to some of the commanders on the ground, I'm sure I'll have more information and will continue to refine my policies" — another loophole, according to Hayden, for allowing American involvement in the Iraq war to drag on.

Obama had begun his campaign for the White House with the repeated warning that "I will disappoint some people." And when the left announced its disappointment once Obama was the Democratic nominee, Obama disputed "this whole notion that I am shifting to the center," adding that "the people who say this apparently haven't been listening to me."

That much was true. Obama already was a moderate. Dating from his prescient opposition to invading Iraq, Obama said at that time he was not opposed to all wars, just "dumb wars." In the U.S. Senate, Obama consistently voted for Bush's war-funding supplemental bills (a trick for keeping the cost of the war off the Pentagon's books), because he was determined to support the troops once they'd been deployed. And as a member of the U.S. Senate Committee on Veterans' Affairs, few legislators in history have fought harder for increased benefits for veterans, a fight that often had him at loggerheads with patriotic-sounding Republican opponents. Obama is a military hardliner, notably against Iran and its nuclear-weapons ambitions and in the search for Osama bin Laden and his al Qaeda confederates, even if that means military missions into an uncooperative Pakistan.

There is little logic to the objections of the pure progressives. If America chose McCain, America, by McCain's stated policy, would have had troops in Iraq at full strength in pursuit of his illusory "victory" in Mesopotamia at least for the duration of McCain's first term and, he said, quite possibly longer. Obama, by contrast, is steadfast that, on being inaugurated, he will begin the process of withdrawing troops as quickly and as carefully as possible — realistically by 2010 or 2011. Even during that period, U.S. military involvement will effectively end with Obama's instruction to his commanders to execute a plan of gradually removing troops immediately, since "force protection" (or self-defense) would now be the U.S. military's primary mission.

What the radical antiwar folks described as loopholes in Obama's Iraq policy are elements of the same admirable flexibility to react to changing conditions on the ground that the outgoing Bush administration ignored in pursuit of ideological, rather than realistic, goals. And that Obama would not act before consulting his generals in the Iraq theater is the sort of conduct most Americans expect of a competent commander-in-chief.

To be sure, it has been interesting, for a change, to watch purist progressives and Republicans, and their media surrogates, wax indignant over an opponent who has outfoxed them. Obama is not going to let either the left or the right define him. And it is revealing that both sides seem to miss the Politics 101 rule that you can't change the character of politics — the "primary cause" Brooks said Obama had sold out — unless you have power. Unless you win.[1] Barbara Ehrenreich, one of the least impressionable of U.S. social-justice advocates, was satisfied with Obama's progressive credentials. "There's no mystery about the direction in which Obama might take us," she wrote on the left-wing Huffington Post website. "He's written a breathtakingly honest autobiography, he has a long legislative history, and now, a meaty economic program." Lauding Obama as "a fresh start" sought by progressives, Ehrenreich said, "That's what 'change' means right now: Get us out of here!"

A glorious defeat in November at the hands of the GOP that successfully smeared Democrats from Michael Dukakis to John Kerry as weak on national security was not Obama's goal in setting out on his presidential quest in late 2006. If anything, as the finish line grew closer, Obama became even more determined to avoid being defined as soft on rogue nations or pedophiles, eager to take away people's guns, and naive enough to throw away the first financial advantage enjoyed by a Democratic presidential candidate in memory in the vain belief that Republicans and their allies would play nice as a result. Obama didn't want a campaign about the four-hundred-dollar haircuts that killed off John Edwards' chances early in the primary season, nor an encore of his own brush with charges of "elitism," when he mangled the answer to a question at a Los Angeles rally about how to win votes in layoff-racked Pennsylvania. Obama said on that occasion, accurately, that in times of distress people tend to cling to church, hunting, and prejudice about immigrants stealing their jobs. That became a mainstream media obsession for almost three precious weeks. No candidate can afford such lengthy distractions and hope to be elected. If he hadn't won the 1932 election, FDR — who became president with far less electoral experience than Obama but had a similar healthy respect for his adversaries — would have been a figure of great promise but a historical footnote.

The debate Obama wanted with McCain was strictly on issues. The two agreed on several concerns, including the threats posed by global warming and nuclear proliferation; campaign-finance reform (an issue McCain advanced in the U.S. Senate and Obama pushed successfully both in Illinois and DC); measures to outlaw U.S. torture of political prisoners; and the need for greater federal financing of stem cell research. Until McCain had his head handed to him in 2007 for his championship of a compassionate, sensible "path to citizenship" for illegal immigrants, Obama and McCain were in agreement on that crucial issue as well. Obama still promotes that policy, while McCain, to secure the support of right-wing Republicans in his second bid for the GOP nomination, shed his maverick ambitions on the issue. McCain's long-time conservatism on social issues (admittedly suspect among many right-wing Republicans) was matched by Obama's similarly consistent support for liberal initiatives to aid the disadvantaged. Yet both men opposed same-sex marriage and believe there are substantial limits to what government can and should do.

Matched with his doctrine of a new "tough diplomacy," in which a President Obama, like John F. Kennedy, Richard Nixon, Gerald Ford, and Ronald Reagan, would talk with America's adversaries as well as its allies, Obama is a military hawk. He wants to increase the size of the U.S. military and boost veterans' benefits. He is committed to using the U.S. Armed Forces to safeguard Israel, destroy al Qaeda in its Afghan and Pakistan bases, and create an international but U.S.-led "no-fly zone" to stop attacks on the Darfur region by the Sudanese government. On Iran, Obama is no less determined than McCain to thwart its nuclear-weapons ambitions, and he sometimes appears to have the same Israel-right-or-wrong mindset as McCain. When Israel was taking criticism worldwide for its attacks on the Lebanese bases of Hezbollah rocket attacks on Israel — a botched 2006 mission in which the Israeli Defense Forces managed to kill more Lebanese civilians than Hezbollah terrorists — Obama was a rare voice supporting the Bush White House resistance to an immediate Israeli cease-fire.

Where Obama and McCain most sharply disagreed was on Iraq, health care, and the Bush tax cuts. This is where their divergence on America's future was clearest. You could see it in their priorities: Obama would spend about one hundred billion dollars a year to subsidize health insurance for all Americans. McCain would spend the same amount to further reduce corporate tax rates after several years of record Fortune 500 profits and outsized CEO bonuses and lucrative golden parachutes for fired CEOs who have mismanaged America's industrial assets.

On Iraq, McCain believed the expected 2009 level of U.S. troops in the country — about 140,000 — must remain until at least the end of his first term, in 2013, in order for Iraq to successfully take over its own security. At a minimum, then, McCain would have spent an additional six hundred billion dollars in Iraq, assuming the current monthly tab of about ten to twelve billion dollars. The total cost to Americans of war in Iraq and Afghanistan is already approaching one trillion dollars, Nobel laureate economist Joseph Stiglitz reported in 2008. And the long-term cost, including lifelong medical treatment and benefits for the thirty-thousand-plus U.S. casualties to date, will top out at about three trillion dollars.

In removing U.S. combat brigades in Iraq within eighteen months of taking office and redeploying at least two brigades to Afghanistan to fight a resurgent Taliban and al Qaeda, Obama will use the freed-up money at home. His focus is on rebuilding or replacing crumbling schools, bridges, and other decaying infrastructure. Independent experts warned in 2007 that America faces a $350-billion "infrastructure deficit" of outdated bridges, highways, and the like in the transportation sector alone.

Six fundamental ways in which Obama aims to change America are universal health care, education reform, energy self-sufficiency, and protecting the U.S. from the impact of global warming. He will also implement a new, more ambitious, and comprehensive foreign policy that restores American goodwill and benevolent influence abroad; and an unprecedented era of government accountability, transparency, and everyday involvement of Americans in a genuine civilian democracy.

The Obama speeches in this book, outlining these goals, are illuminating not only for the passionate commitment he brings to them but the consistency of his objectives, which predate his service in the U.S. Senate. Specific details of Obama's policies — on his central goals and dozens of other issues — are provided in the chapter "Barack Obama on the Major Issues."

The Obama agenda is ambitious yet practical. It's ambitious because Obama wants universal health care for every American, a promise made and not kept by every president since Harry Truman, and because he regards a high-quality education "as the birthright of every American." Obama believes that without a new generation of students with affordable access to the best schools, better training in literacy and numeracy skills that begin in nursery school, as well as better-trained and better-paid teachers and school administrators, the U.S. — and certainly individual Americans — will lose their already shrinking competitive advantage over the emerging economic superpowers in the developing world.

It's ambitious because every U.S. president since Jimmy Carter has at least paid lip service to making America self-sufficient in energy, which Obama proposes to do with bigger investments in research and development into both conventional and alternative fuels; a push by Detroit to build vastly more energy-efficient vehicles; and federal incentives to make new and existing office towers and other commercial buildings more sparing in their energy use.

Ambitious because no presidential candidate has pledged to so thoroughly merge military power with diplomatic intelligence and humanitarian effort to bring existing and new allies to its side in the necessarily international efforts to eradicate terrorism, curb global warming, and find and destroy unaccounted-for nuclear material before it falls into the hands of terrorist groups. Ambitious because Obama seeks to reestablish America's humanitarian reputation with an expanded AmeriCorps and Youth Corps, by reopening shuttered U.S. consulates in neglected parts of the world, and by launching Voice Corps and America House programs that use traveling American ambassadors and fixed locations that showcase America's multicultural realities to counter the anti-Americanism so commonplace in the world — and not just in developing nations.

And ambitious, finally, because after more than two decades of the politics of personal destruction — a divisive politics that pits rich against poor, pro-choice champions against pro-life advocates, and gun owners against the mostly urban dwellers who want guns off the streets — Obama seeks a common ground among Americans of disparate views in order to achieve long-delayed goals that a majority of Americans agree on. This conciliation will require, among other things, draining the cynicism from politics by making elected officials and bureaucrats far more accountable, by publicizing in advance not merely the generalities but the specifics of what Washington proposes and soliciting the views of everyday Americans in policy creation, in the tradition of New England town-hall debates of old. It also means, as Obama has vowed, that his cabinet officers will not only testify on a regular basis to Congress but will talk with the people via quarterly webcasts and solicit their feedback, as will Obama himself.

Yet while it's an ambitious agenda, it's also practical. The American people in 2008 are as never before impatient for overdue reforms in health care, education, and energy self-sufficiency, meaningful accountability of their elected officials, and a foreign policy that serves American interests rather than those of a small group of "neo-conservatives" or any other clutch of ideologues — people who know what works in theory, as a democratic Middle East was supposed to, but not in practice.

It's practical because from electronic medical records to stem cell research, and from the search for alternative energy sources to combining military with humanitarian efforts abroad, a great deal of progress already is underway. About 10 percent of the health-care system has made the transition from paper to electronic records. Stem cell development is underway at university and private-sector research centers across the U.S. Billions of dollars already have been invested in creating jobs in the development of biofuels, wind, solar, and other alternative energy sources. And a new 21st-century military code of practice developed by General David Petraeus was successfully tested in the first year of the Iraq invasion before Petraeus was abruptly reassigned by a Pentagon that was initially anticipating a complete military withdrawal by the end of that year. This code was later put to effective use in General Petraeus's more recent role as chief U.S. commander in Iraq. It combines force with humanitarian relief and rebuilding to win hearts and minds.

It's practical because Obama has a more highly developed skill at bipartisanship than most of the men who have served as president. Partly this owes to Obama's background as a community organizer who had to resolve conflicting aims among the many people with a stake in a given issue. And, later, because in eight of his twelve years as a legislator, Obama served in the minority party. To get any of his proposed legislation passed required him to form allegiances with the other side.

McCain and his surrogates depicted Obama as a traditional Democratic partisan when the opposite is true, as McCain well knew, having cosponsored no fewer than four bills with Obama in the relatively short tenure of the junior U.S. senator from Illinois — most recently in the 2008 campaign itself.

Finally, in capturing the presidency in November, Obama will be working with a Congress and Senate controlled by Obama's fellow Democrats. If that weren't enough, Obama takes with him to the White House the grassroots organization he built for the 2008 election — the largest in U.S. history, with a databank of 10 million donors and volunteers. Its members will hold Obama's feet to the fire on the issues that drew them to him in the first place. They will pressure resistant legislators who balk at needed reforms, and they will mount widely disseminated counterarguments to those made by third parties, such as the powerful insurance, drug, oil, and defense-contractor lobbies.

In the final analysis, though, it's Obama's personal aptitude that will be the deciding issue in the success or failure of an Obama presidency. He is conditioned to setbacks, which are a defining characteristic of grassroots organizing and sitting on the minority side of the aisle in the legislature, which accounts for the calm temperament that would serve him well as chief executive. "I have a very steady temper," Obama has said. "I don't get too high when things are high, I don't get too low when things are low," Obama told *Rolling Stone* in July — an observation confirmed in other accounts — "which has been very helpful during this campaign and is reflected in the people I hire and how we run our organization."

Like Bill Clinton, Obama solicits a wide spectrum of informed and often conflicting expert opinion before shaping a decision based on facts rather than hopes and delusions. And Obama can be dissuaded from his preferred course by a convincing argument. At a critical moment in the primaries, Obama was set on campaigning in delegate-rich California. His campaign manager, David Plouffe, argued that Hillary Clinton was going to win the Golden State and Obama should instead campaign in thinly populated Idaho and Utah. The notion seemed counterintuitive, but Obama went off to Boise and Salt Lake City, where he won most of the delegates in two largely uncontested races, while picking up a hefty number of delegates in California anyway because of the Democratic Party's system of proportional representation.

Unlike Bill Clinton, Obama is decisive and doesn't suffer the liability of a stormy temper. Again, dating from his community-organizing days, Obama listens more than he talks — an irony of sorts for a charismatic figure known mostly for his oratory. And that method of listening extensively before acting has served him so well in his South Side Chicago organizing work, his service in the Illinois and U.S. senates, and his stunning success as a relative unknown in capturing the presidency that he will be unlikely to abandon it at 1600 Pennsylvania Avenue.

Obama is deft at seeing both sides of an issue, which

keeps potential critics off base. He told America's most powerful pro-Israel lobby this year that he will do "everything" to prevent Iran from gaining nuclear weapons. Yet he told the same group that "no one in the region has suffered more than the Palestinians." Asked recently what went wrong with the Bush administration, Obama replied, "It's hard to know where to start." Yet Obama has repeatedly praised Bush for America's five-billion-dollar commitment to fighting the spread of AIDS in Africa. Such is the antipathy of neophyte U.S. Senator Jim Webb (D-Va.) for Bush that Webb refused to shake the president's outstretched hand when they first met at a White House gala. By contrast, Obama's best-selling *The Audacity of Hope*, a blueprint of policies very different from Bush's, begins with praise for Bush's sense of humor and level-headed approach to the enormous challenges of the office. In his late-June 2008 speech celebrating the impending Independence Day festivities, Obama told an Independence, Missouri, crowd that "I believe those who attack America's flaws without acknowledging the singular greatness of our ideals, and their proven capacity to inspire a better world, do not truly understand America." Still, three minutes later, Obama was redefining patriotism to include dissent, echoing Henry David Thoreau's *Civil Disobedience*. "When our laws, our leaders, and our government are out of alignment with our ideals," Obama said, "then the dissent of ordinary Americans may prove to be one of the truest expressions of patriotism." Once asked if God took sides in war, Obama reached back to a question Lincoln had asked — namely, if America was on God's side.

Reinventing government to make it more effective is overdue. "We basically have a New Deal government in a 21st-century economy," says Obama, and "We've got to upgrade it." And in a genuine citizens' democracy where the best ideas flow up from communities rather than being imposed by Washington, "Virtual town-hall meetings, increasing transparency, and accountability on legislation," Obama says, will give Americans "the opportunity to hold me accountable when I'm not following through on promises I've made. It gives me a powerful ally if Congress is resistant to measures that need to be taken."

"I want people to feel connected to their government again," Obama told *Rolling Stone*, "and I want that government to respond to the voices of the people, and not just insiders and special interests. That's real change. I want us to think about the long term and not just the short term, whether it's climate change, energy policy, how we're educating our kids, what kind of investments we're making in our infrastructure, how we're dealing with the federal budget and national debt. I want us to think intergenerationally, something we used to do more of and we have lost. I want us to rediscover our bonds to each other and to get out of this constant petty bickering that's come to characterize our politics" and "doesn't solve problems. I want to get beyond that."

The transformation Obama seeks is to make permanent the grassroots movement he created. Ideally, Obama's would be something of a communal presidency — inspiring the sort of populist support not seen since Andrew Jackson's time — in which the chief executive counts heavily on the same everyday Americans he drew into the political process to enact an agenda largely shaped by them.

Obama "is going to demand that you shed your cynicism," Obama's wife, Michelle, told a February 2008 rally in Los Angeles. "Barack Obama will never allow you to go back to your lives as usual, uninvolved and uninformed."

It's this call to national service by every American, more than his eloquence or youth, that is the most relevant of the many comparisons between Obama and John F. Kennedy. But Obama, the son of the former African goat-herder who helped Chicago public-housing residents get asbestos ripped out of their homes, isn't the next Kennedy, whose sense of irony was a winsome intellectual gift but meant he cared about injustice, only not quite enough to do much about it.

Obama is aiming higher than merely to fulfill a patrician family's dream of placing one of its own in the White House. He will have failed in achieving the greatness he seeks for his mandate if he doesn't create a lasting rejuvenation of the world's most powerful democracy. "This campaign has to be about reclaiming the meaning of citizenship, restoring our sense of common purpose, and realizing that few obstacles can withstand the power of millions of voices calling for change," Obama told a crowd of his supporters last year. "That's why I'm in this race. Not just to hold an office, but to gather with you to transform a nation."

Notes

1. Obama has often ventured further out on a political limb than his peers. In the immediate aftermath of the 9/11 attacks, political and media commentary was uniformly patriotic to the point where even raising the question of what America might have done to provoke the tragedy was unacceptable. Illinois state senator Obama, in the obscure *Hyde Park Herald* distributed in his district, at least hinted at geopolitical realities America has ignored at its peril: "Even as I hope for some measure of peace and comfort to the bereaved families, I must also hope that we as a nation draw some measure of wisdom from this tragedy. Certain immediate lessons are clear, and we must act upon those lessons decisively. We need to step up security at our airports. We must re-examine the effectiveness of our intelligence networks. And we must be resolute in identifying the perpetrators of these heinous acts and dismantling their organizations of destruction.

   "We must also engage, however, in the more difficult task of understandng the sources of such madness. The essence of this tragedy, it seems to me, derives from a fundamental absence of empathy on the part of the attackers: an inability to imagine, or connect with, the humanity and suffering of others. Such a failure of empathy, such a numbness to the pain of a child or the desperation of a parent, is not innate; nor, history tells us, is it unique to a particular culture, religion, or ethnicity. It may find expression in a particular brand of violence, and may be channeled by particular demagogues or fanatics. Most often, though, it grows out of a climate of poverty and ignorance, helplessness and despair.

"We will have to make sure, despite our rage, that any U.S. military action takes into account the lives of innocent civilians abroad. We will have to be unwavering in opposing bigotry or discrimination directed against neighbors and friends of Middle Eastern descent. Finally, we will have to devote far more attention to the monumental task of raising the hopes and prospects of embittered children across the globe — children not just in the Middle East, but also in Africa, Asia, Latin America, Eastern Europe, and within our own shores."

BARACK **OBAMA**

on the Major Issues

The following pages describe where Obama stands on most major issues, from health care and the economy to the Iraq war and the U.S. housing crisis. Where available, cost estimates for Obama's campaign proposals are provided. This information is not speculative but is drawn from Obama's speeches, interviews, and official campaign materials.

While every effort has been made to present Obama's positions and proposals with fairness and accuracy, it is to be expected that some policies and proposals will be altered and others added or dropped in the course of Obama's presidency. For instance, Obama has already modified the conditions under which he would speak to foreign leaders, friend or foe.

For detailed descriptions of the president's positions and proposals, visit BarackObama.com and whitehouse.gov.

DOMESTIC POLICY

Abortion

Obama strongly supports *Roe v. Wade* and opposes restrictions on abortion. An exception is certain late-term abortions, but with a further exception to protect the mother's health. Obama cosponsored the Prevention First Act of 2007, to increase funding for family planning and sex education, and to teach both abstinence and safe-sex methods for preventing unintended pregnancy and sexually transmitted diseases. The bill also expanded access to contraception and compassionate assistance to rape victims.

Affordable housing

Obama will increase America's supply of affordable housing, creating an Affordable Housing Trust Fund to develop affordable housing in mixed-income neighborhoods. He will restore cuts made to public-housing operating subsidies.

After-school programs

Obama will double federal funding for after-school programs with successful track records in reducing youth crime and drug use. He will double funding for the 21st Century Community Learning Centers program, making its services available to an additional one million youth.

Campaign finance reform

Obama does not accept campaign funds from lobbyists. The fundraising champ in the 2008 election cycle — by year-end 2008 Obama had raised more than $600 million, a record, mostly in small-dollar donations of twenty-five and one hundred dollars over the Internet — continued to use private funds in the general-election campaign. In the Illinois and U.S. senates, Obama passed legislation restricting or prohibiting politicians from accepting meals, trips on corporate aircraft, and other gifts from lobbyists.

Capital punishment

Obama supports the death penalty. In the Illinois Senate, he secured bipartisan passage of first-in-the-nation videotaping of confessions in murder cases, so that such confessions could be carefully scrutinized in court, after revelations that Illinois had sent thirteen unjustly accused men to death row. Obama has said, "While the evidence tells me that the death penalty does little to deter crime, I believe there are some crimes — mass murder, the rape and murder of a child — so heinous, so beyond the pale, that the community is justified in expressing the full measure of its outrage by meting out the ultimate punishment."

Child support

Obama will increase funds for child-support enforcement by $4.9 billion over ten years, a measure that he believes will collect twenty billion dollars from spouses negligent in their responsibilities.

Crime and civil rights

Obama will strengthen federal hate-crimes legislation, expand hate-crimes protection by passing the Matthew Shepherd Act, and ban racial profiling by federal law-enforcement agencies.

Obama also believes the sentencing disparity between crack and powder-based cocaine possession should be eliminated. He will give first-time nonviolent offenders a chance to serve their sentence, where appropriate, in drug rehabilitation programs that have proven effective in changing self-destructive behavior. Obama will provide job training and substance abuse and mental-health counseling to ex-offenders, to more successfully reintegrate offenders into society. He will also create a prison-to-work incentive program, to enhance ex-offender employment and job retention rates.

Education

In a June 3, 2008, speech, Obama said, "A first-rate education should not be a privilege, but a birthright of every American."

Obama will spend ten billion dollars to increase enrollment and quality at Head Start preschool programs for poor children and to help make preschool available to all children. At the kindergarten to grade 12 level, he will provide incentives for school districts to recruit and keep highly skilled teachers and provide merit pay to the most effective of them. He estimates the cost of that at eight billion dollars.

Obama supports the spirit of President Bush's No Child Left Behind (NCLB) initiative but says "the money was left behind." Obama will overhaul NCLB to broaden its curriculum, retrain teachers to spend more time teaching and less time calculating test scores, and introduce a mentoring system for teachers. He will further adjust NCLB to support failing schools with additional assistance.

To make college and university more affordable, Obama will provide a tuition tax credit of up to four thousand dollars for students who agree to perform one hundred hours of community service. The credit will begin to phase out at household incomes of more than $135,000. Obama estimates the cost of this initiative at ten billion dollars per year. He will also provide funding to make community college tuition-free for most students.

Obama opposes education vouchers for use at private schools, believing they would undermine public schools.

Energy independence, environment, and climate change

Barack Obama pledges to cut U.S. greenhouse gas emissions by 80 percent below 1990 levels by 2050, using a market-based "cap-and-trade system." (Cap-and-trade requires polluters that exceed caps on their carbon dioxide emissions to purchase emission credits from companies that pollute less.)

Obama proposes a ten-year, $150-billion "Apollo-style"

plan to stimulate development of wind, solar, and other climate-friendly energy sources to contribute to America's energy independence, which would be financed by the proceeds of the cap-and-trade system.

Obama wants to reduce U.S. oil consumption by at least 35 percent by 2030, which he states would more than offset America's OPEC imports; to double fuel-efficiency standards for vehicles within eighteen years; to require that 25 percent of electricity be derived from clean, sustainable energy sources; and to make all buildings carbon neutral by 2030, improving new-building energy efficiency 50 percent and existing building efficiency 25 percent over the next decade. Obama also favors a major expansion of high-speed rail service, especially in high-density areas, which he claims would create jobs and be a fuel-efficient alternative to air transport.

In an Obama administration, the U.S. will join the global fight against climate change and reverse the Bush-era rejection of the Kyoto Protocol. Obama will create a Global Energy Forum of the world's biggest energy-consuming nations to tackle the climate change crisis, consisting of the G-8 nations, Brazil, China, India, Mexico, and South Africa.

Obama wants more civilian nuclear power, but only after safety and storage issues have been resolved. A fair description of Obama on energy is that he wants to try everything — clean-coal technology, alternative sources such as wind and solar, biofuels, nuclear, and conservation. "There is no perfect energy source; everything has some problems, right now; we haven't found it yet," he said December 30, 2007. "I have not ruled out nuclear as part of that package, but only so far as it is clean and safe. I have the same attitude with respect to coal. There is no single optimal solution and we have to try everything to see what works."

Family support

Obama will expand the successful Nurse-Family Partnership program that provides home visits by registered nurses to low-income expectant mothers. He will extend the program to all 570,000 low-income first-mothers each year.

Gay rights

Obama supports civil unions but has a personal aversion to same-sex marriage. However, he will defer to the states in deciding to license same-sex marriages and ask states to recognize each others' unions.

He also supports a law banning employment discrimination against gays and lesbians. He will sign the Employment Non-Discrimination Act that prohibits discrimination based on sexual orientation or gender identity or expression. In the July 2007 CNN/YouTube debate, Obama said: "We've got to make sure that everybody is equal under the law. And the civil unions that I proposed would be equivalent in terms of making sure that all the rights that are conferred by the state are equal for same-sex couples as well as for heterosexual couples."

Gun ownership

Obama supports making guns childproof. He will also close the gun-show loophole. He will revive the lapsed assault weapons ban because "such weapons belong on foreign battlefields and not on our streets." He voted to expose gun makers and dealers to civil suits. In the Illinois Senate, he supported a ban on all forms of semiautomatic weapons.

Health-care reform

Obama wants health insurance for all Americans. Insurers will have to sell coverage at affordable rates to anyone who wants insurance, regardless of preexisting medical conditions, even if the buyer is sick at the time of applying to buy the insurance.

He wants to create a marketplace for health-insurance

plans, a new National Health Insurance Exchange, in which families can select among private plans or a new government-run program, which will operate like Medicare and affordably offer the same coverage available to members of the U.S. Congress and other federal employees under the Federal Employees' Health Benefits Program (FEHBP). The program will use subsidies to cover some of the insurance costs for lower-income households and help cover the cost of insurance for patients requiring the most expensive care.

An Obama administration will invest ten billion dollars a year over five years to move the U.S. health-care system from paper records to electronic data-keeping, including patient records. Privacy will be ensured. Obama believes this will improve patient care, partly by reducing errors, as electronic records are easier for caregivers to read and can be shared among a variety of the patient's caregivers in a matter of seconds. Electronic data is also about half as costly to process as the paper records that still dominate record-keeping. The Rand Corporation estimates that the use of electronic health records by most doctors and hospitals would save up to seventy-seven billion dollars per year in reduced hospital stays, avoidance of duplicative and unnecessary patient testing, and more appropriate drug prescribing.

Obama will allow Americans to buy medicines from other developed nations provided the drugs are safe and the prices lower than in the U.S. Obama will also repeal the ban preventing government from negotiating with drug companies for lower prices, which could result in savings as high as thirty billion dollars. (The Veterans' Administration already uses its enormous buying power to negotiate for lower drug prices.) Obama will encourage the use of lower-cost generic drugs in Medicare, Medicaid and the FEHBP. He opposes drug-company efforts to keep lower-cost generics off the market.

Obama estimates his plan would cost about $110 billion.

Homeland security

Obama will strengthen coordination systems among all levels of government, and he will push for better evacuation plans, learning from the lessons of Hurricane Katrina. He will provide greater technical assistance to local and state first responders and greatly increase funding for communications devices and networks able to "talk" with each other, a deficiency that cost lives on 9/11 and in the Hurricane Katrina crisis.

Housing crisis

On the foreclosure crisis, Obama will reduce and federally insure mortgages for homeowners who owe more than their homes are worth. Obama's plan will permit bankruptcy courts to renegotiate mortgage terms to help owners to keep their homes. Obama will commit twenty billion dollars to help prevent foreclosures and damage to hard-hit communities.

Immigration

Obama proposes strengthening border security, and bringing the estimated twelve to thirteen million illegal, or "undocumented," immigrants "out of the shadows." Illegal immigrants would be required to apply to become legal residents after learning English, paying a fine for entering America illegally, paying back taxes, and clearing background checks to ensure the absence of a criminal record. Obama voted for a 2006 bill with these provisions.

Marijuana

Obama opposes legalization of marijuana. He will, however, reduce punishment for those in possession of small quantities in order to ease pressure on the crowded prison system and "the counterproductive sentencing of non-violent offenders." He supports medicinal marijuana if "scientists, doctors, and patients" show it would be the best method of relief of chronic pain for the patient.

Poverty

Obama believes no working family should live in poverty — most of the thirty-seven million Americans below the poverty line are working poor. He will raise the federal minimum wage to $9.50 an hour by 2011 and index it to inflation.

Obama will expand the Earned Income Tax Credit (EITC) by increasing the number of working parents eligible for the benefit. He will increase the benefit for families with three or more children, reduce the EITC marriage penalty, which hurts low-income families, and increase the benefit for noncustodial parents assisted by child-support programs.

Obama will invest one billion dollars over five years in programs that use "transitional" jobs as a pathway to higher-paying jobs for low-income Americans. He will couple this initiative with successful private-sector and state and local programs that boost levels of fulfilling employment.

He will also create twenty Promise Neighborhoods across the nation, in localities with stubborn intergenerational poverty. They will be modeled on successful programs like the Harlem Children's Zone, which provides comprehensive services from birth to college preparation, improving health standards for infants and youth and preparing students for higher levels of academic achievement.

Obama will reform the Child and Dependent Care Tax Credit, which he believes provides too little relief to families struggling with child-care expenses. He will make the credit refundable and allow low-income families to receive up to a 50 percent credit for their child-care expenses.

Social security

Obama adamantly opposes the "reforms" to Social Security proposed by the Bush administration, and he will strengthen it against its looming revenue shortfall, using the same fairly straightforward measures Congress and then-president Ronald Reagan did in the 1980s.

Stem cell research

Obama favors accelerated medical research using stem cells, but with safeguards on the source. The Stem Cell Research Enhancement Act he cosponsored in 2007 permits research using embryonic stem cells but only from embryos donated, with consent, from in vitro clinics, deemed to be in excess, and created specifically for fertility treatment.

Taxes

Obama claims middle- and low-income Americans would pay less tax than they do currently, while upper-income households would pay more. He will eliminate the Alternative Minimum Tax (AMT) for most middle-class taxpayers. He will also eliminate taxes for Americans over sixty-five earning less than fifty thousand dollars per year. Obama will raise the capital-gains tax rate to between 20 and 28 percent.

Obama will expand retirement accounts, such as IRAS, with matching funds from the government. He will give a five-hundred-dollar tax credit to middle-income households earning up to about $150,000. He will provide a 10 percent tax credit — five hundred dollars on average — to mostly lower-income homeowners who don't itemize.

He will also give the Treasury Department the tools it needs to stop the abuse of tax shelters and offshore tax havens, and he will help close the estimated $350-billion gap between taxes owed and paid. Obama will ensure tax fairness for all businesses by eliminating special-interest loopholes and deductions for selected industrial sectors.

Transparency, trust, and bipartisanship

Negotiations on developing a new health-insurance system will be broadcast live on C-SPAN and via webcasting. Obama will require his national security officials to conduct regular Web town-hall meetings, and Obama himself will deliver "fireside chats" via webcast.

He will create an online database of lobbying reports,

campaign-finance filings, and ethics records. He will also create an independent watchdog agency to monitor congressional ethical violations.

Obama will create a Consultative Group on foreign-policy issues consisting of the congressional leadership of both political parties and the chair and ranking members of the Armed Services, Foreign Relations, Intelligence, and Appropriations committees. This group will meet with the president once a month to review foreign-policy priorities. It will also be consulted in advance of military action. To insulate the director of National Intelligence from political pressure, the director will be given a fixed term of office, as is the case with the chairman of the Federal Reserve Board.

Obama will create a National Declassification Center to make declassification of government documents secure but routine, efficient, and cost-effective. He will require more transparency of special-interest "earmark" spending, which amounts to about $18 billion a year, and he would cut earmarks to 2001 levels or below. With bipartisan support, Obama passed a bill creating an electronic system, USAspending.gov, by which Americans can more easily track government spending. Obama will also ensure that government contracts of more than $25,000 are competitively bid.

Military

Obama will seek to expand and strengthen the U.S. Armed Forces, both to recover from the stresses arising from the Iraq and Afghan conflicts and occupations and to restore and further improve the military's ability to accomplish future missions. He will increase the size of ground forces, adding 65,000 soldiers to the U.S. Army and 27,000 U.S. Marines.

Obama will ensure that soldiers and marines have sufficient training time before they are sent into battle. He will provide U.S. troops the new equipment, armor, training, and language skills they require to carry out the increasingly complex missions of the 21st century. Obama will also reinforce America's civilian capacity abroad, aiming to better link civilian and military capabilities during future missions.

He will restore the readiness of the National Guard and U.S. Army Reserves. He will ensure them adequate time to train and rest between deployments and provide the National Guard with better equipment to meet domestic and foreign emergencies. Obama will also recognize the Guard's importance by making the chief of the National Guard a member of the Joint Chiefs of Staff.

Urban affairs

Obama proposes a sixty-billion-dollar ten-year program of urban infrastructure development, stitching together metropolitan areas with new and repaired roads, rail networks, electrical grids, water systems, and telecommunications networks. Obama will appoint the first White House director of urban policy, who will act as an advocate in Washington for America's cities.

Veterans' benefits

Barack Obama describes America's responsibility to veterans as "a sacred trust." He will reverse the 2003 ban on enrolling modest-income Americans who have served in uniform from the VA, which has deprived one million veterans of care. Obama will hire additional claims workers to speed processing and treatment, and he will ensure fairness of claims assessment in dealing with the 400,000 outstanding VA claims and all future claims. With post-traumatic stress disorder (PTSD) reaching epidemic proportions, Obama will upgrade mental-health screening at every stage of military service. He will also recruit more mental-health professionals to ensure PTSD claims are processed faster. He will create higher standards of care for victims of traumatic brain injury (TBI), one of the most prevalent injuries sustained by U.S. forces in Iraq.

Obama will expand the network and staffing of Vet Centers to improve access to and the quality of counseling to veterans and their families. He will create a "zero tolerance" policy for homeless veterans, who now number approximately one hundred thousand Americans, and those in danger of falling into homelessness. He will provide increased support to proven programs that confront the problem and for innovative new services that spare veterans a life on the streets.

In the Illinois Senate and the U.S. Senate, where he served on the Committee on Veterans' Affairs, Obama has a long-established record as a veterans' advocate. He fought for fair treatment of Illinois veterans' claims and forced the VA to conduct its most extensive outreach program ever for disabled veterans with below-average benefits. In the U.S. Senate, Obama passed legislation to improve treatment and cut red tape at Walter Reed and other veterans' hospitals. He also helped pass laws to guard against veterans' homelessness and an amendment to ensure all military personnel returning from Iraq service are properly screened for traumatic brain injuries, and he led a bipartisan effort in the Senate to stop the military's practice of discharging personnel with service-related psychological injury. Obama and U.S. Senator Jim Webb (D-Va.) cosponsored a two-billion-dollar GI Bill that expands education funding for troops, offering more military service personnel the chance to attend college. President Bush and Senator McCain opposed the measure, but in May 2008 it won passage by a vote of 77–22 and was signed into law by Bush.

Women

Obama would pass the Fair Pay Act to ensure women receive equal pay for equal work. He supports measures to end job discrimination, improve access to quality child care, and guarantee workers at least seven days of paid leave to care for a sick child or other family member. Currently, three in five low-wage workers have no paid sick days.

The Violence Against Women Act, cosponsored by Obama and enacted in 2006, funds community, police, and nonprofit activities to combat domestic violence, sexual assault, and stalking. Legislation introduced by Obama will provide twenty-five million dollars annually to fund the training of local marriage and fatherhood groups to prevent domestic violence and counsel its victims.

FOREIGN POLICY

Diplomacy

Obama has restored his U.N. ambassador to a cabinet-level post, reversing George W. Bush's demotion of the position.

Obama advocates a foreign policy that matches military with diplomatic power, and he pledges a "tough diplomacy" in which he will be prepared to meet and listen to the views of world leaders, friend or foe. In dealing with stubborn challenges like Iran's nuclear-weapons ambitions, Obama has said the Bush policy of not talking with adversaries "doesn't make us look tough — it makes us look arrogant." Obama has said he has no reservations about "telling petty dictators where I stand," and that restoring America's diplomatic goodwill with allies and adversaries alike will strengthen America's influence and its economic and military power.

Breaking with the Bush administration's policy by developing high-level engagements with Iran and Syria in a strategy to stabilize the Middle East, Obama is influenced by a core group of advisers who've spent more than a decade, in both Democratic and Republican administrations, seeking diplomatic openings with the two troublesome nations. Obama's philosophy is to "approach the world, and you approach it through engagement: You shore up alliances, and you engage with enemies," said Daniel Kurtzer, a career diplomat who worked on Mideast policy in the George H.W. Bush administration and was U.S. ambassador to Israel from 2001 to 2005, to the *Wall Street Journal* in June. He added "But occasionally you have to hit them, too."

Obama has said that George W. Bush may be president, but "the position of leader of the free world is open." He believes that, while America cannot solve its geopolitical issues alone, neither can the rest of the world solve them without the U.S. He would stop closing U.S. consulates and begin opening new ones in troubled and neglected parts of the world, particularly in Africa and Latin America. He will expand the U.S. Foreign Service and coordinate the efforts of U.S. military and humanitarian workers to create both security and goodwill.

Obama will also open "America Houses" across the Islamic world, which numbers 1.3 billion people, to showcase U.S. culture and show how American Muslims add strength to U.S. society. These facilities will offer libraries, Internet access, and English lessons, host concerts and lectures, and function as cultural exchanges. They are modeled on the Amerika Haus program the U.S. launched in postwar German cities that was so successful that one Amerika Haus is still operating in western Germany, and the flagship Amerika Haus Berlin closed only last year. Obama will also launch America's Voice Corps to recruit, train, and send into the field talented young Americans who can speak with — and listen to — the people who today only hear about America from its enemies.

Obama will embrace the Millennium Goal of cutting extreme poverty worldwide in half by 2015. He will double U.S. foreign assistance to fifty billion dollars to achieve that goal.

Cuba

Obama will maintain the U.S. embargo as leverage to force the release of political prisoners and the emergence of fair elections and free speech. Obama will break with long-standing policy, however, and engage in direct diplomacy with Cuba. He will also allow unlimited family travel and remittances to the island in order to make Cuban families less reliant on the Castro regime. Obama has said, "bilateral talks would be the best means of promoting Cuban freedom."

As with Iraq and North Korea, Cuba's regard for the U.S., shaped by Fidel Castro and now his brother Raul Castro, has been primarily influenced by a U.S. antipathy that has manifested itself in several covert U.S. attempts to overthrow and even assassinate the Castros. Given the long track record of U.S. interventions in the affairs of Latin American governments, including U.S.-influenced regime changes in Guatemala (1954), Chile (1973), Grenada (1983), and Panama (1989), it would be fair to say that Cuba's foreign policy is grounded in fear of the U.S. By reaching out through open diplomatic channels, Obama hopes to quash this fear and promote Cuba's democratization.

Darfur

Obama believes the U.S. needs to lead a world effort in ending the Darfur genocide. He will apply much tougher sanctions against the Sudanese oil revenues that fund it, and he will lead an international mission to establish and enforce a no-fly zone to protect the internationally displaced people in Darfur from Sudanese government bombings. He will also negotiate with the United Nations to increase the UN-led and UN-funded force, and provide additional U.S. funding and technological assistance to stop the killings.

Obama has been among the leading voices in Congress urging the Bush administration to take stronger measures to end the genocide in Sudan. He worked with U.S. Senator Sam Brownback (R-Kans.) to pass the Darfur Peace and

Accountability Act and with Senator Harry Reid (D-Nev.) to secure twenty million dollars for the joint UN and African Union peacekeeping mission. Obama visited displaced person camps on the Chad-Sudan border to raise awareness of the humanitarian disaster there.

Iran

Obama will not take any military options off the table in preventing Iran from obtaining nuclear weapons, which he believes could trigger a nuclear-arms race in the Middle East. Obama favors tough, direct presidential diplomacy with Iran. He has pledged that if Iran gives up its nuclear ambitions, ends its sponsorship of Hezbollah and Hamas terrorism against Israel, and stops meddling in Iraq, then the U.S. would offer it incentives, including membership in the World Trade Organization (WTO), investments in its economy, and a normalization of U.S.-Iran diplomatic relations, suspended since the ouster of the Shah of Iran in 1979. However, if Iran continues its troubling behavior, the Obama administration will step up economic pressure on Tehran and political isolation from the U.S. and the community of nations.

Interviewed on *Meet the Press* in 2006, Obama said: "I think that military options have to be on the table when you're dealing with rogue states that have shown constant hostility towards the United States. The point that I would make, though, is that we have not explored all of our options. . . . We have not explored any kind of dialogue with either Iran or North Korea, and I think that has been a mistake. As a consequence, we have almost no leverage over them." (In 2007, the Bush administration finally deployed a U.S. State Department envoy to negotiate with North Korea, having for years relied upon China, South Korea, Japan, and other regional neighbors to dissuade Pyongyang from pursuing its nuclear-weapons program, during which time North Korea developed several nuclear weapons and even tested one to signal it had joined the "nuclear club." It was State

Department intervention that resulted in an agreement that North Korea would not develop any further weapons. North Korean strongman Kim Jung-Il and his top officials had indicated from the early days of the Bush administration that, more than anything, they sought a meeting with the U.S., not other nations. They were almost certainly seeking reassurance that the U.S. did not aim to topple their government, which Bush had labeled in his 2002 state of the union address as a member of an "axis of evil," along with Iraq and Iran. A year later, the U.S. invaded its first "axis of evil" country, prompting both North Korea and Iran to step up their nuclear programs.)

Obama described his strategy at a March 2, 2007, meeting of the American Israel Public Affairs Committee (AIPAC) as "direct engagement with Iran similar to the meetings we conducted with the Soviets at the height of the Cold War."

Iraq

Obama publicly opposed the looming Iraq invasion in October 2002, five months before it took place. As president he will remove U.S. combat brigades from Iraq until all are home by 2010, believing only U.S. military withdrawal will force Iraqis to govern themselves. He will, however, leave behind what he describes as an "over-the-horizon" force to attack any bases that al Qaeda attempts to build (the al Qaeda that struck America on September 11, 2001, not the upstart "al Qaeda in Iraq," which is a separate terrorist group that sprung up in Iraq after the invasion), to continue training Iraqi forces, to protect U.S. assets including the U.S. embassy (the Green Zone), and to maintain regional stability. He will redeploy at least two combat brigades to Afghanistan to rout al Qaeda and its Taliban sponsors from their sanctuaries in the Afghan–Pakistan border region.

Obama agrees with General David Petraeus, charged with executing President Bush's "surge" of thirty thousand additional troops announced in January 2007, who warned in his winter 2008 congressional testimony that one year after the surge forces were completely in place, Iraq was no closer to governing itself. Petraeus reported there had been no progress on ethnic reconciliation, the creation of a federated government that commands respect across the ethnically balkanized country, or an oil-revenue-sharing agreement among the main Shia, Sunni, and Kurdish ethnic factions.

Obama will not retain any U.S. forces, and certainly no permanent bases, in Iraq, believing a U.S. presence is a needless provocation to even moderate Muslims worldwide, who bristle at the foreign occupation of a Muslim nation. (It was the presence of U.S. military bases in Saudi Arabia during the Gulf War of 1990–91 that Osama bin Laden cited as his rationale for 9/11 and earlier al Qaeda attacks on U.S. assets in the 1990s.)

During the withdrawal phase, Barack Obama will lead a "diplomatic surge" he describes as one of the most aggressive diplomatic efforts in modern American history. He will meet with Iraqis at every level of society and attempt to draw neighboring Syria and Iran into the task of stabilizing Iraq, asking that they support Iraqi ethnic reconciliation and provide financial aid for Iraq's reconstruction. Obama believes Damascus and Tehran see their own best interests served by an Iraq that does not descend into chaos, given that Syria and Jordan already are coping with roughly two million Iraqi refugees living in tent cities.

Obama will also seek a United Nations role in pressuring Iraqi political and ethnic factions to agree on nation-building steps, including ethnic reconciliation, the creation of a stable federal government, and an oil-revenue-sharing agreement that satisfies the main ethnic groups — with the UN remaining in Iraq until those objectives have been achieved.

While Obama opposed the invasion, he has voted for additional U.S. Senate supplemental funding bills, rather than joining Senate colleagues who sought to end U.S. involvement by starving it of funding — which brought an end to the U.S. role in Vietnam in the mid-1970s. In March 2007, Obama explained his position: "Once we were in, we were going to have some responsibility to try to make it work as best we can." He has said the U.S. has "a moral and a security responsibility" to help alleviate Iraq's humanitarian crisis, and that he would commit two billion dollars to assist Iraqi refugees in neighboring countries and the additional two million internally displaced Iraqis who have been victims of ethnic cleansing.

In its broad outlines, Obama's Iraq strategy aligns with the findings of the bipartisan Iraq Study Group (also known as the Baker-Hamilton Commission), whose December 2006 recommendations were rejected by President Bush in favor of the 2007 surge. Robert Gates, Bush's last defense secretary, was a member of that commission. Obama has nominated Gates to remain as his defense secretary.

Israel and the Palestinian territories

Obama believes America's first commitment in the Middle East is to ensure the security of Israel. He has consistently supported U.S. financial and military-technology aid to Israel and its right to protect its citizens. In the July 2006 Lebanon conflict, when many world leaders were calling for an Israeli cease-fire, Obama insisted Israel should not be pressured into a cease-fire that failed to deal with Hezbollah raids and rocket attacks. He regards both Hezbollah and Hamas, which won control of the Palestinian interim government, as terrorist groups.

Obama denounced former U.S. President Jimmy Carter for meeting with Hamas. And in a June 4, 2008, address, Obama told the American Israel Public Affairs Committee (AIPAC) that "Jerusalem will remain the capital of Israel, and it must remain undivided." Obama later allowed that negotiating a two-state settlement with a widely anticipated one-city-two-capitals formula "will be difficult." But he maintained his commitment to a significant American role in negotiating such a settlement.

At a policy forum in June 2007, Obama said a two-state resolution is "going to require some soul-searching on the Palestinian side. They have to recognize Israel's right to exist; they have to renounce violence and terrorism as a tool to achieve their political ends; they have to abide by agreements. In that context, I think the Israelis will gladly say, 'Let's move forward negotiations that would allow them to live side by side with the Palestinians in peace and security.'"

Latin America

Obama will revive FDR's "Good Neighbor" policy, which sought to advance America's economic and national-security interests by promoting economic growth and political stability south of the Rio Grande. He believes the Bush years have been marked by neglect of the region.

Obama is troubled by the rise of Hugo Chavez, whose "checkbook diplomacy" has made Bolivia and, to a lesser extent, Ecuador more closely allied with Venezuela's radical agenda. Even more worrisome, Obama believes, is the recent de facto undermining of the Monroe Doctrine, which prohibits outside influence in the Western Hemisphere. "While the United States fails to address the changing realities in the Americas," Obama told a Miami audience in May 2008, "others from Europe and Asia — notably China — have stepped up their own engagement. Iran has drawn closer to Venezuela, and just the other day Tehran and Caracas launched a joint bank with their windfall oil profits."

In Mexico, Obama will encourage more investment in drug prevention, community policing, and an independent judiciary. In the Central American drug offensive, he will increase resources to fight drug trafficking measured against benchmarks of drug seizures, corruption prosecutions, crime reduction, and captured traffickers in each country.

In order to avoid what he calls "the globalization of the empty stomach," Obama will increase U.S. financial aid to Latin American nations and embrace the Millennium Goals of cutting global poverty in half by 2015. U.S. aid would be targeted to "bottom-up" growth, that is, to small enterprise development, micro-financing, and vocational training.

To help ensure Latin America's energy security and environmental protection, especially of the rain-forest regions and other ecologically sensitive areas, Obama will increase U.S. funds for research into clean-coal technology, biofuels, and wind and solar energy. He will enlist the joint support of the Organization of American States (OAS), the Inter-American Development Bank, and the World Bank in those initiatives. The U.S. itself will create an Energy Corps of engineers and scientists to assist nations in the region to develop clean energy alternatives to traditional fossil fuels.

To highlight its increased interest in Latin America, the U.S. will open more consulates in "neglected regions of the Americas" and reinstate the Special Envoy for the Americas.

Nuclear weapons

While Obama will maintain a U.S. nuclear-weapons deterrent as long as any nuclear weapons exist, he would begin to move the world "down the long road" toward eliminating nuclear weapons. In addition to halting the development of new U.S. nuclear weapons, he will work with Russia to take American and Russian ballistic missiles off hair-trigger alert. He will also seek major reductions in both U.S. and Russian stockpiles of nuclear weapons and material.

Obama has vowed to secure all "loose," or unaccounted-for, nuclear materials in the world within four years. While doing so, he will negotiate a verifiable global ban on the production of new nuclear-weapons material, denying terrorists the ability to buy or steal nuclear materials. To further curb nuclear proliferation, Obama will strengthen the Nuclear

Non-Proliferation Treaty, so that nations with nuclear ambitions, such as Iran and North Korea, would automatically face severe international sanctions, with the ultimate goal of "a world without nuclear weapons."

Obama will create an international "bank" to store civilian nuclear-power fuel and materials, from which Iran and other nations could draw under supervised conditions. This would remove any nation's excuse for importing weapons-grade materials from the black market or allies — determining the sincerity of Iran, for instance, in its occasional insistence that it seeks nuclear materials for civilian uses only.

Torture

Obama believes torturing suspected enemies of the U.S. is unacceptable under U.S. and international law and an ineffective means of obtaining "actionable," that is, accurate and useful, intelligence.

Trade

Obama has called for a virtual moratorium on new trade agreements. He opposed the Central America Free Trade Agreement (CAFTA) for its lack of labor and environmental standards, but he supported the Peru Free Trade Agreement, which did have such standards. His campaign says he is committed to renegotiating the North American Free Trade Agreement (NAFTA) to ensure enforcement of those standards. Obama opposes pending free-trade deals with Colombia, South Korea, and Panama.

MICHELLE **OBAMA**

The Achiever

She is one of the youngest first ladies since Jacqueline Kennedy, and the first African-American to hold the post. But what makes Michelle Obama remarkable is how she transcended the low expectations set for women and blacks to become an Ivy League–educated lawyer and hospital executive, while clinging to the values of her working-class upbringing: candor about life's hard truths and the overarching importance of family.

In the early laps of the U.S. presidential campaign in 2007, Michelle Obama made her way to the front of a small, crowded hall in a town in all-white New Hampshire. She was soft-spoken at first, praising accomplishments of the local community, then she grew intense, condemning the scourge of deadbeat dads and a society that still pays women scarcely more than seventy cents for every dollar a man earns for the same work. She talked about the "juggling act" for modern mothers, both those who work outside the home and those who don't. She described a network of women relatives and friends without whom her own life would be impossible. "Thank God for Grandma!" Michelle said, gesturing to her mother, Marian Robinson, seventy-one, who was sitting in a row close to the front, and often accompanies Michelle on the campaign trail. Last year Marian quit her job at a Chicago bank to help care for the Obama children, Malia, ten, and Natasha, or "Sasha," seven.

Michelle leaned over the podium for emphasis, her long arms outstretched and hands curved toward the audience, as if to embrace it. "I don't know how you do it. How do you cope?" The room was filled with nodding heads, the occasional hushed "She gets it" and not infrequent laughter, especially when the potential First Lady held out Barack Obama as an example of a man who could do a little more work around the house. "I mean, I love Barack. He's got my back, you know. And he's a gifted man, but in the end, he's just a man." Twenty minutes into her talk, Michelle Obama qualified for membership in the local women's group sponsoring the event, so strongly had she bonded with these folks.

Early on, Obama campaign strategists thought Michelle would connect with African-American audiences. That constraint was quickly abandoned. In a high-school gym in Pennsylvania last spring, by which point Michelle's audiences were electrified because Obama's campaign was in the lead, she made the obligatory thank yous to the organizers then settled the mostly white crowd with an almost whispered, "Now let's talk." The cavernous gym fell silent, the students anticipating a candid, intimate chat with a woman poised to become the first descendant of slaves to be first lady. She talked about college tuition rates that have become unaffordable, a job market where the best-paying work has been outsourced abroad, and how living expenses — for everything from health care to gasoline — have spiraled out of control. Her voice rising without losing any of its authority, she demanded to know why our politics seem powerless to help the many Americans trying to make ends meet. She had been interrupted by waves of applause even before getting to her main point: young people are going to be the generation that reclaims the American Dream.

At a giant outdoor rally in California last spring, Michelle's buoyant side was on display. As emcee, Michelle introduced a parade of celebrity endorsers of her absent husband's candidacy, including fellow Chicagoan Oprah Winfrey and Maria Shriver, the extended Kennedy family member and wife of the state's (Republican) governor, Arnold Schwarzenegger. Michelle is particularly comfortable with crowds. Before this jubilant audience of thousands of "Obamaniacs," Michelle was an exuberant cheerleader, exhorting supporters to sing and sway with her to the music.

Michelle generally gives a forty-five-minute "stump speech" she writes herself and delivers without notes. It covers the gamut of issues from Middle-East diplomacy and national and energy security to shortcomings in education policy and health-care reform. Michelle has called her husband "the fact guy" for his polymath curiosity, but Michelle herself easily summons detailed data on an astonishing breadth of topics to make her points. What she does not do at public events is play either the race or gender cards. She connects with people on issues and anxieties, not the "identity politics" of ethnic, religious, or income-group affiliation that have been a divisive force in U.S. politics since the 1960s.

Campaigning in the South Carolina primary in January — the first big test of whether Barack Obama could win the votes of African-Americans who came into 2008 still believing America wasn't ready to elect a black president — Michelle rejected the obvious ploy of exploiting black victimhood, long a staple of African-American politics. At a small Methodist church in Orangeburg, South Carolina, where the largely African-American audience invited her to enumerate black injustices ("Tell it like it is, sister!"), Michelle was indignant about the economic suffering of the working class, crumbling schools, the corrosive effect of gangs and drugs on inner-city neighborhoods. But then she said, "What we have to understand in this race is that this is true regardless of the color of your skin, regardless of your gender. This is the truth about living in America."

When it was first brought to Michelle Obama's attention that she was a rival to her husband as a public speaker, her response was "Why's everybody surprised?" Well, it was a surprise to those who don't know the Obamas. Michelle has no formal speech training. She's neither a veteran pol (as late as August she was reiterating to a *People* magazine reporter her distaste for conventional party politics), nor a national figure steeped in the arcana of every corner of the nation. But for Michelle the compliment stung. No less a social-justice advocate than her husband, she is a Princeton University graduate cum laude in sociology, and she landed a job handling intellectual-property law at the top-drawer Chicago firm of Sidley Austin after graduating from Harvard Law School, also Barack Obama's alma mater.

Later, as an assistant to the deputy chief of staff to Chicago Mayor Richard Daley, Michelle was notably efficient in expediting solutions to problems brought to her by city businesses. She was then recruited to start from scratch the Chicago branch of Public Allies, which finds paid internships at nonprofit groups for young adults from diverse backgrounds. Michelle scouted widely for young potential leaders, including visits to Cabrini-Green, the notorious public-housing project so violent and dilapidated that it has since been largely demolished. One of her recruits, an alienated Mexican immigrant named José A. Rico, worked with Michelle at her insistence on his improbable dream of launching a Latino high school. Today, Rico is president and cofounder of Chicago's Multicultural Arts High School. Finally, as vice president for community and external affairs at the University of Chicago Hospitals — a post from which she is on leave during the Obama campaign — Michelle has taken on both an entrenched U of C bureaucracy and hardened attitudes among the school's low-income neighbors, who've long believed U of C willfully isolates itself from the surrounding community. To local acclaim, Michelle opened more neighborhood health clinics with a focus on preventive care to relieve the strain on the hospital's emergency ward. And her revisions to the hospital's contracting practices directed so much business to suppliers owned by women and minorities that University of Chicago earned awards for enlightened community engagement.

After a career negotiating with every kind of intellect and malcontent and a home life spent with a walking encyclopedia, had she come this far with her skills still in doubt? At Princeton, where Michelle was one of ninety-four African-American frosh in a class of more than 1,100, her white roommate's mother badgered school officials for months to get her daughter a white roommate. Her guidance counselors at the Whitney M. Young Magnet High School — one of the best schools in Chicago's public system, where Michelle consistently made the honor roll — had tried to talk her out of applying to Princeton and subjecting herself to the rigors of an Ivy League school. And her advisers at Princeton tried to dissuade her from Harvard Law. "What minority communities go through still represents the challenges, the legacies, of oppression and racism," Michelle told the *New Yorker* in March. "You know, when you have cultures that feel like second-class citizens at some level . . . there's this natural feeling within the community that we're not good enough . . . we can't be as smart or prepared — and it's that internal struggle that is always the battle."

At all costs, the Obama campaign was determined that Barack Obama not become "the black candidate" for president. The media largely cooperated, instead debating whether Obama was the first "post-racial" presidential prospect. But for Michelle, race is central to the contest, even if she's careful not to share that view at campaign events. "One of the things I hope happens through our involvement in this campaign," she told the *Chicago Tribune* last year, "is that this country and this world sees yet another image of what it means to be black."

In contrast with her husband, the self-confessed "hope-monger," there is an African-American fatalism to Michelle Obama, a sense that hard-won gains must be fought for over and over. Barack Obama captured this vulnerability in his 2006 book, *The Audacity of Hope*. He wrote of Michelle that there was "a glimmer that danced across her round, dark eyes whenever I looked at her, the slightest hint of uncertainty, as if, deep inside, she knew how fragile things really were, and that if she ever let go, even for a moment, all her plans might quickly unravel."

Barack Obama did not grow up in the racial cauldron of Chicago (or Boston, Philly, or South Central L.A.), but in Hawaii, America's most multicultural state. Obama did not encounter severe racism until venturing to the U.S. mainland in his late teens. The polyglot milieu of Honolulu and his four years in Jakarta to this day make Barack Obama not merely frustrated but on some level mystified by the staying power of America's original sin. It's a world view that life-long Chicago resident Michelle has only gradually absorbed.

The couple first met in 1989, when Obama was a summer intern at a prestigious Chicago law firm now known as Sidley Austin, and Michelle was assigned to be his mentor. Michelle thought colleagues had too much praise for Obama's good looks and outstanding first-year marks at Harvard Law. Here comes another skirt-chaser, Michelle believed — the sort of man, as her brother Craig recalled, that Michelle so routinely "fired" that the Robinson family began to wonder if Michelle, two years Craig's junior and his only sibling, would ever marry. Yet, "later I was just shocked to find out that he really could communicate with people," Michelle told Obama biographer David Mendell, "and that he had some depth to him. He turned out to be an elite individual with strong moral values."

Michelle and Craig were raised in a rented four-room bungalow in the South Shore district of Chicago's mostly African-American South Side. It would be an exaggeration to say Michelle was looking for her father in a mate, but Craig Robinson did once warn her that no beau was going to measure up to Fraser Robinson. Michelle's affection for her father was so strong that she would curl up in his lap even as an adult. Despite a decades' long disability thought to be multiple sclerosis (though it was never formally diagnosed), Robinson seldom missed a day's work running the boilers at the city's water filtration plant. Nor did he miss time with his children even as his health deteriorated.

Robinson's paycheck carried the family and helped finance, along with summer jobs, scholarships, and student loans, the Ivy League education of both Craig and Michelle. Their mother, Marian, did not take a job outside the home until Michelle entered high school, becoming an administrative assistant in the trust department of a Chicago bank.

The home life of the Robinson children revolved around reading, athletics, chess matches, Chinese checkers, and a dinnertime ritual of debating current affairs. TV viewing was limited to one hour a night. Marian Robinson advised Craig and Michelle to challenge the views of authority figures about which they were skeptical, including those expressed by herself and their father. Both parents insisted that only by accepting the low ambitions that others might impose on them would Craig and Michelle be held back from whatever they wanted to do with their lives. Fraser attached so much importance to education that when Craig was attracted to the basketball program of a state college, Fraser insisted he apply to Princeton with the family helping cover the expense. Craig became one of the top basketball players in Ivy League history; this year he was appointed head coach of men's basketball at Oregon State, after having held that post at Brown University.

"My parents told us time and again, 'Don't tell us what you can't do,'" Michelle said in a *New York Times* interview. "'And don't worry about what can go wrong.'" Michelle told an Atlanta audience early this year that, "I realized that gnawing sense of self-doubt that lies within all of us is within our own heads. The truth is we are more ready and more prepared than we even know. My own life is proof of that."

Michelle offered Obama the family stability he had never experienced. With an often-absent mother and a father who had abandoned him at age two to return to Kenya — and whom Barack would meet just once, briefly and unhappily, at age ten — Obama was given to describing himself, without self-pity, as "an orphan." Obama had taken readily to Fraser Robinson, who died in 1992. Of Robinson, Obama wrote in his 1995 memoir, *Dreams from My Father*, he was "as good and decent a man as I've ever known." Barack describes his brother-in-law Craig as "simply one of the finest men anyone could know." While Craig didn't work on the Obama campaign, he felt its every twitch. "It's much harder watching Barack in this race than watching my own team," he told the *New York Times* in February 2008. "It's much harder to watch someone you love go through a close game."

Barack Obama didn't show much promise as boyfriend material when Michelle finally consented to a lunch date with her Sidley Austin protégé. He was a smooth talker in an ill-fitting sport jacket and with an ever-present cigarette perched on his lips. Obama was smitten immediately, but Michelle's initial reaction was that this Hawaiian emigré was "nerdy, strange, off-putting." While she did find him "cute," Michelle hesitated over Obama's unusual name, skinny frame, and big ears. She thought it unprofessional to date a protégé and "tacky" for the only two African-Americans at the firm to be dating. Michelle tried to set Obama up with a couple of her girlfriends, but he was interested only in her. Obama understood what he was up against. In *Dreams from My Father*, published three years after his marriage, Obama wrote that Michelle still wondered if her new husband was too influenced by the carefree ways of his maternal grandfather and father. "She doesn't always know what to make of me," Obama wrote. "She worries that, like Gramps and the Old Man, I am something of a dreamer."

So it was to be a cautious four-year courtship. It helped that, for once, the statuesque, five-foot-eleven Michelle was not looking down at her date. (Obama is six foot two.) The penny finally dropped for Michelle when Obama took her to revisit one of his old haunts as a community organizer, in a gritty corner of the South Side. She was impressed as he listened carefully to the stories of the public-housing residents. He then gave an impassioned talk reminding them of what they had already achieved after years of near-resignation, thus proving themselves capable of the challenges ahead.

One night at Gordon, a posh restaurant on Chicago's Clark Street, Obama was indulging his annoying habit of itemizing the overrated merits of marriage. Michelle had finally heard enough. It was time, she said, for Obama to get serious about this relationship. Soon dessert arrived along with a box containing an engagement ring. "That kind of shuts you up, doesn't it?" Obama said. Michelle now can't remember what the accompanying dessert was. "I was so shocked and a little embarrassed because he did shut me up."

Michelle LaVaughn Robinson and Barack Hussein Obama were married in 1992 in the sanctuary of Chicago's Trinity United Church of Christ by its pastor, Reverend Jeremiah Wright Jr. It was Wright's mission of social justice, particularly in Africa, that had first attracted Obama to Trinity United and, ultimately, in his late twenties, to Christ. (Obama's childhood was spent in a secular home in Hawaii, and as a young adult he shared his parents' aversion to organized religion.)

The chief source of friction in the Obamas' marriage would be Barack's long absences in Springfield, the Illinois state capital, during his eight years as a state senator. In *The Audacity of Hope*, Obama writes that Michelle told him more than once, "I never thought I'd have to raise a family alone." In his thirties Obama was a workaholic. In 1992 alone, he ran a successful voter-registration drive that helped Bill Clinton carry Illinois in that year's presidential contest and send the nation's second elected African-American to the U.S. Senate (Carol Mosely Braun), even as he was burning the midnight oil drafting his 400-page memoir.

Obama has repeatedly cited his tendency to overdrive as a major personal failing, although friends find him more relaxed and convivial in his forties. "There are times when I want to do everything and be everything," Obama told David Mendell, a *Chicago Tribune* reporter who covered Obama's career in state politics. "I want to have time to read and swim with my kids and not disappoint my voters and do a really careful job on each and every thing that I do. And that can get me into trouble." For her part, Michelle described how Obama's order of priorities left her as the heavy lifter at home. She had already experienced the "mommy track" phenomenon. Michelle was overqualified for her University of Chicago Hospitals post, but she stepped a few rungs down the career ladder to be closer to her young children. The Obamas' home was only a few blocks from the hospital. "What I notice about men, all men, is that their order is me, my family, God is in there somewhere, but 'me' is first," she told Mendell. "And for women, 'me' is fourth, and that's not healthy."

Yet Michelle had held out, after all, for a partner of intellectual substance and ambition. She gave her husband the green light when he told her he wanted to give up his civil-rights law practice for a political career. Michelle told him he would "be great at it. You are everything people say they want in their public officials." Ten years later, the Obama presidential campaign put out the story that in discussing a bid for the White House, Michelle imposed only one condition, that Barack finally quit smoking. The smoking edict is true: Obama now has a Nicorette habit. The Obamas' older daughter, Malia, is asthmatic, and Michelle had been trying for years to get her husband to give up cigarettes, though he never smoked in the presence of Michelle or the children. "To me it's a role model thing," Michelle said. "You can smoke or you can be president."[1]

But Michelle also needed assurance that the unlikely presidential bid of a first-term U.S. senator was at least halfway realistic. Before giving her blessing to what would be a joint venture of the entire Obama family, Michelle — no slouch at organizing herself — demanded to see a convincing campaign blueprint. And she attended all of the late-2006 strategy meetings for taking on Hillary Clinton, who was the prohibitive favorite to win the Democratic presidential nomination, right up until Obama's upset January 3, 2008, victory in the lead-off Iowa caucuses, where he established a delegate lead he would retain for the balance of the race. Michelle's nickname in the campaign was "The Closer," for her ability to persuade undecided voters to sign Obama pledge cards.

Michelle's one significant campaign gaffe was to tell a rally in Wisconsin in February 2008 that "For the first time in my adult lifetime, I am really proud of my country, and not just because Barack has done well, but because I think people are hungry for change." It was a slip of which adversaries would make copious use. Could it be that only now was this privileged forty-four-year-old product of America's finest schools, who pulled down a $316,962 salary at University of Chicago Hospitals in 2005, proud of her country? Cindy McCain, wife of presumptive Republican presidential nominee John McCain, soon made a point of saying she had always been proud of America, as did ordinary Americans recruited for a Republican TV ad campaign.

And there was, even among more generous observers, a feeling that Michelle conveyed a sense of entitlement. In the early phase of the campaign, some voters were put off by Michelle's description of her husband as a once-in-a-lifetime opportunity for America to find its bearings, and by her statements that they should be grateful she was willing to share him with 303 million Americans. "The man . . . who I am willing to sacrifice," Michelle called her husband at an Iowa event. In Harlem, it was "I am married to the solution" to America's problems. "There is a hectoring, buy-one-while-supplies-last quality to Obama's frequent admonitions that Americans will have only one chance to elect her husband President," Lauren Collins wrote in a March 2008 profile of Michelle in the *New Yorker.* "Someone who has spent a good portion of her life gaining purchase has suddenly been asked to sell something, and she seemed to find it slightly beneath her."[2]

After Hillary Clinton was eased from the scene, with an assist from her own perceived sense of entitlement and a not infrequently misogynist media ("Where's her broom?" was the terribly original line of one right-wing radio talker), Michelle Obama became the new target in what *New York Times* columnist Maureen Dowd called the "sulphurous national game of Kill the Witch." Conservative columnist Michelle Malkin branded Michelle Obama her husband's "bitter half." The right-wing *National Review* tagged Michelle as "Mrs. Grievance." And on the June night that Obama clinched the Democratic presidential nomination, Michelle gave her husband a thumbs-up and a "fist bump" — a light victory punch on the knuckles indulged in by the likes of Tiger Woods, Prince Charles, and even the Dalai Lama. A Fox News commentator labeled the gesture a "terrorist fist jab," necessitating the first of back-to-back apologies by the network. (It later ran a "crawl" at the bottom of the screen during a panel discussion on Michelle Obama that read, "Outraged liberals: Stop picking on Obama's baby mama," baby mama being slang for unwed mother.)

But to resonate, even the silliest attacks need something tangible to feed on. As it happened, a video clip of Barack Obama appearing to refuse to place his hand over his heart during a group recital of the Pledge of Allegiance was making the rounds. And while many of his Democratic rivals and the prominent TV news anchors who moderated the two dozen or so candidates' debates didn't wear a U.S. flag pin, Obama alone had offered an explanation for why he did not do so, which made his decision an issue. Obama had removed the pin he had been wearing since the terrorist attacks of September 11, 2001, when its appearance on the lapels of politicians who had acted to slash veterans' benefits struck him as a symbol of false patriotism. And there was the fact that in late 2006, when calls for Obama to run for the presidency had reached fever pitch, he told interviewers that his misgivings included the sacrifice of "giving every bit of yourself to your country for four or eight years."

Meanwhile, Michelle, a confessed unenthusiastic voter in the past, was obviously reluctant to embrace the rituals of conventional party politics, even if she was raised in a Democratic household. (Fraser Robinson was a longtime Democratic precinct captain.) Michelle often said she would have given more full-throated support to Obama's fast-track political ambitions if he'd been a neighbor and not the father of her children. In a March 2007 interview with Associated Press reporter Eric Tucker, Michelle explained, "I'm one of the skeptics Barack often talks about. Like most people my view about politics — and it has evolved, but it had been — that politics is for dirty, nasty people who aren't trying to do much in the world. I think I had become cynical like many people."

The Obamas pointedly did not move to DC after Obama's 2004 U.S. Senate victory, which kept him grounded not only in his family but real-life community issues during his weekly commutes back to Chicago. Michelle is keenly aware that her husband attracts more than his share of attention from female admirers and political groupies, and she gives him a sharp stare when a conversation with a female stranger has gone on long enough. An epiphany of sorts was a warning from a friend of Michelle's who had overheard two young women excitedly talking about Obama at his health club: "Let's go down and see Barack Obama work out," one of the women said to the other. Michelle's friend Valerie Jarrett, who had hired her at Richard Daley's office and is now an Obama administration official, told Obama biographer David Mendell how Michelle has dealt with marriage to a political celebrity. "He knows that if he messes up, she'll leave him," Jarrett said. "You know, she'll kill him first — and then she'll leave him. And I think there is a subtle element of fear on his part, which is good."

While she leaves the campaign combat to the warriors, Michelle does indeed have a sense of grievance. She rejects the conventional wisdom that the slight narrowing of the gap between rich and poor during the economic boom of the Clinton era, since reversed under President Bush, did anything to relieve the suffering of the millions of Americans in poverty — even as mediocre corporate CEOs are collecting millions of dollars in pay and pocketing severance packages north of a hundred million dollars when they're fired for incompetence. "The life that I'm talking about that most people are living has gotten progressively worse since I was a little girl," Obama told the *New Yorker* in March 2008, "so if you want to pretend like there was some point over the last couple of decades when your lives were easy, I want to hear from you!"

It's fitting that American universities and colleges long ago appropriated "Land of Hope and Glory" from British composer Edward Elgar's *Pomp and Circumstance* for their commencement send-off rituals. Hope has always been the great elixir of the American condition, and the belief that tomorrow can be a better day is central to Barack Obama's message. But Michelle, whose default facial expression is a frown, has some facts on her side in her comparatively "downer" stump speeches. Real incomes of America's working and middle classes have stagnated over the past two decades. The number of poor people in America is a record thirty-seven million — almost nine million of whom are children, and one hundred thousand of whom are homeless military veterans. There were about thirty-two million Americans without health-care coverage when Bill Clinton first came to office. That number is now forty-seven million. At a New York City fundraiser in the summer of 2008, Michelle talked about the challenge of moving from "the way things are" to "the way things should be." To judge from her speeches, Michelle prefers to dwell on the former, knowing her husband, the erstwhile dreamer, is best suited to convincing voters that a path can be plotted to the latter.

As the 2008 primaries progressed, Michelle eased off her efforts to depict her husband as a regular guy, with putdowns of his housekeeping skills and how he could be a "snorey and stinky" cuddling companion. It was beginning to seem as though no previous would-be presidential spouse had gone to such lengths to publicly find fault with a partner. It was a hard habit to break. "He's one of the few men I've met who is not intimidated by strong women," Michelle told the *Chicago Tribune* in April 2007, perhaps unmindful of President George W. Bush's close working relationship with Condoleezza Rice, his first national security adviser and later his secretary of state. "He relishes the fact that I'm not impressed by him." It's true Obama often cites Michelle's useful role in keeping his head from swelling — "I'm an imperfect man, as my wife will tell you," he often says — but the image of an aspiring Commander-in-Chief who doesn't impress his own wife might not sit well with Americans. Barack Obama's conciliatory manner already had inspired *New York Times* columnist Maureen Dowd to stick Obama with the moniker "Obambi."

Neither did Michelle choose to master the adoring gaze of the political spouse on the campaign trail, preferring to introduce her husband and then make an abrupt getaway with the girls to visit a local museum or zoo rather than stare, apparently spellbound, at her husband as he delivered the same speech for the fifth time that day. Michelle has kept audiences waiting with phone calls to her "little people," Malia and Sasha. In the manner of most children, they aren't shy about deflating Dad's ego. When Obama told the girls this year how much he looked forward to taking them for a walk in Manhattan's Central Park, Malia pointed out that he would surely be recognized. Obama said he'd wear a fake moustache. Without skipping a beat, seven-year-old Sasha said, "What about your ears?"

The Obama campaign, like Bill Clinton's in the early summer of 1992, discovered in its June polling that after a year and a half of campaigning, the majority of Americans still had no real idea of who their candidate was. It follows they knew even less about Michelle Obama. And so, in June the Obama campaign assigned a veteran strategist, Stephanie Cutter, to be Michelle's chief of staff and cope with, among other things, the fallout from what the *New York Times* described that month as Michelle's "brutally honest approach to talking about race."

Joel McNally, columnist at the *Capital Times*, the newspaper serving the Wisconsin capital of Madison, was incensed that "racist attacks on Michelle have been going on for some time on the Internet on conservative Republican Web sites. That's where Fox News originally got that absurd reference to a terrorist fist jab." McNally was convinced that "if it were not for race, instead of trashing these admirable people, the media would be preparing us for the kind of fairy tale first family this country enjoyed when Jackie Kennedy was reshaping fashion and John-John was crawling under the president's desk."

The candidate himself was uncharacteristically livid about GOP ads that made hay of Michelle's apparently qualified patriotism. In a joint interview at a Kentucky ABC affiliate, Michelle was beginning to respond to a question about her controversial Wisconsin remarks when Obama cut in, asserting that she was among the most patriotic of

Americans. And that while he was fair game, "I also think these folks should lay off my wife."

After taking her own shot at Obama's patriotism, Cindy McCain, fifty-four, called a truce. "I do not think that spouses and family members . . . are fair game," McCain told CNN in mid-June. Cindy McCain went on to praise Michelle Obama as a fine woman and a good mother, adding, "We both are in an interesting line of work right now." Michelle Obama, now more careful about the impact of her words, vowed to "go down every dark road" before saying anything that might blow up in her face.

One of the complaints about Hillary Clinton in the early 1990s, when her husband gave her the enormous task of health-care reform, is that no one elects the First Lady, a post that does not appear in the U.S. Constitution and the holder of which effectively is accountable to no one. Yet while the names Michelle Obama and Cindy McCain didn't appear on ballots in November, the impressions they created did weigh on the electoral outcome. A June survey by the U.S. polling firm Rasmussen found that 61 percent of respondents said the candidates' spouses would influence their vote.

In contrast with the McCains, the Obamas are the more familiar nuclear family. Michelle and Barack Obama each boast Ivy League educations, to be sure, while the Obama girls are enrolled in a private school. And Michelle, a fitness demon who rises at 4:30 a.m. for her daily workout, uses a personal trainer about three times a week. But the Obamas otherwise present a tableau of Rockwellian normality. Michelle's own childhood was conventional enough that Barack Obama describes her as "being raised by Ozzie and Harriet," after the 1950s sitcom of suburban American domestic tranquility.

The Obamas themselves aren't that far removed from Ozzie and Harriet. One of Michelle's favorite comfort foods is macaroni and cheese. Michelle and Barack Obama are both lifelong Stevie Wonder fans (the Obama campaign song is "Signed, Sealed, Delivered"), while Barack also favors the similarly inoffensive Earth, Wind & Fire. Crediting Ronald Reagan with returning a sense of normalcy to America after the 1970s era of oil shocks, double-digit inflation, and the psychodrama of the Nixon resignation, Obama wrote in *The Audacity of Hope* that Reagan's appeal "was related to the pleasure that I still get from watching a well-played baseball game, or my wife gets from watching reruns of *The Dick Van Dyke Show*."

Michelle's candor and unorthodox refusal to sugarcoat issues has won her an appreciative audience. After a June fundraiser in New York's Chelsea district sponsored by Seventh Avenue power brokers, where she elicited several standing ovations with her unscripted remarks, Francisco Costa of Calvin Klein Collection told fashion industry bible *Women's Wear Daily* that Michelle was "brilliant. She spoke so well you get chills."

"Can Michelle Obama Be First Lady No Matter What?" pleaded a 2008 post on the political website Wonkette, from a correspondent who approvingly noted Michelle's inability to suppress rolling her eyes at a comment made by a fellow guest on a panel of presidential candidates' spouses. "I love Michelle," the controversial author Camille Paglia, professor at the University of Arts in Philadelphia, told a British interviewer in June. "She's fabulous. She has an instinct for combat and goes for the jugular. Barack Obama is much more genial. It would be a dream to have them as president and first lady."

Michelle's other Obama campaign sobriquet was "The Taskmaster," earned from her complaints each time her husband's image takes an unreciprocated hit. "I know that my caricature out there is sort of the bad-ass wife who is sort of keeping it real, which is fine," Michelle has said. But her competitive streak, dating from childhood, has lately been tempered by mirth. Michelle demurred at first when a *New*

Yorker reporter asked her opinion of Bill Clinton's assertion that Barack Obama's 2002 opposition to the looming war in Iraq was a "fairy tale" — one of several misstatements by which the former president helped undermine his wife's campaign. A few seconds later, though, Michelle was clawing the air in front of her with her fingers. "I want to rip his eyes out!" she said. She quickly turned to an alarmed handler, "Kidding!" she said, and added, "See, this is what gets me into trouble."

By late spring 2008, Michelle was making news in safe, traditional ways. She dutifully entered *Family Circle*'s quadrennial contest in which readers vote for their favorite cookie recipe submitted by the two potential first ladies. (Michelle offered shortbread cookies with orange and lemon zest with a dash of Amaretto.) Michelle used to duck out of her own events soon after speaking, but with smaller groups she now lingers to chat with everyone present. She invariably is described as gracious.

Her wardrobe runs the gamut from avant-garde designer Isabel Toledo to the sleeveless $148 black-and-white dress she wore for an appearance on *The View*, one of America's most popular morning TV shows. (The garment quickly sold out at White House | Black Market, a retailer that sells only black-and-white apparel.) But Obama's fashion loyalty is to fellow Chicagoan Maria Pinto, fifty-one, a designer who was relatively unknown beyond the Windy City until 2007, when Michelle hit the campaign trail in Pinto's streamlined pieces. These included the elegant nine-hundred-dollar purple silk shift she wore the night her husband secured the presidential nomination. Michelle has eclipsed another Chicagoan, billionaire Oprah Winfrey, as Pinto's most prominent client. But Pinto is reticent about riding Michelle's coattails into postelection prosperity, as Oleg Cassini did after client Jacqueline Kennedy became first lady. Early on, Pinto admitted that she had an Obama inaugural gown "in the incubation stage," but in order not to jinx the electoral outcome, she kept her plans "on the lowdown." Obama eventually wore a Toledo-designed brocade coat and shift-dress for Inauguration Day, and a white gown by Taiwan-born Jason Wu to the inaugural balls.

In her June appearance on *The View*, Obama thanked First Lady Laura Bush for her encouraging words after the Wisconsin patriotism flap. She hinted at emulating the back-seat role that Laura Bush adopted in her husband's administration. "I'm taking cues" from Laura Bush, Michelle said. "There's a reason why people like her. It's because she doesn't fuel the fire." Michelle repeated the Obama campaign talking point that it was America's political process and not the country itself in which she had earlier lacked pride. But in a playful riposte to her critics, Michelle gave each of her five co-hosts a fist bump.

Overwhelmingly, Michelle Obama has been an asset to her husband's campaign: a symbol of grit and grace under the everyday pressures of caring for an extended family. Neither she nor Obama is the radical the Clintons seemed to be in 1992. Especially in their home life, they are, instead, deeply conservative. Michelle is so wistful about the days when one paycheck carried a family, and children had the benefit of a full-time parent, as she did, that one has the sense she'd like to see a return to that era.

Asked if there's one issue she would press for more than any other as first lady, Michelle without hesitation cited the unprecedented strains on modern-day mothers and the need to strike a healthier balance between the workplace and family. "The attention that [Barack has] focussed on work-family balance . . ." Michelle told the *New Yorker*, "that is our life. To the extent we have challenges and struggles, headaches that everybody is going through . . . those are our conversations."[3] That struggle has fully played out in a hectic two-year-long campaign, where the tug-of-war between the campaign and family and friends has been greatly accentuated. And in which a certain mother of two preadolescent girls doesn't mind letting you know occasionally that she's not having a great day.

No one appreciates the leap Michelle has made from Chicago homebody, caregiver, and executive to national political campaigner more than her husband. "There's something about Michelle that projects such honesty and strength," Obama told his hometown *Chicago Tribune*. "It's what makes her such an unbelievable professional, and partner, and mother, and wife."

Writing in *The Audacity of Hope* about the second-hand reports he gets from those who have heard or worked with Michelle, Obama noted that people tell him, "You know I think the world of you, Barack, but your wife . . . wow!"

Campaigning on her own, Michelle rapidly evolved in 2007–08 into a political natural, especially with audiences of women and college students, with whom she struck a quick rapport. Increasingly described as an orator no less gifted than her husband, Michelle would be a political recruiter's dream if her estimation of politics ever changes. Her hope that it will is why Michelle Obama committed so much of herself to her husband's candidacy.

Notes

1. Soon after Obama's presidential victory, he allowed in a TV interview that he had slipped off the bandwagon occasionally, seeking absolution given the stress of the campaign. Michelle's reaction has yet to be reported.
2. Michelle Obama is quick to assert that questions about her steep career trajectory are sexist and perhaps racist as well. But it's hard to argue that her career hasn't benefited from her association with Barack Obama. Not long after his voter-registration efforts that helped Bill Clinton become president in 1992, Obama was invited to become a founding director of Public Allies, which was created under the umbrella of Clinton's new AmeriCorps initiative. It was board member Obama, according to Public Allies' current president, Paul

Schmitz, who recommended his wife, with her background in intellectual-property law and just eighteen months' experience handling community issues at city hall, to launch Public Allies' Chicago branch. Two months after Obama took office as a U.S. senator, Michelle was promoted at University of Chicago Hospitals, more than doubling her pay, from $121,910 in 2004 to $316,962 in 2005. The hospital's then-president, Michael Riordan, said he feared Michelle would be recruited away, disrupting the effective programs she had put in place. Michelle was also invited to join the board of TreeHouse Foods, a specialty foods maker in suburban Westchester, where her 2006 compensation was $101,083. TreeHouse is a private-label supplier of pickles and other packaged foods whose largest client by far is Wal-Mart Stores Inc., a company frequently criticized by Obama for its business and labor practices. Still, in 2005, the Obamas' total income of $1.67 million was more than they earned in the previous seven years combined, enabling them finally to pay off their student loans. On the strength of his growing celebrity, Obama signed a three-book deal in 2004. Sales of the first volume, *The Audacity of Hope* (2006), set a record for U.S. political tomes of its kind and raised the Obamas' household income to $4.2 million in 2007. That year, the Obamas made $240,370 in charitable donations, including $50,000 to the United Negro College Fund, $35,000 to the global poverty charity CARE, and $26,270 to their church, Trinity United Church of Christ. In April 2008, Bill and Hillary Clinton reported joint income of $109 million over the previous eight years. In his individual tax returns, John McCain reported total income of $741,000 in 2006–07. McCain's wife, Cindy, who has reported her income separately since she and McCain were married, in 2008 publicly released only a partial return, reporting income of $6 million for 2006.

3. After her husband's November 4, 2008, victory, Michelle Obama said as a White House cause she would take on the challenges faced by the spouses of active military service personnel, whose difficulties had moved her during the campaign.

A note on BARACK **OBAMA**'s Oratorical Style and its Impact

Barack Obama is not the first U.S. politician propelled to contention for the highest office in the land by soaring rhetoric. Northern abolitionists impressed by the powerful logic of the oratory of a one-term Illinois congressman and recently failed candidate for the U.S. Senate lured Abraham Lincoln to New York's Cooper Union. There the obscure, lanky railroad lawyer became a national figure and prohibitive favorite to win his party's presidential nomination with a brilliant eight-thousand-word speech condemning the slavery that was making a mockery of the U.S. Constitution and creating a divided America that could not stand.

Obama became a de facto presidential candidate with his compelling personal story intertwined with the blessings and promise of America itself at the 2004 Democratic National Convention in Boston that nominated John Kerry as its presidential candidate. "In ten minutes, America watched [Obama] rip off the rumpled suit of anonymous, mild-mannered state-senatorhood and squeeze into the gaudy cape and tights of our national oratorical superhero — a honey-tongued Frankenfusion of Lincoln, Gandhi, Cicero, Jesus, and all our most cherished national acronyms (MLK, JFK, RFK, FDR)," wrote Sam Anderson in *New York* magazine in June 2008. "Although he may have been canonized a little too quickly, Obama has since managed to justify much of the hype."

Obama proved words do matter, as Marc Antony, Churchill, FDR, and Nelson Mandela had done before him. He toppled Hillary Clinton, the heavily financed, nationally known prohibitive favorite for the 2008 Democratic presidential nomination with erudite speeches that somehow touched the everyday American — with hope backed by facts, a futuristic vision of a better America grounded in the nation's earlier triumphs, and a convention-breaking decision to showcase his intellectual gifts rather than hide them for fear of giving offense. "He seems to be actually thinking about what he is saying," one U.S. political strategist said in early 2008. Obama's decision not to dumb down his message for widespread consumption prompted a somewhat amazed British newspaper columnist to write last spring that Obama "treats the American people as adults."

It's difficult to date with precision the beginning of the decline of American political speech-making. Some argue it began when the likes of Theodore Roosevelt, a prolific author, and Woodrow Wilson, the former Princeton president, who both wrote their own speeches, ultimately gave way to the era of Ronald Reagan, by which point presidents usually did not know the names of their speechwriters. Even JFK's greatest speeches, notably his 1961 inaugural address, were drafted principally by someone else — in the case of the inaugural address, by longtime confidante Theodore Sorensen (now an Obama supporter) with an assist from other top aides Arthur Schlesinger Jr. and the Canadian-born economist John Kenneth Galbraith. The latter contributed the line "We must never negotiate out of fear, but we must never fear to negotiate," which Obama has adopted as the centerpiece of his proposed new foreign policy of "tough diplomacy" over reliance solely on military might.

Television and its demand for sound bites accelerated the deterioration of political oratory, of course. But a bigger culprit was simply the demand on contemporary politicians to give more speeches than their predecessors, increasing their reliance on hired hands and robbing them of time for contemplative speech crafting.

Hillary Clinton argued during the 2008 primary season that oratory was overrated, and accused Obama of lacking the hands-on experience to transform words into action. Her line of reasoning backfired, appearing to downplay the work of Martin Luther King Jr., who was in Clinton's estimation merely the inspiration for Lyndon Johnson's civil rights and voting rights legislative breakthroughs of the mid-1960s. Quite apart from diminishing the stature of a Nobel laureate and one of the few Americans honored with a statutory holiday, Clinton's mistake was either failing to grasp or refusing to acknowledge that it was King's relentless shaming of America's betrayal of its founding creed, which powerfully shifted public opinion, that finally allowed LBJ to realize his own long-held legislative ambitions. Segregationist lawmakers in LBJ's own party then had no choice but to accede to the new public will, which King and other civil-rights leaders had brought about through nonviolent protests and, especially, with words.

Churchill, for his part, used words and the power of a cogent argument to convince a British cabinet favoring capitulation to the seemingly unstoppable Nazis to instead stand and fight, again with public backing, which he had created with his stirring oratory. Obama accumulated an insurmountable delegate lead in the Democratic primaries with speech after speech. He rejected traditional Democratic themes of rich versus poor (easily dismissed as "class warfare"). He used America's origin stories, from Lexington and Concord to Patton's army sweeping Hitler's Thousand-Year Reich into the dustbin of history. His call for change resonated with an American public described in 1992 by another skilled orator, Bill Clinton, as being "sick and tired of being sick and tired." With words alone — few in Hillary Clinton's camp or the media had yet taken the measure of Obama's legislative record — Obama was able to depict himself as the genuine agent of change who would experiment with solutions to long-standing problems, including inadequate health care, deficient educational standards, manufacturing job losses, and an obsolete post–Cold War foreign policy forged when the Soviet Union was a menace.

Obama's eloquent New Hampshire concession speech became a song by will.i.am of the Black Eyed Peas and a clutch of celebrities, including Scarlett Johansson and John Legend, that was downloaded more than three million times within days of its release — the first U.S. political speech set to music. And when the anti-American ranting of his long-time pastor, Jeremiah Wright Jr., threatened Obama's candidacy, the candidate turned again to words to right the ship with a widely praised five-thousand-word Philadelphia address that examined the origins and evolution of race in the American story.

It helps, of course, that Obama is a masterful writer who in his twenties contemplated a writing career. Obama's *Dreams from My Father* is an almost lyrical recounting of his father's tragic story and his own youthful struggle to transcend the societal forces that still work powerfully against minority advancement. In his game-changing New Hampshire speech, Obama took that sense of injustice and, improbably, turned it into a message of racial unity and hope. "It was a creed written into the founding documents that declared the destiny of a nation. Yes we can," Obama said. "It was whispered by slaves and abolitionists as they blazed a trail toward freedom through the darkest of nights. "Yes we can."

In his *New York* magazine article, Sam Anderson reports on a Moroccan waiter in the central plaza of Marrakech reciting that and other passages of Obama's New Hampshire speech to him. In America and abroad, Anderson wrote, "The signature project of [Obama's] candidacy — before health care or housing or Iraq — seems to be the reuniting of presidential discourse with actual, visible thought. It is not a trivial achievement."

IRAQ WAR

Obama's prescient warning about an Iraq invasion

"Even a successful war against Iraq will require a U.S. occupation of undetermined length, at undetermined cost, with undetermined consequences."

More than five months before the U.S. invasion of Iraq, in March 2003, Barack Obama, then an Illinois state senator who had just launched a race for a seat in the U.S. Senate, spoke out against the war at an antiwar rally in Chicago's Federal Plaza. The looming conflict was then supported by 65 percent of Americans, and Obama's advisors warned that if the war went well, he would have thrown away his political career.

While a handful of prominent Democrats including former vice-president Al Gore and U.S. senators Ted Kennedy, Robert Byrd, Bob Graham, and Illinois' Dick Durbin, a future Obama mentor, were to oppose U.S. President George W. Bush's war plans in the Middle East, Obama was going against the Democratic grain. A majority of Senate Democrats, including Obama rivals for the presidency in 2008 such as Hillary Clinton and John Edwards, would ultimately vote to give Bush the war-authorization powers to invade Iraq.

"AGAINST GOING TO WAR WITH IRAQ"

October 2, 2002

Chicago, IL

Good afternoon. Let me begin by saying that although this has been billed as an antiwar rally, I stand before you as someone who is not opposed to war in all circumstances. The Civil War was one of the bloodiest in history, and yet it was only through the crucible of the sword, the sacrifice of multitudes, that we could begin to perfect this union, and drive the scourge of slavery from our soil. I don't oppose all wars.

My grandfather signed up for a war the day after Pearl Harbor was bombed, fought in Patton's[1] army. He saw the dead and dying across the fields of Europe; he heard the stories of fellow troops who first entered Auschwitz[2] and Treblinka.[3] He fought in the name of a larger freedom, part of that arsenal of democracy that triumphed over evil, and he did not fight in vain. I don't oppose all wars.

After September 11th, after witnessing the carnage and destruction, the dust and the tears, I supported this administration's pledge to hunt down and root out those who would slaughter innocents in the name of intolerance, and I would willingly take up arms myself to prevent such tragedy from happening again. I don't oppose all wars. And I know that in this crowd today, there is no shortage of patriots, or of patriotism.

What I am opposed to is a dumb war. What I am opposed to is a rash war. What I am opposed to is the cynical attempt by Richard Perle[4] and Paul Wolfowitz[5] and other armchair, weekend warriors in this administration to shove their own ideological agendas down our throats, irrespective of the costs in lives lost and in hardships borne.

What I am opposed to is the attempt by political hacks like Karl Rove[6] to distract us from a rise in the uninsured, a rise in the poverty rate, a drop in the median income — to distract us from corporate scandals and a stock market that has just gone through the worst month since the Great Depression. That's what I'm opposed to. A dumb war. A rash war. A war based not on reason but on passion, not on principle but on politics. Now let me be clear — I suffer no illusions about Saddam Hussein. He is a brutal man. A ruthless man. A man who butchers his own people to secure his own power. He has repeatedly defied UN resolutions, thwarted UN inspection teams, developed chemical and biological weapons, and coveted nuclear capacity. He's a bad guy. The world, and the Iraqi people, would be better off without him.

But I also know that Saddam poses no imminent and direct threat to the United States, or to his neighbors, that the Iraqi economy is in shambles, that the Iraqi military is a fraction of its former strength, and that in concert with the international community he can be contained until, in the way of all petty dictators, he falls away into the dustbin of history. I know that even a successful war against Iraq will require a U.S. occupation of undetermined length, at undetermined cost, with undetermined consequences. I know that an invasion of Iraq without a clear rationale and without strong international support will only fan the flames of the Middle East, and encourage the worst, rather than best, impulses of the Arab world, and strengthen the recruitment arm of al Qaeda. I am not opposed to all wars. I'm opposed to dumb wars.

So for those of us who seek a more just and secure world for our children, let us send a clear message to the president today. You want a fight, President Bush? Let's finish the fight with bin Laden and al Qaeda, through effective, coordinated intelligence, and a shutting down of the financial networks that support terrorism, and a homeland security program that involves more than color-coded warnings. You want a fight, President Bush?

Let's fight to make sure that the UN inspectors can do their work, and that we vigorously enforce a non-proliferation treaty, and that former enemies and current allies like Russia safeguard and ultimately eliminate their stores of nuclear material, and that nations like Pakistan and India never use the terrible weapons already in their possession, and that the arms merchants in our own country stop feeding the countless wars that rage across the globe. You want a fight, President Bush? Let's fight to make sure our so-called allies in the Middle East, the Saudis and the Egyptians, stop oppressing their own people, and suppressing dissent, and tolerating corruption and inequality, and mismanaging their economies so that their youth grow up without education, without prospects, without hope, the ready recruits of terrorist cells. You want a fight, President Bush? Let's fight to wean ourselves off Middle East oil, through an energy policy that doesn't simply serve the interests of

Exxon and Mobil.[7] Those are the battles that we need to fight. Those are the battles that we willingly join. The battles against ignorance and intolerance. Corruption and greed. Poverty and despair.

The consequences of war are dire, the sacrifices immeasurable. We may have occasion in our lifetime to once again rise up in defense of our freedom, and pay the wages of war. But we ought not — we will not — travel down that hellish path blindly. Nor should we allow those who would march off and pay the ultimate sacrifice, who would prove the full measure of devotion with their blood, to make such an awful sacrifice in vain.

Notes

1. General George S. Patton (1885–1945), leading U.S. military commander in the World War II theaters of North Africa, Sicily, southern France, and Germany.
2. Auschwitz-Birkenau, Nazi concentration and extermination camp in German-occupied southern Poland.
3. Treblinka I and II, adjoining facilities in German-occupied Poland, the first an extermination camp, the latter a forced labor camp.
4. Richard N. Perle (b. 1941), assistant defense secretary in the Reagan administration and chairman of the Defense Policy Board Advisory Committee (2001–03) that counselled Defense Secretary Donald Rumsfeld in the Bush administration. Perle was a leading "neo-conservative," or neo-con, advocate of the Iraq war.
5. Paul Dundes Wolfowitz (b. 1943), U.S. deputy defense secretary, second-ranking Pentagon official (2001–05), a leading champion of the Iraq war.
6. Karl Christian Rove (b. 1950), chief political strategist in George W. Bush's gubernatorial campaigns in Texas and two presidential campaigns in 2000 and 2004. In the White House, he served as Bush's deputy chief of staff from 2001 to 2007.

7. The reference is to Exxon Mobil Corporation, formed in the 1999 merger of Exxon Corporation and Mobil Corporation.

NATIONAL UNITY

Obama denounces false divisions among Americans

"There are patriots who opposed the war in Iraq and patriots who supported it. We are one people, all of us pledging allegiance to the stars and stripes, all of us defending the United States of America."

Citing core American values of political and cultural unity, shared sacrifice, ingenuity, and communal compassion, Barack Obama became a national figure for the first time with his 2004 keynote address at the Democratic National Convention in Boston that selected U.S. Senator John Kerry as its presidential nominee. At a time of divisiveness in the nation over a controversial war in Iraq, Obama's evocation of America's past triumphs as a united people in meeting tremendous challenges won praise from conservative and liberal commentators alike. While Obama was careful not to upstage Kerry's later acceptance speech, he nonetheless enthralled the crowd gathered at Boston's Fleet Center arena with a personal-life story that is a realization of the American Dream. These two themes — the need for unity to tackle America's urgent concerns, and Obama as an embodiment of that Dream — would be central to Obama's own presidential bid four years later.

"KEYNOTE ADDRESS AT THE 2004 DEMOCRATIC NATIONAL CONVENTION"

July 27, 2004

Boston, MA

On behalf of the great state of Illinois, crossroads of a nation, land of Lincoln, let me express my deep gratitude for the privilege of addressing this convention. Tonight is a particular honor for me because, let's face it, my presence on this stage is pretty unlikely. My father was a foreign student, born and raised in a small village in Kenya. He grew up herding goats, went to school in a tin-roof shack. His father, my grandfather, was a cook, a domestic servant.

But my grandfather had larger dreams for his son. Through hard work and perseverance my father got a scholarship to study in a magical place: America, which stood as a beacon of freedom and opportunity to so many who had come before. While studying here, my father met my mother. She was born in a town on the other side of the world, in Kansas. Her father worked on oil rigs and farms through most of the Depression. The day after Pearl Harbor he signed up for duty, joined Patton's army and marched across Europe. Back home, my grandmother raised their baby and went to work on a bomber assembly line. After the war, they studied on the GI Bill,[1] bought a house through FHA,[2] and moved west in search of opportunity.

And they, too, had big dreams for their daughter, a common dream, born of two continents. My parents shared not only an improbable love; they shared an abiding faith in the possibilities of this nation. They would give me an African name, Barack, or "blessed," believing that in a tolerant America your name is no barrier to success. They imagined me going to the best schools in the land, even though they weren't rich, because in a generous America you don't have to be rich to achieve your potential. They are both passed away now. Yet, I know that, on this night, they look down on me with pride.

I stand here today, grateful for the diversity of my heritage, aware that my parents' dreams live on in my precious daughters. I stand here knowing that my story is part of the larger American story, that I owe a debt to all of those who came before me, and that, in no other country on earth, is my story even possible. Tonight, we gather to affirm the greatness of our nation, not because of the height of our skyscrapers, or the power of our military, or the size of our economy. Our pride is based on a very simple premise, summed up in a declaration made over two hundred years ago, "We hold these truths to be self-evident, that all men are created equal. That they are endowed by their Creator with certain inalienable rights. That among these are life, liberty and the pursuit of happiness."

That is the true genius of America, a faith in the simple dreams of its people, the insistence on small miracles. That we can tuck in our children at night and know they are fed and clothed and safe from harm. That we can say what we think, write what we think, without hearing a sudden knock on the door. That we can have an idea and start our own business without paying a bribe or hiring somebody's son. That we can participate in the political process without fear of retribution, and that our votes will be counted — or at least, most of the time.

This year, in this election, we are called to reaffirm our values and commitments, to hold them against a hard reality and see how we are measuring up, to the legacy of our forebears, and the promise of future generations. And fellow Americans — Democrats, Republicans, Independents — I say to you tonight: we have more work to do. More to do for the workers I met in Galesburg, Illinois, who are losing their union jobs at the Maytag plant that's moving to Mexico, and now are having to compete with their own children for jobs that pay seven bucks an hour. More to do for the father I met who was losing his job and choking back tears, wondering how he would pay $4,500 a month for the drugs his son needs without the health benefits he counted on. More to do for the young woman in East St. Louis, and thousands more like her, who has the grades, has the drive, has the will, but doesn't have the money to go to college.

Don't get me wrong. The people I meet in small towns and big cities, in diners and office parks, they don't expect government to solve all their problems. They know they have to work hard to get ahead and they want to. Go into the collar counties around Chicago, and people will tell you they don't want their tax money wasted by a welfare agency or the Pentagon. Go into any inner city neighborhood, and folks will tell you that government alone can't teach kids to learn. They know that parents have to parent, that children can't achieve unless we raise their expectations and turn off the television sets and eradicate the slander that says a black youth with a book is acting white. No, people don't expect government to solve all their problems. But they sense, deep in their bones, that with just a change in priorities, we can make sure that every child in America has a decent shot at life, and that the doors of opportunity remain open to all. They know we can do better. And they want that choice.

In this election, we offer that choice. Our party has chosen a man to lead us who embodies the best this country has to offer. That man is John Kerry. John Kerry understands the ideals of community, faith, and sacrifice, because they've defined his life. From his heroic service in Vietnam to his years as prosecutor and lieutenant governor, through two decades in the United States Senate, he has devoted himself to this country. Again and again, we've seen him make tough choices when easier ones were available. His values and his record affirm what is best in us.

John Kerry believes in an America where hard work is rewarded. So instead of offering tax breaks to companies shipping jobs overseas, he'll offer them to companies creating jobs here at home. John Kerry believes in an America where all Americans can afford the same health coverage our politicians in Washington have for themselves. John Kerry believes in energy independence, so we aren't held hostage to the profits of oil companies or the sabotage of foreign oil fields. John Kerry believes in the constitutional freedoms that have made our country the envy of the world, and he will never sacrifice our basic liberties nor use faith as a wedge to divide us. And John Kerry believes that in a dangerous world, war must be an option, but it should never be the first option.

A while back, I met a young man named Shamus at the VFW Hall[3] in East Moline, Illinois. He was a good-looking kid, six-two or six-three, clear-eyed, with an easy smile. He told me he'd joined the Marines and was heading to Iraq the following week. As I listened to him explain why he'd enlisted, his absolute faith in our country and its leaders, his devotion to duty and service, I thought this young man was all any of us might hope for in a child. But then I asked myself: are we serving Shamus as well as he was serving us? I thought of more than nine hundred service men and women, sons and daughters, husbands and wives, friends and neighbors, who will not be returning to their hometowns. I thought of families I had met who were struggling to get by without a loved one's full income, or whose loved ones had returned with a limb missing or with nerves shattered, but who still lacked long-term health benefits because they were reservists. When we send our young men and women into harm's way, we have a solemn obligation not to fudge the numbers or shade the truth about why they're going, to care for their families while they're gone, to tend to the soldiers upon their return, and to never ever go to war without enough troops to win the war, secure the peace, and earn the respect of the world.

Now let me be clear. We have real enemies in the world. These enemies must be found. They must be pursued and they must be defeated. John Kerry knows this. And just as Lieutenant Kerry did not hesitate to risk his life to protect the men who served with him in Vietnam, President Kerry will not hesitate one moment to use our military might to keep America safe and secure. John Kerry believes in America. And he knows it's not enough for just some of us to prosper. For alongside our famous individualism, there's another ingredient in the American saga.

A belief that we are connected as one people. If there's a child on the South Side of Chicago who can't read, that matters to me, even if it's not my child. If there's a senior citizen somewhere who can't pay for her prescription and has to choose between medicine and the rent, that makes my life poorer, even if it's not my grandmother. If there's an Arab-American family being rounded up without benefit of an attorney or due process, that threatens my civil liberties. It's that fundamental belief — I am my brother's keeper, I am my sister's keeper — that makes this country work. It's what allows us to pursue our individual dreams, yet still come together as a single American family. *E pluribus unum.* Out of many, one.

Yet even as we speak, there are those who are preparing to divide us, the spin masters and negative ad peddlers who embrace the politics of anything goes. Well, I say to them tonight, there's not a liberal America and a conservative America — there's the United States of America. There's not a black America and white America and Latino America and Asian America; there's the United States of America. The pundits like to slice-and-dice our country into Red States and Blue States; Red States for Republicans, Blue States for Democrats. But I've got news for them, too. We worship an awesome God in the Blue States, and we don't like federal agents poking around our libraries in the Red States. We coach Little League in the Blue States and have gay friends in the Red States. There are patriots who opposed the war in Iraq and patriots who supported it. We are one people, all of us pledging allegiance to the stars and stripes, all of us defending the United States of America.

In the end, that's what this election is about. Do we participate in a politics of cynicism or a politics of hope? John Kerry calls on us to hope. John Edwards calls on us to hope. I'm not talking about blind optimism here — the almost willful ignorance that thinks unemployment will go away if we just don't talk about it, or the health care crisis will solve itself if we just ignore it. No, I'm talking about something more substantial. It's the hope of slaves sitting around a fire singing freedom songs; the hope of immigrants setting out for distant shores; the hope of a young naval lieutenant bravely patrolling the Mekong Delta;[4] the hope of a mill-worker's son who dares to defy the odds;[5] the hope of a skinny kid with a funny name who believes that America has a place for him, too. The audacity of hope!

In the end, that is God's greatest gift to us, the bedrock of this nation; the belief in things not seen;[6] the belief that there are better days ahead. I believe we can give our middle class relief and provide working families with a road to opportunity. I believe we can provide jobs to the jobless, homes to the homeless, and reclaim young people in cities across America from violence and despair. I believe that as we stand on the crossroads of history, we can make the right choices, and meet the challenges that face us. America!

Tonight, if you feel the same energy I do, the same urgency I do, the same passion I do, the same hopefulness I do — if we do what we must do, then I have no doubt that all across the country, from Florida to Oregon, from Washington to Maine, the people will rise up in November, and John Kerry will be sworn in as president, and John Edwards will be sworn in as vice president, and this country will reclaim its promise, and out of this long political darkness a brighter day will come. Thank you and God bless you.

Notes

1. Among the last initiatives of Franklin Roosevelt's New Deal era, the GI Bill (formally the Servicemen's Readjustment Act of 1944) provided free college or vocational training for returning U.S. veterans of World War II, as well as loans for returning vets to purchase homes and launch businesses. The spike in post-secondary enrolment triggered by the bill caused a vast expansion in the U.S. education system, and often is credited with laying the foundation for America's postwar middle class. "GI," or general issue, was adopted by front-line soldiers as a self-identifying sobriquet, referring to their "general issue" kit of uniform and equipment.
2. The Federal Housing Administration, another legacy of Franklin Roosevelt's New Deal era, was created in 1934 to improve housing standards, provide affordable home financing, and stabilize a mortgage market debilitated by foreclosures in

the early years of the Great Depression.

3. Veterans of Foreign Wars (VFW), one of the world's largest organizations for military personnel, founded in 1899, with a mandate similar to that of the American Legion (1919), the Vietnam Veterans of America (1978), the Royal British Legion (1921), the Royal Canadian Legion (1925), the Returned and Services League of Australia (1916), and the Royal New Zealand Returned and Services' Association (1916). To a greater degree than in other countries above, U.S. candidates for elected office are attentive to the concerns raised by groups representing veterans, an important voting constituency.
4. Mekong Delta, region in southern Vietnam where U.S. Senator John Kerry (D-Mass.), a decorated serviceman, captained a "swift" boat patrolling for enemy Vietcong.
5. Millworker's son: a reference to Kerry's running mate, U.S. Senator John Edwards (D-N.C.).
6. An allusion to one of Robert F. Kennedy's best-known quotes: "There are those who look at things the way they are, and ask why . . . I dream of things that never were, and ask why not?"

PROSPERITY AND FAIRNESS

Obama calls for a middle-class revival

"These are the challenges we face at the beginning of the 21st century . . . It cannot be denied that families face more risk and greater insecurity than we have known since FDR*'s time, even as those families have fewer resources available to help pull themselves through the tough spots."*

Privatizing Social Security was one of President George W. Bush's signature goals, a way of shifting a government burden onto pensioners, who would manage their own retirement planning by investing directly in the markets for stocks, bonds, commodities, and real estate.

In this 2005 address, Obama uses the Social Security debate to highlight a larger issue — the growing gap between rich and poor in America, and the struggle of middle- and working-class Americans with higher costs for everything from health care to tuition, even in the midst of a robust economy in which a selected few at the top were reaping extraordinary personal gains. Democrats who address this issue often are accused by Republicans of engaging in "class warfare," successfully evoking the American cultural sentiment of rugged individualism.

Obama was thus careful to frame his enumeration of middle- and working-class burdens as a simple matter of fairness. The America he describes is experiencing a largely unseen revolution, in which the postwar "social contract" between corporate employers and their workers — where employers provided health and other benefits in exchange for worker loyalty — is rapidly unwinding in a new era of globalization and outsourcing.

"A HOPE TO FULFILL"

April 26, 2005

Washington, DC

Thank you. It's great to be here at the National Press Club — I want to thank the club as well as the FDR Institute for arranging this luncheon together. I'd also like to thank Anne Roosevelt and Jim Roosevelt, who inspire us all by carrying on the proud legacy of their grandfather.

By the time the Senate Finance Committee holds the first Senate hearing on the President's Social Security Plan today, we'll have heard just about everything there is to be said about the issue. We've heard about privatization and benefit cuts, about massive new debt and huge new risks, and we've even been scared into thinking the system will go broke when our kids retire, even though we know there'll be enough money then to pay the vast majority of benefits.

I'm happy to address some of these issues in the Q and A after the speech. But aside from the usual back-and-forth of this debate, I can't help but think about the larger issue at stake here.

Think about the America that Franklin Roosevelt saw when he looked out the windows of the White House from his wheelchair — an America where too many were ill-fed, ill-clothed, ill-housed, and insecure. An America where more and more Americans were finding themselves on the losing end of a new economy, and where there was nothing available to cushion their fall.

Some thought that our country didn't have a responsibility to do anything about these problems, that people would be better off left to their own devices and the whims of the market. Others believed that American capitalism had failed and that it was time to try something else altogether.

But our President believed deeply in the American idea.

He understood that the freedom to pursue our individual dreams is made possible by the promise that if fate causes us to stumble or fall, our larger American family will be there to lift us up. That if we're willing to share even a small amount of life's risks and rewards with each other, then we'll all have the chance to make the most of our God-given potential.

And because Franklin Roosevelt had the courage to act on this idea, individual Americans were able to get back on their feet and build a shared prosperity that is still the envy of the world.

The New Deal gave the laid-off worker a guarantee that he could count on unemployment insurance to put food on his family's table while he looked for a new job. It gave the young man who suffered a debilitating accident assurance that he could count on disability payments to get him through the tough times. A widow might still raise her children without the indignity of charity. And Franklin Roosevelt's greatest legacy promised the couple who put in a lifetime of sacrifice and hard work that they could retire in comfort and dignity because of Social Security.

Today, we're told by those who want to privatize that promise how much things are different and times have changed since Roosevelt's day.

I couldn't agree more.

A child born in this new century is likely to start his life with both parents — or a single parent — working full-time jobs. They'll try their hardest to juggle work and family, but they'll end up needing child care to keep him safe, cared for, and educated early.

They'll want to give him the best education possible, but unless they live in a wealthy town with good public schools, they'll have to settle for less or find the money for private schools.

This student will study hard and dream of going to the best colleges in the country, but with tuition rising higher and faster than ever before, he may have to postpone those dreams or start life deeper in debt than any generation before him.

When he graduates from college, this young man will find a job market where middle-class manufacturing jobs with good benefits have long been replaced with low-wage, low-benefit service sector jobs and high-skill, high-wage jobs of the future.

To get those good jobs, he'll need the skills and knowledge to not only compete with other workers in America, but with highly skilled and highly knowledgeable workers all over the world who are being recruited by the same companies that once made their home in this country.

When he finally starts his job, he'll want health insurance, but rising costs mean that fewer employers can afford to provide that benefit, and when they do, fewer employees can afford the record premiums.

When he starts a family, he'll want to buy a house and a car and pay for child care and college for his own children, but as he watches the lucky few benefit from lucrative bonuses and tax shelters, he'll see his own tax burden rise and his own paycheck barely cover this month's bills.

And when he retires, he'll hope that he and his wife have saved enough, but if there wasn't enough to save, he'll hope that there will still be two Social Security checks that come to the house every month.

These are the challenges we face at the beginning of the 21st century. We shouldn't exaggerate; we aren't seeing the absolute deprivation of the Great Depression. But it cannot be denied that families face more risk and greater insecurity than we have known since FDR's time, even as those families have fewer resources available to help pull themselves through the tough spots. Whereas people were once able to count on their employer to provide health care, pensions, and a job that would last a lifetime, today's worker wonders if suffering a heart attack will cause his employer to drop his coverage, worries about how much he can contribute to his own pension fund, and fears the possibility that he might walk into work tomorrow and find his job outsourced.

Yet, just as the naysayers in Roosevelt's day told us that there was nothing we could do to help people help themselves, the people in power today are telling us that instead of sharing the risks of the new economy, we should shoulder them on our own.

In the end, this is what the debate over the future of Social Security is truly about.

After a lifetime of hard work and contribution to this

country, do we tell our seniors that they're on their own, or that we're here for them to provide a basic standard of living? Is the dignity of life in their latter years their problem, or one we all share?

Since this is Washington, you won't hear them answer those questions directly when they talk about Social Security. Instead, they will use the word reform when they mean privatize, and they will use strengthen when they really mean dismantle. They tell us there's a crisis to get us all riled up so we'll sit down and listen to their plan to privatize.

But we know what the whole thing's really about.

It's not just about cutting guaranteed benefits by up to 50 percent — though it certainly does that.

It's not just about borrowing five trillion dollars from countries like China and Japan to finance the plan — after all, we know how fiscal conservatives hate debt and deficit.

And it's not even about the ability of private accounts to finance the gap in the system — because even the privatization advocates admit they don't.

What this whole thing is about, and why conservatives have been pushing it so hard for so long now, is summed up in one sentence in one White House memo that somehow made its way out of the White House: for the first time in six decades, the Social Security battle is one we can win — and in doing so, we can help transform the political and philosophical landscape of the country.

And there it is. Since Social Security was first signed into law almost seventy years ago, at a time when FDR's opponents were calling it a hoax that would never work and some likened it to communism, there has been movement after movement to get rid of the program for purely ideological reasons. Because some still believe that we can't solve the problems we face as one American community; they think this country works better when we're left to face fate by ourselves.

I understand this view. There's something bracing about the Social Darwinist idea, the idea that there isn't a problem that the unfettered free market can't solve. It requires no sacrifice on the part of those of us who won life's lottery — and it doesn't consider who our parents were, or the education we received, or the right breaks that came at the right time.

But I couldn't disagree more. If we privatize Social Security, what will we tell retirees whose investments in the stock market went badly? We're sorry? Keep working? You're on your own?

When people's expected benefits get cut and they have to choose between their groceries and their prescriptions, what will we say to them? That's not our problem?

When our debt climbs so high that our children face sky-high taxes just as they're starting their first job, what will we tell them? Deal with it yourselves?

This isn't how America works. This isn't how we saved millions of seniors from a life of poverty seventy years ago. This isn't how we sent the greatest generation of veterans to college so they could build the greatest middle-class in history. And this isn't how we should face the challenges of this new century either.

And yet, this is the direction they're trying to take America on almost every issue. Instead of trying to contain the skyrocketing cost of health care and expand access to the uninsured, the idea behind the President's Health Savings Accounts are to leave the system alone and give you a few extra bucks to go find a plan you can afford on your own. You deal with the double-digit inflation by going to the doctor less. Instead of strengthening a pension system that provides defined benefits to employees who've worked a lifetime, we'll give you a tax break and hope that you invest well and save well in your own little account. And if none of this works — if you couldn't find affordable insurance and suffer an illness that leaves you thousands of dollars in debt — then you should no longer count on being able to start over by declaring bankruptcy because they've changed the law to put the burden of debt squarely on your shoulders.

Taking responsibility for oneself and showing individual initiative are American values we all share. Frankly, they're values we could stand to see more of in a culture where the buck is too often passed to the next guy. They are values we could use more of here in Washington too.

But the irony of this all-out assault against every existing form of social insurance is these safety nets are exactly what encourage each of us to be risk-takers and entrepreneurs who are free to pursue our individual ambitions. We get into a car knowing that if someone rear-ends us, they will have insurance to pay for the repairs. We buy a house knowing that our investment is protected by homeowners insurance. We take a chance on start-ups and small businesses because we know that if they fail, there are protections available to cushion our fall. Corporations across America have limited liability for this very reason. Families should too — and that's why we need social insurance. This is how the market works.

This is how America works. And if we want it to keep working, we need to develop new ways for all of us to share the new risks of a 21st-century economy, not destroy what we already have.

The genius of Roosevelt was putting into practice the idea that America doesn't have to be a place where our individual aspirations are at war with our common good; it's a place where one makes the other possible.

I think we will save Social Security from privatization this year. And in doing so, we will affirm our belief that we are all connected as one people — ready to share life's risks and rewards for the benefit of each and the good of all.

Let me close by suggesting that Democrats are absolutely united in the need to strengthen Social Security and make it solvent for future generations. We know that, and we want that. And I believe that both Democrats and Republicans can work together to do that. While we're at it, we can begin a debate about the real challenges America faces as the baby boomers begin to retire.

About getting a handle on the growing cost of health care and prescription drugs. About increasing individual and national savings. About strengthening our pension system for the 21st century.

These are important questions that require us to work together, not in a manufactured panic about a genuine but solvable problem, but with the spirit of pragmatism and innovation that will offer every American the secure retirement they have earned.

You know, there are times in the life of this nation where we are individual citizens going about our own business, enjoying the freedoms we've been blessed with.

And then there are times when we are one America, linked by the dignity of each and the destiny of all.

The debate over the future of Social Security must be one of these times.

The people I've met since starting my campaign tell me they don't want a big government that's running their lives, but they do want an active government that will give them the opportunity to make the most of their lives.

Starting with the child born today and the senior moving into the twilight of life, together we can provide that opportunity.

The day Franklin Roosevelt signed the Social Security Act of 1935 into law, he began by saying that, "Today, a hope of many years' standing is in large part fulfilled."

It is now time to fulfill our hope for an America where we're in this together — for our seniors, for our children, and for every American in the years and generations yet to come. Thank you.

EDUCATION REFORM

America can't afford to fall behind in the 21st-century economy

"We have a mutual responsibility to make sure our schools are properly funded, our teachers are properly paid, and our students have access to an affordable college education. And if we don't do something about all that, then nothing else matters."

Invited to celebrate triumphs of the civil rights movement, Obama instead dwells on a new civil-rights challenge that cuts across races and cultures — the declining standards in U.S. education, and the perilous consequences for future American generations in a 21st-century economy of hyper-competitive globalization. Obama of course honors giants of the 1950s and 1960s civil-rights struggles in this 2005 Detroit address to an audience of the National Association for the Advancement of Colored People (NAACP), America's leading black advocacy group. But in detailing the remarkable, courageous confrontations with those who resisted racial inequality, Obama repeatedly draws parallels with modern-day, unresolved inequalities — of education, income, and career opportunity — that continue to hold America back. For Americans accustomed to hearing that everything from their health care to education systems is world-class and universally envied, Obama's recitation of abysmal U.S. drop-out rates, student test scores, and crumbling schools is a harsh reality check.

"REMARKS AT NAACP FIGHT FOR FREEDOM FUND DINNER"

May 2, 2005

Detroit, MI

Half a century after the first few hundred people sat for justice and equality at these tables, I am honored to be here with this crowd of thousands at the fiftieth NAACP Fight for Freedom Fund Dinner.

Founded at a time when we were constantly reminded how the world around us was separate and unequal . . . when the idea of legal rights for black folks was almost a contradiction in terms . . . when lunch counters and bus seats and water fountains were luxuries you had to fight for and march for, the fiftieth anniversary of the Fight for Freedom Dinner reminds us of just how far our struggle has come.

I was reminded of this last month, when I had the honor of going to Atlanta to speak at John Lewis's sixty-fifth birthday celebration. Many of the luminaries of the civil rights movement were down there, and I had the great honor of sitting between Ethel Kennedy and Coretta Scott King, who both turned to me and said, "We're really looking forward to hearing you speak." Now that's a really intimidating thing!

And as I stood up there next to John Lewis, not a giant in stature, but a giant of compassion and courage, I thought to myself, never in a million years would I have guessed that I'd be serving in Congress with John Lewis.

And then I thought, you know, there was once a time when John Lewis might never have guessed that he'd be serving in Congress. And there was a time not long before that when people might never have guessed that someday, black folks would be able to go to the polls, pick up a ballot, make their voice heard, and elect that Congress.

But we can, and many of us are here because people like John Lewis believed. Because people feared nothing and risked everything for those beliefs. Because they saw injustice and endured pain in order to right what was wrong. We're here tonight because of them, and to them we owe the deepest gratitude.

The road we have taken to this point has not been easy. But then again, the road to change never is.

Some of you might know that I taught Constitutional law at the Chicago Law school for awhile. And one of the courses I taught was a course in race and law, where we chronicled the history of race in this country and people's struggle to achieve freedom in the courts and on the streets. And often times my students would come up to me and say things like, "Boy I wish I could've been around at the height of the civil rights movement. Because things seemed so clear at the time. And while there may have been room for debate on some things, the clarity of the cause and the need for the movement were crystal clear, and you didn't have the ambiguities you have today.

"Because it's one thing to know that everyone has a seat at the lunch counter, but how do we figure out how everyone can pay for the meal? It was easy to figure out that blacks and whites should be able to go to school together, but how do we make sure that every child is equipped and ready to graduate? It was easy to talk about dogs and fire hoses, but how do we talk about getting drugs and guns off the streets?" This is what they told me.

And of course, I reminded them that it wasn't very easy at all. That the moral certainties we now take for granted — that separate can never be equal, that the blessings of liberty enshrined in our Constitution belong to all of us, that our children should be able to go to school together and play together and grow up together — were anything but certain in 1965.

I reminded them that even within the African-American community, there was disagreement about how much to stir things up. We have a church in Chicago that's on what used to be known as State Park Way. After Dr. King's assassination, the street was renamed to Martin Luther King Jr. Drive. But the pastor of the church — a prominent African-American in the community — hated Dr. King so bad that he actually changed the address of the church.

And so it's never been clear. And it's never been easy. To get to where we are today it took struggle and sacrifice, discipline and tremendous courage.

And sometimes, when I reflect on those giants of the civil rights movement, I wonder — where did you find that courage? John Lewis, where did you find that courage? Dorothy Height, where did you find that courage? Rosa Parks, where did you find that courage?

When you're facing row after row of state troopers on

horseback armed with billy clubs and tear gas . . . when they're coming toward you spewing hatred and violence, how do you simply stop, kneel down, and pray to the Lord for salvation?

Where do you find that courage?

I don't know. But I do know that it's worth examining because the challenges we face today are going to require this kind of courage. The battle lines may have shifted and the barriers to equality may be new, but what's not new is the need for everyday heroes to stand up and speak out for what they believe is right.

Fifty years ago this country decided that Linda Brown shouldn't have to walk miles and miles to school every morning when there was a white school just four blocks away because when it comes to education in America, separate can never be equal.

Now that ruling came about because the NAACP was willing to fight tirelessly and risk its reputation; because everyday Americans — black and white — were willing to take to the streets and risk their freedom. Because people showed courage.

Fifty years later, what kind of courage are we showing to ensure that our schools are foundations of opportunity for our children?

In a world where kids from Detroit aren't just competing with kids from Macomb for middle-class jobs, but with kids from Malaysia and New Delhi, ensuring that every American child gets the best education possible is the new civil-rights challenge of our time.

A student today armed with only a high school diploma will earn an average of only $25,000 a year — if you're African-American, it's 14 percent less than that. Meanwhile, countries like China are graduating twice as many students with a college degree as we do. We're falling behind, and if we want our kids to have the same chances we had in life, we must work harder to catch up.

So what are we doing about it?

When we see that America has one of the highest high school dropout rates in the industrialized world — even higher for African-Americans and Hispanics — what are we doing about it?

When we see that our high school seniors are scoring lower on their math and science tests than almost any other students in the world at a time when expertise in these areas is the ticket to a high-wage job, what are we doing about it?

When we see that for every hundred students who enter ninth grade, only eighteen — eighteen — will earn any kind of college degree within six years of graduating high school, what are we doing about it?

And when we see broken schools, old textbooks, and classrooms bursting at the seams, what are we doing about that?

I'll tell you what they've been doing in Washington. In Washington, they'll talk about the importance of education one day and sign big tax cuts that starve our schools the next. They'll talk about Leaving No Child Behind but then say nothing when it becomes obvious that they've left the money behind.[1] In the budget they passed this week in Congress, they gave out over one hunded billion dollars in tax cuts, on top of the trillions they've already given to the wealthiest few and most profitable corporations.

One hundred billion dollars. Think about what that could do for our kids if we invested that in our schools. Think of how many new schools we could build, how many great teachers we could recruit, what kind of computers and technology we could put in our classrooms. Think about how much we could invest in math and science so our kids could be prepared for the 21st-century economy. Think about how many kids we could send to college who've worked hard, studied hard, but just can't afford the tuition.

Think about all that potential and all that opportunity. Think about the choice Washington made instead. And now think about what you can do about it.

I believe we have a mutual responsibility to make sure our schools are properly funded, our teachers are properly paid, and our students have access to an affordable college education. And if we don't do something about all that, then nothing else matters.

But I also believe we have an individual responsibility as well.

Our grandparents used to tell us that being black means you have to work twice as hard to succeed in life. And so I ask today, can we honestly say our kids are working twice as hard as the kids in India and China who are graduating ahead of us, with better test scores and the tools they need to kick our butts on the job market? Can we honestly say our teachers are working twice as hard, or our parents?

One thing's for sure, I certainly know that Washington's not working twice as hard — and that's something each of us has a role in changing. Because if we want change in our education system — if we want our schools to be less crowded and funded more equitably; if we want our children to take the courses that will get them ready for the 21st century; if we want our teachers to be paid what they're worth and armed with the tools they need to prepare our kids; then we need to summon the same courage today that those giants of the civil rights movement summoned half a century ago.

Because more than anything else, these anniversaries — of the Voting Rights Act and the Civil Rights Act and Fight for Freedom Fund Dinner — they remind us that in America, ordinary citizens can somehow find in their hearts the courage to do extraordinary things. That change is never easy, but always possible. And it comes not from violence or militancy or the kind of politics that pits us against each other and plays on our worst fears; but from great discipline and organization, and from a strong message of hope.

And when we look at these challenges and think, how can we do this? How can we cut through the apathy and the partisanship and the business-as-usual culture in Washington? When we wonder this, we need to rediscover the hope that people have been in our shoes before and they've lived to cross those bridges.

Personally, I find that hope in thinking about a trip I took during my campaign for the U.S. Senate.

About a week after the primary, Dick Durbin and I embarked on a nineteen-city tour of southern Illinois. And one of the towns we went to was a place called Cairo, which, as many of you might know, achieved a certain notoriety during the late sixties and early seventies as having one of the worst racial climates in the country. You had an active white citizens' council there, you had cross burnings, Jewish families were being harassed, you had segregated schools, race riots, you name it — it was going on in Cairo.

And we're riding down to Cairo and Dick Durbin turns to me and says, "Let me tell you about the first time I went to Cairo. It was about thirty years ago. I was twenty-three years old and Paul Simon, who was lieutenant governor at the time, sent me down there to investigate what could be done to improve the racial climate in Cairo."

And Dick tells me how he diligently goes down there and gets picked up by a local resident who takes him to his motel. And as Dick's getting out of the car, the driver says, "Excuse me, let me just give you a piece of advice. Don't use the phone in your motel room because the switchboard operator is a member of the white citizens' council, and they'll report on anything you do."

Well, this obviously makes Dick Durbin upset, but he's a brave young man, so he checks in to his room, unpacks his bags and a few minutes later he hears a knock on the door. He opens up the door and there's a guy standing there who just stares at Dick for a second, and then says, "What the hell are you doing here?" and walks away.

Well, now Dick is really feeling concerned and so am I because as he's telling me this story, we're pulling in to

Cairo. So I'm wondering what kind of reception we're going to get. And we wind our way through the town and we go past the old courthouse, take a turn and suddenly we're in a big parking lot and about three hundred people are standing there. About a fourth of them are black and three-fourths are white and they all are about the age where they would have been active participants in the epic struggle that had taken place thirty years earlier.

And as we pull closer, I see something. All of these people are wearing these little buttons that say "Obama for U.S. Senate." And they start smiling. And they start waving. And Dick and I looked at each other and didn't have to say a thing. Because if you told Dick thirty years ago that he — the son of Lithuanian immigrants born into very modest means in east St. Louis — would be returning to Cairo as a sitting United States Senator, and that he would have in tow a black guy born in Hawaii with a father from Kenya and a mother from Kansas named Barack Obama, no one would have believed it.

But it happened. And it happened because John Lewis and scores of brave Americans stood on that bridge and lived to cross it.

You know, two weeks after Bloody Sunday, when the march finally reached Montgomery, Martin Luther King Jr. spoke to the crowd of thousands and said, "The arc of the moral universe is long, but it bends towards justice." He's right, but you know what? It doesn't bend on its own. It bends because we help it bend that way. Because people like John Lewis and Martin Luther King and Rosa Parks and thousands of ordinary Americans with extraordinary courage have helped bend it that way. And as their examples call out to us from across the generations, we continue to progress as a people because they inspire us to take our own two hands and bend that arc.

Congratulations to all of you here at the NAACP who are busy bending that arc. Thank you.

Note

1. No Child Left Behind, one of President George W. Bush's earliest initiatives and an intended centerpiece of his administration, passed the U.S. Congress with enthusiastic, bipartisan support. Its stated goal was to improve student test scores and teacher performance, rewarding improved schools with extra funding, and closing schools deemed to be failing. In the implementation of NCLB, however, it was evident that the program's real intent was to force teachers to adhere to a constricted curriculum focused on literacy and numeracy at the expense of music, art, and other programs. And they were to do so, most conspicuously in inner-city schools, in facilities that still lacked new books and equipment and remained in physical disrepair for continued lack of adequate funding.

LITERACY

Improved literacy is the key to American competitiveness

"Literacy is the most basic currency of the knowledge economy we're living in today."

Parents and librarians are in the front lines of America's continued claim on economic and technological leadership in this new century, Barack Obama argues in this 2005 address to the American Library Association. Obama lauds librarians for standing fast against locals routinely seeking the removal of controversial classics from the shelves, and especially for fighting off the post-9/11 federal efforts to snoop into the reading habits of American citizens. But addressing the librarians as parents, Obama asserts that advanced literacy skills must begin at home before a child commences school. He proposes a stronger partnership between parents and librarians, and innovations to make reading more accessible and a larger and more routine part of a young person's life.

"ADDRESS TO THE AMERICAN LIBRARY ASSOCIATION"

June 27, 2005

Boston, MA

Thank you. It's an honor to be here with the hundreds of dedicated librarians who make up the American Library Association. Before we begin, I'd like to say a special hello to ALA member Nancy Gibbs, who is the mother of my communications director, Robert Gibbs. Believe me, I have no idea how the biggest mouth in our office came from a family of two librarians, but we're proud to have him on board and I'm sure you are too.

I'd also like to give a shout-out to my librarians from the Punahou School in Hawaii — Molly Lyman, Joan Kaaua, and Lillian Hiratani. I'd like to offer them an apology too, for all those times I couldn't keep myself out of trouble and ended up sitting in their library on a timeout, trying to cause even more trouble there. Sorry ladies.

It is a pleasure to address you today because of what libraries represent. More than a building that houses books and data, the library has always been a window to a larger world — a place where we've always come to discover big ideas and profound concepts that help move the American story forward.

And at a time when truth and science are constantly being challenged by political agendas and ideologies; a time where so many refuse to teach evolution in our schools, where fake science is used to beat back attempts to curb global warming or fund life-saving research; libraries remind us that truth isn't about who yells the loudest, but who has the right information. Because even as we're the most religious of people, America's innovative genius has always been preserved because we also have a deep faith in facts.

And so the moment we persuade a child, any child, to cross that threshold into a library, we've changed their lives forever, and for the better. This is an enormous force for good.

So I'm here to gratefully acknowledge the importance of libraries and the work you do. I also want to work with you to insure that libraries continue to be sanctuaries for learning, where we are free to read and consider what we please, without the fear of Big Brother peering menacingly over our shoulders.

Now, some of you might have heard about this speech I gave at the Democratic Convention last summer. It ended up making some news here and there, and one of the lines that people seem to remember was when I said that "We don't like federal agents poking around our libraries in the Red States."

What many people don't remember is that for years, librarians are the ones who've been on the front lines of this fight for privacy and freedom. There have always been dark times in our history where America has strayed from the ideals that make us a great nation. But the question has always been, can we overcome? And you have always been a group of Americans who have answered a resounding "yes" to that question.

When political groups try to censor great works of literature, you're the ones putting Huck Finn and *Catcher in the Rye* back on the shelves, making sure that our right to free thought and free information is protected. And ever since we've had to worry about our own government looking over our shoulders in the library, you've been there to stand up and speak out on privacy issues. You're full-time defenders of the most fundamental American liberties, and for that, you deserve America's deepest gratitude.

You also deserve our protection. That's why I've been working with Republicans and Democrats to make sure we have a Patriot Act that helps us track down terrorists without trampling on our civil liberties. This is an issue that Washington always tries to make "either-or." Either we protect our people from terror or we protect our most cherished principles. But this kind of choice asks too little of us and assumes too little about America. We can harness new technologies and a new toughness to find terrorists before they strike while still protecting the very freedoms we're fighting for in the first place.

I know that some of you here have been subject to FBI or other law enforcement orders asking for reading records. And so I hope we can pass a provision like the House of Representatives did that would require federal agents to get these kinds of search warrants from a real judge in a real court, just like everyone else does. In the Senate, the bipartisan bill that we're working on, known as the SAFE Act, will prevent the federal government from freely rifling through e-mails and library records without first obtaining such a warrant. Giving law enforcement the tools they need to investigate suspicious activity is one thing; but doing it without the approval of our judicial system seriously jeopardizes the rights of all Americans and the ideals America stands for.

Now, in addition to the line about federal agents poking around in our libraries, there was also another line in the convention speech that received a lot of attention — a line I'd like to talk more about today. At one point in the speech, I mentioned that the people I've met all across Illinois know that government can't solve all their problems. They know that, quote, ". . . parents have to parent, that children can't achieve unless we raise their expectations and turn off the television sets and eradicate the slander that says a black youth with a book is acting white."

I included this line in the speech because I believe that we have a serious challenge to meet. I believe that if we want to give our children the best possible chance in life; if we want to open doors of opportunity while they're young and teach them the skills they'll need to succeed later on, then one of our greatest responsibilities as citizens, as educators, and as parents is to ensure that every American child can read and read well.

This isn't just another education debate where the answer lies somewhere between more money and less bureaucracy. It's a responsibility that begins at home — one that we need to take on before our kids ever step foot in a classroom; one that we need to carry through well into their teenage years.

That's because literacy is the most basic currency of the knowledge economy we're living in today. Only a few generations ago, it was okay to enter the workforce as a high school dropout who could only read at a third-grade level. Whether it was on a farm or in a factory, you could still hope to find a job that would allow you to pay the bills and raise your family.

But that economy is long gone. As revolutions in technology and communication began breaking down barriers between countries and connecting people all over the world, new jobs and industries that require more skill and knowledge have come to dominate the economy. Whether it's software design or computer engineering or financial analysis, corporations can locate these jobs anywhere there's an Internet connection. And so as countries like China and India continue to modernize their economies and educate their children longer and better, the competition American workers face will grow more intense; the necessary skills more demanding.

These new jobs are about what you know and how fast you can learn what you don't know. They require innovative thinking, detailed comprehension, and superior communication.

But before our children can even walk into an interview for one of these jobs; before they can ever fill out an application or earn the required college degree; they have to be able to pick up a book, read it, and understand it. Nothing is more basic; no ability more fundamental.

Reading is the gateway skill that makes all other learning possible, from complex word problems and the meaning of our history to scientific discovery and technological proficiency. In a knowledge economy where this kind of learning is necessary for survival, how can we send our kids out into the world if they're only reading at a fourth-grade level?

I don't know, but we do. Day after day, year after year.

Right now, one out of every five adults in the United States can't read a simple story to their child. During the last twenty years or so, over ten million Americans reached the twelfth grade without having learned to read at a basic level.

But these literacy problems start far before high school. In 2000, only 32 percent of all fourth graders tested as reading proficient. And the story gets worse when you take race and income into consideration. Children from low-income families score 27 points below the average reading level, while students from wealthy families score 15 points above the average. And while only one in twelve white seventeen-year-olds has the ability to pick up the newspaper and understand the science section, for Hispanics the number jumps to one in fifty, for African-Americans it's one in one hundred.

In this new economy, teaching our kids just enough so that they can get through *Dick and Jane* isn't going to cut it. Over the next ten years, the average literacy required for all American occupations is projected to rise by 14 percent. It's not enough just to recognize the words on the page anymore — the kind of literacy necessary for 21st-century employment requires detailed understanding and complex comprehension. But too many kids simply aren't learning at that level.

And yet, every year we pass more of these kids through school or watch as more drop out. These kids who will pour through the help wanted section and cross off job after job that requires skills they just don't have. And others who will have to take that help wanted section, walk it over to someone else, and find the courage to ask, "Will you read this for me?"

We have to change our whole mindset in this country. We're living in a 21st-century knowledge economy, but our schools, our homes, and our culture are still based around 20th-century expectations. It might seem like we're doing kids a favor by teaching them just enough to count change and read a food label, but in this economy, it's doing them a huge disservice. Instead, we need to start setting high standards and inspirational examples for our children to follow. While there's plenty that can be done to improve our schools and reform education in America, this isn't just an issue where we can turn to the government and ask for help. Reading has to begin at home.

We know that children who start kindergarten with an awareness of letters and basic language sounds become better readers and face fewer challenges in the years ahead. We also know that the more reading material kids are exposed to at home, the better they score on reading tests throughout their lives. So we need to make investments in family literacy programs and early childhood education so that kids aren't left behind before they even go to school. And we need to get books in our kids' hands early and often.

I know that this is often easier said than done. Parents today still have the toughest job in the world — and no one ever thanks you enough for doing it. You're working longer and harder than ever, juggling job and family responsibilities, and trying to be everywhere at once. When you're home, you might try to get your kids to read, but you're competing with the other byproducts of the technological revolution: video games and DVDs that they just have to have; TVs in every room of the household. Children eight to eighteen now spend three hours a day watching TV, while they only spend forty-three minutes reading.

Our kids aren't just seeing these temptations at home — they're everywhere. Whether it's their friends or the people they see on TV or a general culture that glorifies anti-intellectualism, it's too easy for kids today to put down a book and turn their attention elsewhere. And it's too easy for the rest of us to make excuses for it — pretending that putting a baby in front of a DVD is educational, letting a twelve-year-old skip reading as long as he's playing good video games, or substituting dinner in front of the TV for family conversation.

We know that's not what our kids need. We know that's not what's best for them. And so as parents, we need to find the time and the energy to step in and find ways to help our kids love reading. We can read to them, talk to them about what they're reading, and make time for this by turning off the TV ourselves.

Libraries can help parents with this. Knowing the constraints we face from busy schedules and a TV culture, we need to think outside the box here — to dream big like we always have in America. Right now, children come home from their first doctor's appointment with an extra bottle of formula. But imagine if they came home with their first library card or their first copy of *Goodnight Moon*?

What if it was as easy to get a book as it is to rent a DVD

or pick up McDonald's? What if instead of a toy in every Happy Meal, there was a book? What if there were portable libraries that rolled through parks and playgrounds like ice cream trucks? Or kiosks in stores where you could borrow books? What if during the summer, when kids often lose much of the reading progress they've made during the year, every child had a list of books they had to read and talk about and an invitation to a summer reading club at the local library?

Libraries have a special role to play in our knowledge economy. Your institution has been and should be the place where parents and kids come to read together and learn together. We should take our kids here more, and we should make sure politicians aren't closing libraries down because they had to spend a few extra bucks on tax cuts instead.

Each of you has a role here too. You can get more kids to walk through your doors by building on the ideas so many of you are already pursuing — book clubs and contests, homework help, and advertising your services throughout the community.

In the years ahead, this is our challenge — and this must be our responsibility.

As a librarian or as a parent, every one of you here today can probably remember the look on a child's face after finishing a first book. They turn that last page and stare up at you with those wide eyes, and in that look you find such a sense of accomplishment and pride; of great potential and so much possibility.

And in that moment, there's nothing we want more than to nurture that hope; to make all those possibilities and all those opportunities real for our children; to have the ability to answer the question, "What can I be when I grow up?" with "Anything you want — anything you can dream of."

It's a hope that's as old as the American story itself. From the moment the first immigrants arrived on these shores, generations of parents have worked hard and sacrificed whatever is necessary so that their children could have the same chances they had; or the chances they never had. Because while we could never ensure that our children would be rich or successful; while we could never be positive that they would do better than their parents, America is about making it possible to give them the chance. To give every child the opportunity to try.

Education is still the foundation of this opportunity. And the most basic building block that holds that foundation together is still reading. At the dawn of the 21st century, in a world where knowledge truly is power and literacy is the skill that unlocks the gates of opportunity and success, we all have a responsibility as parents and librarians, educators and citizens, to instill in our children a love of reading so that we can give them the chance to fulfill their dreams. Thank you.

VETERANS

Obama condemns neglect of military veterans

"Veterans already have difficulty accessing VA *care, and none of us want those who are still fighting to be greeted by a system that tells them, 'Thanks for fighting for your country — now take a number.'"*

With barely concealed anger, Barack Obama cites the experience of his grandfather's benefits from the GI Bill on returning home from European service in World War II, and contrasts that with a current federal government that consistently short-changes veterans in underfunding benefit programs managed by the U.S. Department of Veterans Affairs (VA). "The benefits are still too low and the waits are still too long," Obama told an American Legion Conference in 2005. "It's not enough to simply wave a flag and welcome our veterans with words of praise. We need to get serious about solving these problems and honoring their service."

"ADDRESS TO THE AMERICAN LEGION CONFERENCE"

July 15, 2005

Springfield, IL

Thank you. It's an honor to be here today with all of you Legionnaires.

Over the last few months and throughout the campaign, I've been able to travel the state and meet veterans from all across Illinois. And no matter how many stories of heroism I hear, I constantly find myself in awe of your service and inspired by your sacrifice.

Oliver Wendell Holmes once said that, "To fight out a war, you must believe in something and want something with all your might."

In America, we must never forget how lucky we are to have so many men and women who believe — who are willing to put aside their own pursuit of happiness, to subordinate their own sense of survival, for something bigger, something greater.[1]

When many of you joined the Armed Forces, you had your whole lives ahead of you — birthdays and weddings, holidays with family and friends, successes not yet achieved. And yet, you were willing to leave all that behind — perhaps forever — because you believed that your service would make it possible for the rest of us to live happily, safely, and freely.

And so it's this sense of obligation — of responsibility to one's fellow American — that we must honor when our veterans return and need our care and support. Since I joined the Veterans Committee, I've heard a lot of debate over funding and budget numbers — about what we can afford and where we can save money. But I know those aren't the first things that come to your mind when you think about taking care of America's veterans. And they're not the first things that come to my mind either.

I think about my grandfather, who signed up for duty in World War II the day after Pearl Harbor. He marched across Europe in Patton's army, and when he came home, it was the education and opportunity offered by the GI Bill that allowed his family to build their own American Dream.

I think about stories like the one I heard from a veteran named Bill Allen, who told me that on a trip to Chicago, he actually saw homeless veterans fighting over access to the dumpsters.

And so I ask: are we serving our veterans as well as they've served us when we find out that veterans' health care has been short-changed by at least one billion dollars? A shortfall that could have meant veterans turned away from doctors' visits, veterans unable to pay their medical bills, or veterans refused the prosthetics they need to live normal lives?

Thankfully, we restored the funding in Congress so that none of this would happen. But let me be clear — the Department of Veterans Affairs should never be funded as an afterthought. Republicans and Democrats warned the administration that there may be a shortfall months ago, and so we shouldn't have to be scraping for change now to care for those who risked their lives to defend ours. It should be America's first priority.

And yet, you've all seen how we keep falling short. How disabled veterans are waiting hundreds of days just to get their claim processed. How wounded veterans in Illinois receive fewer disability benefits than those in New Mexico or Maine. When I first arrived in the Senate, and saw the *Chicago Sun-Times* report that ranked Illinois forty-ninth in how much disability pay our veterans received, we decided to hold town hall meetings here in Springfield and in Chicago to hear directly from you. Well, you spoke, we relayed your concerns to VA Secretary Nicholson, he came out to see the problem for himself, and now we've increased our VA staff by 27 percent so there are more caseworkers for each veteran.

But the benefits are still too low and the waits are still too long, and so we've got a ways to go. It's not enough to simply wave a flag and welcome our veterans with words of praise[2] — we need to get serious about solving these problems and honoring their service. We held a hearing in Chicago about these issues just the other week, and I heard from a veteran whose hands had been crushed in an accident. Twenty years later he's still caught in the VA bureaucracy, trying to obtain disability benefits. Twenty years later. Meanwhile, we just learned that the VA's latest solution on disability disparities is to stop ranking which states are the best and worst. I don't know about you, but I don't think that burying bad news is any way to deal with it.

If this is the best we can do for veterans who've already come home, what will we do for the hundreds of thousands who will, God-willing, return from Iraq and Afghanistan? Veterans already have difficulty accessing VA care, and none of us want those who are still fighting to be greeted by a system that tells them, "Thanks for fighting for your country — now take a number."

We know that soldiers are already coming home with post-traumatic stress disorder, and we know that a recent Army study showed that one in six soldiers in Iraq reported symptoms of major depression. Some experts predict that more than one hundred thousand soldiers may need some kind of mental health treatment when they come home. For tens of thousands of others, the wounds they suffered in battle will need care that could last a lifetime. These brave men and women may not have survived earlier wars, but thanks to advances in technology, these young people not only have the chance to survive, but to live normal lives. But it's up to us to provide the resources to make that a reality.

It is not only our patriotic duty to provide this care, it is our moral duty at the most fundamental level — and we must rise to that challenge.

We've made some progress already. In Congress, with the help of the American Legion, I worked to ensure that our hospitalized soldiers don't get billed for their meals. And I've also sponsored the Sheltering All Veterans Everywhere Act, which would strengthen the VA programs our homeless vets need to get back on their feet. The American Legion has endorsed this bill, and so I hope we can work together on this and other initiatives in the future.

Over half a century ago, it was American Legion National Commander Harry Colmery[3] who first sat down and wrote the legislation that would become the GI Bill of Rights — a bill that has since provided education and training for nearly eight million Americans, housing for nearly two million families, and led to the creation of the great American middle class. That was a bill that told our heroes, "When you come home, we're here for you, because we're all in this together."

Today, we shouldn't be scraping to find the bare minimum in benefits and health care for our veterans. And with the largest deployment of troops since Vietnam fighting for freedom in an increasingly dangerous world, we should be talking about a GI Bill for the 21st century.[4]

When veterans look to Congress for help, this is the kind of legislation they should hear about — not budget cuts and funding shortfalls.

It's time to reassess our priorities. We never hesitate to praise the service of our veterans and to acknowledge the debt we owe them for their service, but now we must renew our commitment to them by increasing funding for the VA, and ensure that our veterans receive more than just words of praise, but also the health care and benefits they've earned.[5]

George Washington once said, "The willingness with which our young people are likely to serve in any war, no matter how justified, shall be directly proportional to how they perceive veterans of earlier wars were treated and appreciated by our nation."

Washington understood then what every veteran here knows now — that when we make the decision to send our troops to war, we also make the decision to care for them, to speak for them, and to think of them — always — when they come home. Thank you and God bless you.

Notes

1. In May 2008, President George W. Bush was asked in a television interview if he had made any personal sacrifices during the Iraq and Afghan wars. Bush said yes, he had given up his golf game. "It's not good that soldiers at a time like this should see pictures of their president playing golf," Bush said. Actually, as photographs later shown by MSNBC revealed, Bush was still golfing months after the date at which he told the interviewer he had quit.
2. It was at about this time that Obama, who began wearing a flag pin in his lapel after the September 11, 2001, terrorist attacks, stopped doing so, although he continued to carry one — along with his Bible — at all times. By his own account, the sight of flag pins worn by Bush and too many legislators whose patriotism struck him as hollow prompted the decision. By

May 2008, in the midst of his presidential run, the pin reappeared on Obama's suit lapel. "People keep giving them to me," Obama said. "And one older woman, obviously a supporter with all the 'Obama '08' buttons she was wearing, asked why I 'refused' to wear the pin. 'It would cost you so little [to do so],' she said." Obama sensed that his private misgivings with a relative handful of flag-brandishers was needlessly hurtful to the sensibilities of a wider public.

3. Drafted by Colmery, the GI Bill of Rights was an FDR initiative with an intended scope more limited than what Colmery devised and gained approval of. It was Colmery, too, who insisted on the extension of GI benefits to African-American veterans.
4. In 2008, U.S. Senator Jim Webb secured passage of a new GI Bill for Veterans of the Iraq and Afghan conflicts, over the opposition of John McCain and President Bush, who ultimately signed the GI Bill provision as part of a larger Iraq-War funding bill. Obama was a chief cosponsor of Webb's bill.
5. After years of criticism that the VA wasn't doing enough to help soldiers returning from Iraq and Afghanistan, the VA finally launched a suicide hotline in July 2007. In its first year, the hotline fielded 22,000 calls from anguished vets. The VA estimates taht 6,500 veterans take their own lives each year, or 18 per day. A Rand Corp. study in 2008 estimated that roughly one in five soldiers returning from Iraq and Afghanistan show symptoms of post-traumatic stress disorder (PTSD), putting them at greater risk of suicide. Each year, the VA reported in July 2008, 12,000 vets under its care attempt to take their own lives.

A CARING SOCIETY

Obama's pragmatic approach to progressive politics

"[RFK] still inspires our debate with his words, animates our politics with his ideas, and calls us to make gentle the life of a world that's too often coarse and unforgiving."

In commemoration of the eightieth anniversary of Robert F. Kennedy's birth, Obama pays tribute to RFK in all his dimensions — Kennedy as the erstwhile Cold Warrior whose evolution into a pragmatic progressive inspired Americans to fight injustice at home and abroad, a vision much needed today.

"ADDRESS AT THE ROBERT F. KENNEDY HUMAN RIGHTS AWARD CEREMONY"

November 16, 2005

Washington, DC

Thank you. It's an honor to be here today, and I'd also like to congratulate Stephen Bradbury on his award and on all the wonderful work he's been doing on behalf of the people of New Orleans.

I come to this with tremendous humility. I was only seven when Bobby Kennedy died. Many of the people in this room knew him as brother, as husband, as father, as friend.

I knew him only as an icon. In that sense, it is a distance I share with most of the people who now work in this Capitol — many of whom were not even born when Bobby Kennedy died. But what's interesting is that if you go throughout the offices in the Capitol, everywhere you'll find photographs of Kennedy, or collections of his speeches, or some other memento of his life.

Why is this? Why is it that this man who was never President, who was our Attorney General for only three years, who was New York's junior Senator for just three and a half, still calls to us today? Still inspires our debate with his words, animates our politics with his ideas, and calls us to make gentle the life of a world that's too often coarse and unforgiving?

Obviously, much has to do with charisma and eloquence — that unique ability, rare for most but common among Kennedys, to sum up the hopes and dreams of the most diverse nation on earth with a simple phrase or sentence; to inspire even the most apathetic observers of American life.

Part of it is his youth — both the time of life and the state of mind that dared us to hope that even after John was killed; even after we lost King; there would come a younger, energetic Kennedy who could make us believe again.

But beyond these qualities, there's something more.

Within the confines of these walls and the boundaries of this city, it becomes very easy to play small-ball politics. Somewhere between the partisan deadlock and the twenty-four hour news cycles, the contrived talking points and the focus on the sensational over the substantive, issues of war and poverty, hopelessness and lawlessness become problems to be managed, not crises to be solved. They become fodder for the Sunday show scrum, not places to find genuine consensus and compromise. And so, at some point, we stop reaching for the possible and resign ourselves to that which is most probable.

This is what happens in Washington.

And yet, as this goes on, somewhere another child goes hungry in a neighborhood just blocks away from one where a family is too full to eat another bite. Somewhere another hurricane survivor still searches for a home to return to or a school for her daughter. Somewhere another twelve-year-old is gunned down by an assailant who used to be his kindergarten playmate, and another parent loses their child on the streets of Tikrit.

But somewhere, there have also always been people who believe that this isn't the way it was supposed to be — that things should be different in America. People who believe that while evil and suffering will always exist, this is a country that has been fueled by small miracles and boundless dreams — a place where we're not afraid to face down the greatest challenges in pursuit of the greater good; a place where, against all odds, we overcome.

Bobby Kennedy was one of these people.

In a nation torn by war and divided against itself, he was able to look us in the eye and tell us that no matter how many cities burned with violence, no matter how persistent the poverty or the racism, no matter how far adrift America strayed, hope would come again.

It was an idealism not based in rigid ideology. Yes, he believed that government is a force for good — but not the only force. He distrusted big bureaucracies, and knew that change erupts from the will of free people in a free society; that it comes not only from new programs, but new attitudes as well.

And Kennedy's was not a pie-in-the-sky-type idealism either. He believed we would always face real enemies, and that there was no quick or perfect fix to the turmoil of the 1960s.

Rather, the idealism of Robert Kennedy — the unfinished legacy that calls us still — is a fundamental belief in the continued perfection of American ideals.

It's a belief that says if this nation was truly founded on the principles of freedom and equality, it could not sit idly by while millions were shackled because of the color of their skin. That if we are to shine as a beacon of hope to the rest of the world, we must be respected not just for the might of our military, but for the reach of our ideals. That if this is a land where destiny is not determined by birth or circumstance, we have a duty to ensure that the child of a millionaire and the child of a welfare mom have the same chance in life. That if out of many, we are truly one, then we must not limit ourselves to the pursuit of selfish gain, but that which will help all Americans rise together.

We have not always lived up to these ideals and we may fail again in the future, but this legacy calls on us to try. And the reason it does — the reason we still hear the echo of not only Bobby's words, but John's and King's and Roosevelt's and Lincoln's before him — is because they stand in such stark contrast to the place in which we find ourselves today.

It's the timidity of politics that's holding us back right now — the politics of can't-do and oh-well. An energy crisis that jeopardizes our security and our economy? No magic wand to fix it, we're told. Thousands of jobs vanishing overseas? It's actually healthier for the economy that way. Three days late to the worst natural disaster in American history? Brownie, you're doing a heck of a job.[1]

And of course, if nothing can be done to solve the problems we face, if we have no collective responsibility to look out for one another, then the next logical step is to give everyone one big refund on their government — divvy it up into individual tax breaks, hand 'em out, and encourage everyone to go buy their own health care, their own retirement plan, their own child care, their own schools, their own roads, their own levees. . . .

We know this as the Ownership Society. But in our past there has been another term for it — Social Darwinism — every man or woman for him- or herself. It allows us to say to those whose health care or tuition may rise faster than they can afford — tough luck. It allows us to say to the child who was born into poverty — pull yourself up by your bootstraps. It lets us say to the workers who lose their job when the factory shuts down — you're on your own.

But there is a problem. It won't work. It ignores our history. Yes, our greatness as a nation has depended on individual initiative, on a belief in the free market. But it has also depended on our sense of mutual regard for each other, the idea that everybody has a stake in the country, that we're all in it together and everybody's got a shot at opportunity.

Robert Kennedy reminded us of this. He reminds us still. He reminds us that we don't need to wait for a hurricane to know that Third World living conditions in the middle of an

American city make us all poorer. We don't need to wait for the three thousandth death of someone else's child in Iraq to make us realize that a war without an exit strategy puts all of our families in jeopardy. We don't have to accept the diminishment of the American Dream in this country, now or ever.

It's time for us to meet the whys of today with the why nots we often quote but rarely live — to answer "why hunger" and "why homeless," "why violence" and "why despair," with "why not good jobs and living wages," "why not better health care and world class schools," "why not a country where we make possible the potential that exists in every human being?"

If he were here today, I think it would be hard to place Robert F. Kennedy into any of the categories that so often constrain us politically. He was a fervent anti-communist but knew diplomacy was our way out of the Cuban Missile Crisis. He sought to wage the war on poverty but with local partnerships and community activism. He was at once both hard-headed and big-hearted.

And yet, his was not a centrism in the sense of finding a middle road or a certain point on the ideological spectrum. His was a politics that, at its heart, was deeply moral — based on the notion that in this world, there is right and there is wrong, and it's our job to organize our laws and our lives around recognizing the difference.

When RFK made his famous trip to the Mississippi Delta with Charles Evers[2] in 1967, the story is often told about the destitute people they encountered as they walked from shack to shack. As they walk into one with hardly a ceiling and a floor full of holes, Kennedy sees a small child with a swollen stomach sitting in the corner. He tries and tries to talk to this child again and again, but he gets no response, no movement, not even a look of awareness. Just a blank stare from cold, wide eyes so battered by poverty that they're barely alive.

And at that point we're told that Kennedy begins to cry.

And he turns to Evers and asks, "How can a country like this allow it?" and Evers responds, "Maybe they just don't know."

Bobby Kennedy spent his life making sure that we knew — not only to wake us from indifference and face us with the darkness we let slip into our own backyard, but to bring us the good news that we have it within our power to change all this; to write our own destiny. Because we are a people of hope. Because we are Americans.

This is the good news we still hear all these years later — the message that still points us down the road that Bobby Kennedy never finished traveling. It's a road I hope our politics and our country begin to take in the months and years to come. Thank you.

Notes

1. The reference is to Michael D. Brown (b. 1954), head to the Federal Emergency Management Agency at the time of the Katrina disaster. In the immediate aftermath of the hurricane damage that destroyed much of New Orleans, and for which FEMA was obviously unprepared given its incompetent handling of the crisis in the first few days of the massive flooding, President George W. Bush, while visiting Katrina-relief workers at the Mobile (Alabama) Regional Airport, singled out Brown for special praise, saying, "Again, I want to thank you all for — and Brownie, you're doing a heck of a job." Brown, a lifelong Republican who had failed in a 1988 congressional bid, had no emergency management experience, had been Judges and Standards Commissioner for the International Horse Association before joining FEMA as general counsel in 2001, where he was hired by a longtime friend. Seven days after his praise from Bush, Brown was relieved of all on-site relief duties along the Gulf Coast, and three days later, on September 12, 2005, resigned as director of FEMA. His boss, Michael Chertoff, head of the Department of Homeland Security, was similarly unaware of the magnitude of the

Katrina damage for at least three days after the New Orleans levees broke.

2. Medgar Willy Evers (1925–1963), African-American Civil rights leader from Mississippi, assassinated by Ku Klux Klan member Byron De La Beckwith.

GLOBAL WARMING

The climate-change threat requires urgent action

"Greenland is dumping into the ocean an amount of water fifty-four times greater than the city of Los Angeles uses in an entire year. All in all, Greenland has enough ice to raise the global sea level twenty-three feet, making a New Orleans out of nearly every coastal city imaginable."

There is a marked difference between Obama's hope-laced orations at rallies and his deliberative, almost stern style in formal addresses. Often accused of dealing in lofty generalities, Obama tells this annual luncheon of the Associated Press in detail about the damage already wrought by climate change; the future calamities to be anticipated if humanity's contribution to global warming isn't soon curbed; examples of progress already underway in heading off the threat to American cities and the heartland; and his own ideas for bringing the crisis under control.

"ENERGY INDEPENDENCE AND THE SAFETY OF OUR PLANET"

April 3, 2006

Chicago, IL

In April of 2005, Elizabeth Kolbert did a series of articles for *The New Yorker* about climate change. In one of those articles, she tells a very interesting story about some of the effects we're already seeing from global warming.

About fifteen years ago, in the furthest reaches of Alaska, the people of a small, thousand-year-old, oceanfront hunting village noticed something odd. The ice that surrounded and protected the village, which is only twenty feet above sea level, began to grow slushy and weak. Soon, it began to freeze much later in the fall and melt much earlier in the spring.

As the ice continued to melt away at an alarming pace during the 1990s, the village began to lose the protection it offered and became more vulnerable to storm surges. In 1997, the town completely lost a 125-foot-wide strip of land at its northern edge. In 2001, a storm with twelve-foot waves destroyed dozens of homes. And finally, in the summer of 2002, with the storms intensifying, the ice melting, and the land shrinking all around them, the residents of Shishmaref were forced to move their entire town miles inland — abandoning their homes forever.

The story of the Village That Disappeared is by no means isolated. And it is by no means over.

All across the world, in every kind of environment and region known to man, increasingly dangerous weather patterns and devastating storms are abruptly putting an end to the long-running debate over whether or not climate change is real. Not only is it real, it's here, and its effects are giving rise to a frighteningly new global phenomenon: the man-made natural disaster.

For decades, we've been warned by legions of scientists and mountains of evidence that this was coming — that we couldn't just keep burning fossil fuels and contribute to the changing atmosphere without consequence. And yet, for decades, far too many have ignored the warnings, either dismissing the science as a hoax or believing that it was the concern of enviros looking to save polar bears and rainforests.

But today, we're seeing that climate change is about more than a few unseasonably mild winters or hot summers. It's about the chain of natural catastrophes and devastating weather patterns that global warming is beginning to set off around the world — the frequency and intensity of which are breaking records thousands of years old.

In Washington, issues come and go with the political winds. And they are generally covered through that prism: Who's up and who's down? Which party benefits? Which party loses?

But in these superficial exchanges, we often lose sight of the real and lasting meaning of the decisions we make and those we defer.

The issue of climate change is one that we ignore at our own peril. There may still be disputes about exactly how much we're contributing to the warming of the earth's atmosphere and how much is naturally occurring, but what we can be scientifically certain of is that our continued use of fossil fuels is pushing us to a point of no return. And unless we free ourselves from a dependence on these fossil fuels and chart a new course on energy in this country, we are condemning future generations to global catastrophe.

Just think about some of the trends we've seen.

Since 1980, we've experienced nineteen of the twenty hottest years on record — with 2005 being the hottest ever.

These high temperatures are drying up already dry land, causing unprecedented drought that's ruining crops, devastating farmers, and spreading famine to already poor parts of the world. Over the last four decades, the percentage of the earth's surface suffering drought has more than doubled. In the United States, the drought we experienced in 2002 was the worst in forty years. And in Africa, more rivers are beginning to dry up, threatening the water supply across the continent.

As more land becomes parched, more forests are starting to burn. Across Indonesia, throughout Alaska, and in the western United States, wildfires have raged in recent years like never before. A new record was set in 2002, as more than seven million acres burned from Oregon down to Arizona.[1]

And while the situation on the land may look ugly, what's going on in the oceans is even worse. Hurricanes and typhoons thrive in warm water, and as the temperature has risen, so has the intensity of these storms. In the last thirty-five years, the percentage of Category Four and Five hurricanes has doubled, and the wind speed and duration of these storms has jumped 50 percent. A hurricane showed up in the South Atlantic recently when scientists said it could never happen. Last year, Japan set a new record when it suffered its tenth typhoon and the United States set a record for the most tornadoes we've ever had. And at one point, Hurricane Wilma was the most powerful storm ever measured.

These are all frightening situations, but perhaps none more so than what is beginning to occur at the North and South Poles. There, a satellite image from space or a trip to the region shows indisputable evidence that the polar ice caps are melting. But it's not just a slow, steady thaw that's been occurring over centuries, it's a rapidly accelerating meltdown that may eventually dump enough water into the ocean to annihilate coastal regions across the globe.

In 1996, a melting Greenland dumped about twenty-two cubic miles of water into the sea. Today, just ten years later, it's melting twice as fast. In real terms, this means that every single month, Greenland is dumping into the ocean an amount of water fifty-four times greater than the city of Los Angeles uses in an entire year. All in all, Greenland has enough ice to raise the global sea level twenty-three feet, making a New Orleans out of nearly every coastal city imaginable.

Indeed, the Alaskan village of Shishmaref could be just the beginning.

And yet, despite all the ominous harbingers of things to come, we do not have to stand by helplessly and accept this future. In fact, we can't afford to. Climate change may be unleashing the forces of nature, but we can't forget that this has been accelerated by man and can be slowed by man too.

By now, the culprit of this climate change is a familiar one, as is the solution. Last September, when I gave my first speech on energy, I talked about how our dependence on oil is hurting our economy, decimating our auto industry, and costing us millions of jobs. A few months ago, I discussed how the oil we import is jeopardizing our national security by keeping us tied to the world's most dangerous and unstable regimes. And when it comes to climate change, it's the fossil fuels we insist on burning — particularly oil — that are the single greatest cause of global warming and the damaging weather patterns that have been its result.

You'd think by now we'd get the point on energy

dependence. Never has the failure to take on a single challenge so detrimentally affected nearly every aspect of our well-being as a nation. And never have the possible solutions had the potential to do so much good for so many generations to come.

Of course, many Americans have gotten this point, and it's true that the call for energy independence is now coming from an amazingly diverse coalition of interests. From farmers and businesses, military leaders and CIA officials, scientists and Evangelical Christians, auto executives and unions, and politicians of almost every political persuasion, people are realizing that an oil future is not a secure future for this country.

And yet, when it comes to finding a way to end our dependence on fossil fuels, the greatest vacuum in leadership, the biggest failure of imagination, and the most stubborn refusal to admit the need for change is coming from the very people who are running the country.

By now, the Bush administration's record on climate change is almost legendary. This is the administration that commissioned government experts and scientists to do a study on global warming, only to omit the part from the final report that said it was caused by humans. This is the administration that didn't try to improve the Kyoto Treaty by trying to include oil guzzlers like China and India, but walked away from the entire global effort to stem climate change. And just recently, this is the administration that tried to silence a NASA scientist for letting the rest of us know that yes, climate change is a pretty big deal.

Meanwhile, it's pretty tough to make any real progress on this issue in Congress when the chairman of the committee in charge of the environment thinks that, in the face of literally thousands of scientists and studies that say otherwise, global warming is the "greatest hoax ever perpetrated on the American people."[2] And you know it's bad when the star witness at his global warming hearing is a science fiction writer.

Now, after the President's last State of the Union, when he told us that America was addicted to oil, there was a brief moment of hope that he'd finally do something on energy.

I was among the hopeful. But then I saw the plan.

His funding for renewable fuels is at the same level it was the day he took office. He refuses to call for even a modest increase in fuel-efficiency standards for cars. And his latest budget funds less than half of the energy bill he himself signed into law — leaving hundreds of millions of dollars in under-funded energy proposals.

This is not a serious effort. Saying that America is addicted to oil without following a real plan for energy independence is like admitting alcoholism and then skipping out on the twelve-step program. It's not enough to identify the challenge — we have to meet it.

See, there's a reason that some have compared the quest for energy independence to the Manhattan Project or the Apollo moon landing. Like those historic efforts, moving away from an oil economy is a major challenge that will require a sustained national commitment.

During World War II, we had an entire country working around the clock to produce enough planes and tanks to beat the Axis powers. In the middle of the Cold War, we built a national highway system so we had a quick way to transport military equipment across the country. When we wanted to pull ahead of the Russians into space, we poured millions into a national education initiative that graduated thousands of new scientists and engineers.

America now finds itself at a similar crossroads. As gas prices keep rising, the Middle East grows ever more unstable, and the ice caps continue to melt, we face a now-or-never, once-in-a-generation opportunity to set this country on a different course.

Such a course is not only possible, it's already being pursued in other places around the world. Countries like Japan are creating jobs and slowing oil consumption by churning out and buying millions of fuel-efficient cars. Brazil, a nation that once relied on foreign countries to import 80 percent of its crude oil, will now be entirely self-sufficient in a few years thanks to its investment in biofuels.

So why can't we do this? Why can't we make energy security one of the great American projects of the 21st century?

The answer is, with the right leadership, we can. We can do it by partnering with business, not fighting it. We can do it with technology we already have on the shelf. And we can do it by investing in the clean, cheap, renewable fuels that American farmers grow right here at home.

To deal directly with climate change, something we failed to do in the last energy bill, we should use a market-based strategy that gradually reduces harmful emissions in the most economical way. John McCain and Joe Lieberman are continuing to build support for legislation based on this approach, and Senators Bingaman and Domenici are also pursuing proposals that will cut carbon emissions. Right here in Chicago, the Chicago Climate Exchange is already running a legally binding greenhouse gas trading system.

The idea here is simple: if you're a business that can't yet meet the lower cap we'll put on harmful carbon emissions, you can either purchase credits from other companies that have achieved more than their emissions goal, or you can temporarily purchase a permit from the government, the money from which will go towards investments in clean energy technology. As Fred Krupp, the president of Environmental Defense has said, "Once you put a value on carbon reductions, you make winners out of innovators."

Any strategy for reducing carbon emissions must also deal with coal, which is actually the most abundant source of energy in this country. To keep using this fossil fuel, I believe we need to invest in the kind of advanced coal technology that will keep our air cleaner while still keeping our coal mines in business. Over the next two decades, power companies are expected to build dozens of new coal-fired power plants, and countries like India and China will build hundreds. If they use obsolete technology, these plants will emit over sixty billion tons of heat-trapping pollution into the atmosphere. We need to act now and make the United States a leader in putting in place the standards and incentives that will ensure that these plants use available technology to capture carbon dioxide and dispose of it safely underground.

But of course, one of the biggest contributors to our climate troubles and our energy dependence is oil, and so any plan for the future must drastically reduce our addiction to this dirty, dangerous, and ultimately finite source of energy.

We can do this by focusing on two things: the cars we drive and the fuels we use.

The President's energy proposal would reduce our oil imports by 4.5 million barrels per day by 2025. Not only can we do better than that, we must do better than that if we hope to make a real dent in our oil dependency. With technology we have on the shelves right now and fuels we can grow right here in America, by 2025 we can reduce our oil imports by over 7.5 million barrels per day — an amount greater than all the oil we are expected to import from the entire Middle East.

For years, we've hesitated to raise fuel economy standards as a nation in part because of a very legitimate concern — the impact it would have on Detroit. The auto industry is right when they argue that transitioning to more hybrid and fuel-efficient cars would require massive investment at a time when they're struggling under the weight of rising health care costs, sagging profits, and stiff competition.

But it's precisely because of that competition that they don't have a choice. China now has a higher fuel economy standard than we do, and Japan's Toyota is doubling production of the popular Prius to sell 100,000 in the U.S. this year.

There is now no doubt that fuel-efficient cars represent the future of the auto industry. If American car companies hope to be a part of that future — if they hope to survive —

they must start building more of these cars. This isn't just about energy — this is about the ability to create millions of new jobs and save an entire American industry.

But that's not to say we should leave the industry to face the transition costs on its own. Yes, we should raise fuel economy standards by 3 percent a year over the next fifteen years, starting in 2008. With the technology they already have, this should be an achievable goal for automakers. But we can help them get there.

Right now, one of the biggest costs facing auto manufacturers isn't the cars they make, it's the health care they provide. Health care costs make up $1,500 of the price of every GM car that's made — more than the cost of steel. Retiree health care alone cost the Big Three automakers nearly $6.7 billion just last year.

I believe we should make the auto companies a deal that could solve this problem. It's a piece of legislation I introduced called "Health Care for Hybrids," and it would allow the federal government to pick up part of the tab for the auto companies' retiree health care costs. In exchange, the auto companies would then use some of that savings to build and invest in more fuel-efficient cars. It's a win-win proposal for the industry — their retirees will be taken care of, they'll save money on health care, and they'll be free to invest in the kind of fuel-efficient cars that are the key to their competitive future.

But building cars that use less oil is only one side of the equation. The other involves replacing the oil we use with the home-grown biofuels that will finally slow the warming of the planet. In fact, one study shows that using cellulosic ethanol fuel instead of oil can reduce harmful emissions by up to 75 percent.

Already, there are hundreds of fueling stations that use a blend of ethanol and gasoline known as E85, and there are millions of cars on the road with the flexible-fuel tanks necessary to use this fuel — including my own right here in Illinois.

But the challenge we face with these biofuels is getting them out of the labs, out of the farms, and onto the wider commercial market.

The federal government can help in a few ways here, and recently, I introduced the American Fuels Act with Senator Dick Lugar to get us started.

First, this legislation would reduce the risk of investing in renewable fuels by providing loan guarantees and venture capital to those entrepreneurs with the best plans to develop and sell biofuels on a commercial market.

Second, it would let the private sector know that there will always be a market for renewable fuels by creating an alternative diesel standard in this country that would blend millions of more gallons of renewable fuels into the petroleum supply each year.

Third, it would help make sure that every single new car in America is a flexible-fuel vehicle within a decade. Currently it costs manufacturers just one hundred dollars to add these tanks to each car. But we can do them one better. If they install flexible-fuel tanks in their cars before the decade's up, we will provide them a one hundred dollar tax credit to do it — so there's no excuse for delay. And we'd also give consumers a bargain by offering a thirty-five cents tax credit for every gallon of E85 they use.

Fourth, this legislation calls for a Director of Energy Security to oversee all of our efforts. Like the Chairman of the Joint Chiefs and the National Intelligence Director, this person would be an advisor to the National Security Council and have the full authority to coordinate America's energy policy across all levels of government. He or she would approve all major budget decisions and provide a full report to Congress and the country every year detailing the progress we're making toward energy independence.

Finally, while it's not in the bill, we should also make sure that every single automobile the government purchases is a flexible-fuel vehicle — starting today. When it becomes possible in the coming years, we should also make sure that every government car is the type of hybrid that you can plug in to an outlet and recharge.

As the last few residents of Shishmaref pack up their homes and leave their tiny seaside village behind, I can't help but think that right now, history is testing our generation.

Will we let this happen all over the world? Will we stand by while drought and famine, storms and floods overtake our planet? Or will we look back at today and say that this was the moment when we took a stand? That this was the moment when we began to turn things around?

The climate changes we are experiencing are already causing us harm. But in the end, it will not be us who deal with its most devastating effects. It will be our children, and our grandchildren.

I have two daughters, aged three and seven. And I can't help but think that they are the reason I wanted to make a difference in this country in the first place — to give them a better, more hopeful world to raise their children.

This is our generation's chance to give them that world. It's a chance that will not last much longer, but if we work together and seize this moment, we can change the course of this nation forever. I hope we can start today.

Notes

1. Author Paul Roberts describes the devastating impact of changing weather patterns on declining food production in *The End of Food* (Houghton Mifflin, 2008).
2. U.S. Senator James (Jim) Inhofe (b. 1934), R-Okla., Chairman of the Senate Environment and Public Works Committee, 2003–07. Inhofe once compared the U.S. Environmental Protection Agency to the Gestapo and its head, Carol Browner, to Tokyo Rose, and said the Weather Channel was behind the global-warming hoax in a bid to raise its viewership ratings.

RELIGION AND POLITICS

Religious faith should not be divorced from politics

"Americans are a religious people. Ninety percent of us believe in God, 70 percent affiliate themselves with an organized religion, 38 percent call themselves committed Christians, and substantially more people in America believe in angels than they do in evolution."

In one of his most provactive speeches, Obama takes his own Democratic Party to task for bleaching spirituality out of American political discourse. Called to Christ in his late twenties, Obama faults Democrats for failing to grasp the central role of faith in the lives of most Americans at this "Call to Renewal" gathering of religious activists. It has made no sense, he argues, to grant Republicans a monopoly on religious discourse in the public square, fostering a disconnect between Democrats and the people they seek to represent.

"CALL TO RENEWAL KEYNOTE ADDRESS"

June 28, 2006

Washington, DC

Good morning. I appreciate the opportunity to speak here at the Call to Renewal's Building a Covenant for a New America conference. I've had the opportunity to take a look at your Covenant for a New America. It is filled with outstanding policies and prescriptions for much of what ails this country. So I'd like to congratulate you all on the thoughtful presentations you've given so far about poverty and justice in America, and for putting fire under the feet of the political leadership here in Washington.

But today I'd like to talk about the connection between religion and politics and perhaps offer some thoughts about how we can sort through some of the often bitter arguments that we've been seeing over the last several years.

I do so because, as you all know, we can affirm the importance of poverty in the Bible; and we can raise up and pass out this Covenant for a New America. We can talk to the press, and we can discuss the religious call to address poverty and environmental stewardship all we want, but it won't have an impact unless we tackle head-on the mutual suspicion that sometimes exists between religious America and secular America.

I want to give you an example that I think illustrates this fact. As some of you know, during the 2004 U.S. Senate General Election I ran against a gentleman named Alan Keyes. Mr. Keyes is well-versed in the Jerry Falwell[1]–Pat Robertson[2] style of rhetoric that often labels progressives as both immoral and godless.

Indeed, Mr. Keyes announced towards the end of the campaign that "Jesus Christ would not vote for Barack Obama. Christ would not vote for Barack Obama because Barack Obama has behaved in a way that it is inconceivable for Christ to have behaved."

Jesus Christ would not vote for Barack Obama.

Now, I was urged by some of my liberal supporters not to take this statement seriously, to essentially ignore it. To them, Mr. Keyes was an extremist, and his arguments not worth entertaining. And since at the time, I was up forty points in the polls, it probably wasn't a bad piece of strategic advice.

But what they didn't understand, however, was that I had to take Mr. Keyes seriously, for he claimed to speak for my religion, and my God. He claimed knowledge of certain truths.

Mr. Obama says he's a Christian, he was saying, and yet he supports a lifestyle that the Bible calls an abomination.

Mr. Obama says he's a Christian, but supports the destruction of innocent and sacred life.

And so what would my supporters have me say? How should I respond? Should I say that a literalist reading of the Bible was folly? Should I say that Mr. Keyes, who is a Roman Catholic, should ignore the teachings of the Pope?

Unwilling to go there, I answered with what has come to be the typically liberal response in such debates — namely, I said that we live in a pluralistic society, that I can't impose my own religious views on another, that I was running to be the U.S. Senator of Illinois and not the Minister of Illinois.

But Mr. Keyes's implicit accusation that I was not a true Christian nagged at me, and I was also aware that my answer did not adequately address the role my faith has in guiding my own values and my own beliefs.

Now, my dilemma was by no means unique. In a way, it reflected the broader debate we've been having in this country for the last thirty years over the role of religion in politics.

For some time now, there has been plenty of talk among pundits and pollsters that the political divide in this country has fallen sharply along religious lines. Indeed, the single biggest "gap" in party affiliation among white Americans today is not between men and women, or those who reside in so-called Red States and those who reside in Blue, but between those who attend church regularly and those who don't.

Conservative leaders have been all too happy to exploit this gap, consistently reminding evangelical Christians that Democrats disrespect their values and dislike their church, while suggesting to the rest of the country that religious Americans care only about issues like abortion and gay marriage, school prayer and intelligent design.

Democrats, for the most part, have taken the bait. At best, we may try to avoid the conversation about religious values altogether, fearful of offending anyone and claiming that — regardless of our personal beliefs — constitutional principles tie our hands. At worst, there are some liberals who dismiss religion in the public square as inherently irrational or intolerant, insisting on a caricature of religious Americans that paints them as fanatical, or thinking that the very word "Christian" describes one's political opponents, not people of faith.

Now, such strategies of avoidance may work for progressives when our opponent is Alan Keyes. But over the long haul, I think we make a mistake when we fail to acknowledge the power of faith in people's lives — in the lives of the American people — and I think it's time that we join a serious debate about how to reconcile faith with our modern, pluralistic democracy.

And if we're going to do that then we first need to understand that Americans are a religious people. Ninety percent of us believe in God, 70 percent affiliate themselves with an organized religion, 38 percent call themselves committed Christians, and substantially more people in America believe in angels than they do in evolution.

This religious tendency is not simply the result of successful marketing by skilled preachers or the draw of popular mega-churches. In fact, it speaks to a hunger that's deeper than that — a hunger that goes beyond any particular issue or cause.

Each day, it seems, thousands of Americans are going about their daily rounds — dropping off the kids at school, driving to the office, flying to a business meeting, shopping at the mall, trying to stay on their diets — and they're coming to the realization that something is missing. They are deciding that their work, their possessions, their diversions, their sheer busyness, is not enough.

They want a sense of purpose, a narrative arc to their lives. They're looking to relieve a chronic loneliness, a feeling supported by a recent study that shows Americans have fewer close friends and confidants than ever before. And so they need an assurance that somebody out there cares about them, is listening to them — that they are not just destined to travel down that long highway towards nothingness.

And I speak with some experience on this matter. I was not raised in a particularly religious household, as undoubtedly many in the audience were. My father, who returned to Kenya when I was just two, was born Muslim but as an adult became an atheist. My mother, whose parents were non-practicing Baptists and Methodists, was probably one of the most spiritual and kindest people I've ever known, but grew up with a healthy skepticism of organized religion herself. As a consequence, so did I.

It wasn't until after college, when I went to Chicago to work as a community organizer for a group of Christian churches, that I confronted my own spiritual dilemma.

I was working with churches, and the Christians who I worked with recognized themselves in me. They saw that I knew their Book and that I shared their values and sang their songs. But they sensed that a part of me that remained removed, detached, that I was an observer in their midst.

And in time, I came to realize that something was missing as well — that without a vessel for my beliefs, without a commitment to a particular community of faith, at some level I would always remain apart, and alone.

And if it weren't for the particular attributes of the historically black church, I may have accepted this fate. But as the months passed in Chicago, I found myself drawn — not just to work with the church, but to be in the church.

For one thing, I believed and still believe in the power of the African-American religious tradition to spur social change, a power made real by some of the leaders here today. Because of its past, the black church understands in an intimate way the Biblical call to feed the hungry and clothe the naked and challenge powers and principalities. And in its historical struggles for freedom and the rights of man, I was able to see faith as more than just a comfort to the weary or a hedge against death, but rather as an active, palpable agent in the world. As a source of hope.

And perhaps it was out of this intimate knowledge of hardship — the grounding of faith in struggle — that the church offered me a second insight, one that I think is important to emphasize today.

Faith doesn't mean that you don't have doubts.

You need to come to church in the first place precisely because you are first of this world, not apart from it. You need to embrace Christ precisely because you have sins to wash away — because you are human and need an ally in this difficult journey.

It was because of these newfound understandings that I was finally able to walk down the aisle of Trinity United Church of Christ on 95th Street in the South Side of Chicago one day and affirm my Christian faith. It came about as a choice, and not an epiphany. I didn't fall out in church. The questions I had didn't magically disappear. But kneeling beneath that cross on the South Side, I felt that I heard God's spirit beckoning me. I submitted myself to His will, and dedicated myself to discovering His truth.

That's a path that has been shared by millions upon millions of Americans — evangelicals, Catholics, Protestants, Jews, and Muslims alike; some since birth, others at certain turning points in their lives. It is not something they set apart from the rest of their beliefs and values. In fact, it is often what drives their beliefs and their values.

And that is why, if we truly hope to speak to people where they're at — to communicate our hopes and values in a way that's relevant to their own — then as progressives, we cannot abandon the field of religious discourse.

Because when we ignore the debate about what it means to be a good Christian or Muslim or Jew; when we discuss religion only in the negative sense of where or how it should not be practiced, rather than in the positive sense of what it tells us about our obligations towards one another; when we shy away from religious venues and religious broadcasts because we assume that we will be unwelcome — others will fill the vacuum, those with the most insular views of faith, or those who cynically use religion to justify partisan ends.

In other words, if we don't reach out to evangelical Christians and other religious Americans and tell them what we stand for, then the Jerry Falwells and Pat Robertsons and Alan Keyeses will continue to hold sway.

More fundamentally, the discomfort of some progressives with any hint of religion has often prevented us from effectively addressing issues in moral terms. Some of the problem here is rhetorical — if we scrub language of all religious content, we forfeit the imagery and terminology through which millions of Americans understand both their personal morality and social justice.

Imagine Lincoln's Second Inaugural Address without reference to "the judgments of the Lord." Or King's "I Have a Dream" speech without references to "all of God's children." Their summoning of a higher truth helped inspire what had seemed impossible, and move the nation to embrace a common destiny.

Our failure as progressives to tap into the moral underpinnings of the nation is not just rhetorical, though. Our fear of getting "preachy" may also lead us to discount the role that values and culture play in some of our most urgent social problems.

After all, the problems of poverty and racism, the uninsured and the unemployed, are not simply technical problems in search of the perfect ten-point plan. They are rooted in both societal indifference and individual callousness — in the imperfections of man.

Solving these problems will require changes in government policy, but it will also require changes in hearts and a change in minds. I believe in keeping guns out of our inner cities, and that our leaders must say so in the face of the gun manufacturers' lobby — but I also believe that when a gang-banger shoots indiscriminately into a crowd because he feels somebody disrespected him, we've got a moral problem. There's a hole in that young man's heart — a hole that the government alone cannot fix.

I believe in vigorous enforcement of our non-discrimination laws. But I also believe that a transformation of conscience and a genuine commitment to diversity on the part of the nation's CEOs could bring about quicker results than a battalion of lawyers. They have more lawyers than us anyway.

I think that we should put more of our tax dollars into

educating poor girls and boys. I think that the work that Marian Wright Edelman[3] has done all her life is absolutely how we should prioritize our resources in the wealthiest nation on earth. I also think that we should give them the information about contraception that can prevent unwanted pregnancies, lower abortion rates, and help assure that that every child is loved and cherished.

But, you know, my Bible tells me that if we train a child in the way he should go, when he is old he will not turn from it. So I think faith and guidance can help fortify a young woman's sense of self, a young man's sense of responsibility, and a sense of reverence that all young people should have for the act of sexual intimacy.

I am not suggesting that every progressive suddenly latch on to religious terminology — that can be dangerous. Nothing is more transparent than inauthentic expressions of faith. As Jim has mentioned, some politicians come and clap — off rhythm — to the choir. We don't need that.

In fact, because I do not believe that religious people have a monopoly on morality, I would rather have someone who is grounded in morality and ethics, and who is also secular, affirm their morality and ethics and values without pretending that they're something they're not. They don't need to do that. None of us need to do that.

But what I am suggesting is this — secularists are wrong when they ask believers to leave their religion at the door before entering into the public square. Frederick Douglass, Abraham Lincoln, Williams Jennings Bryan,[4] Dorothy Day,[5] Martin Luther King — indeed, the majority of great reformers in American history — were not only motivated by faith, but repeatedly used religious language to argue for their cause. So to say that men and women should not inject their "personal morality" into public policy debates is a practical absurdity. Our law is by definition a codification of morality, much of it grounded in the Judeo-Christian tradition.

Moreover, if we progressives shed some of these biases,

we might recognize some overlapping values that both religious and secular people share when it comes to the moral and material direction of our country. We might recognize that the call to sacrifice on behalf of the next generation, the need to think in terms of "thou" and not just "I," resonates in religious congregations all across the country. And we might realize that we have the ability to reach out to the evangelical community and engage millions of religious Americans in the larger project of American renewal.

Some of this is already beginning to happen. Pastors, friends of mine like Rick Warren[6] and T.D. Jakes,[7] are wielding their enormous influences to confront AIDS, Third World debt relief, and the genocide in Darfur. Religious thinkers and activists like our good friend Jim Wallis[8] and Tony Campolo[9] are lifting up the Biblical injunction to help the poor as a means of mobilizing Christians against budget cuts to social programs and growing inequality.

And by the way, we need Christians on Capitol Hill, Jews on Capitol Hill, and Muslims on Capitol Hill talking about the estate tax. When you've got an estate tax debate that proposes a trillion dollars being taken out of social programs to go to a handful of folks who don't need and weren't even asking for it, you know that we need an injection of morality in our political debate.

Across the country, individual churches like my own and your own are sponsoring day care programs, building senior centers, helping ex-offenders reclaim their lives, and rebuilding our gulf coast in the aftermath of Hurricane Katrina.

So the question is, how do we build on these still-tentative partnerships between religious and secular people of good will? It's going to take more work, a lot more work than we've done so far. The tensions and the suspicions on each side of the religious divide will have to be squarely addressed. And each side will need to accept some ground rules for collaboration.

While I've already laid out some of the work that progressive leaders need to do, I want to talk a little bit about what conservative leaders need to do — some truths they need to acknowledge.

For one, they need to understand the critical role that the separation of church and state has played in preserving not only our democracy, but the robustness of our religious practice. Folks tend to forget that during our founding, it wasn't the atheists or the civil libertarians who were the most effective champions of the First Amendment. It was the persecuted minorities, it was Baptists like John Leland[10] who didn't want the established churches to impose their views on folks who were getting happy out in the fields and teaching the scripture to slaves. It was the forebears of the evangelicals who were the most adamant about not mingling government with religion, because they did not want state-sponsored religion hindering their ability to practice their faith as they understood it.

Moreover, given the increasing diversity of America's population, the dangers of sectarianism have never been greater. Whatever we once were, we are no longer just a Christian nation; we are also a Jewish nation, a Muslim nation, a Buddhist nation, a Hindu nation, and a nation of nonbelievers.

And even if we did have only Christians in our midst, if we expelled every non-Christian from the United States of America, whose Christianity would we teach in the schools? Would we go with James Dobson's,[11] or Al Sharpton's?[12] Which passages of Scripture should guide our public policy? Should we go with Leviticus, which suggests slavery is okay and that eating shellfish is abomination? How about Deuteronomy, which suggests stoning your child if he strays from the faith? Or should we just stick to the Sermon on the Mount — a passage that is so radical that it's doubtful that our own Defense Department would survive its application? So before we get carried away, let's read our Bibles. Folks haven't been reading their Bibles.

This brings me to my second point. Democracy demands that the religiously motivated translate their concerns into universal, rather than religion-specific, values. It requires that their proposals be subject to argument, and amenable to reason. I may be opposed to abortion for religious reasons, but if I seek to pass a law banning the practice, I cannot simply point to the teachings of my church or evoke God's will. I have to explain why abortion violates some principle that is accessible to people of all faiths, including those with no faith at all.

Now this is going to be difficult for some who believe in the inerrancy of the Bible, as many evangelicals do. But in a pluralistic democracy, we have no choice. Politics depends on our ability to persuade each other of common aims based on a common reality. It involves the compromise, the art of what's possible. At some fundamental level, religion does not allow for compromise. It's the art of the impossible. If God has spoken, then followers are expected to live up to God's edicts, regardless of the consequences. To base one's life on such uncompromising commitments may be sublime, but to base our policy making on such commitments would be a dangerous thing. And if you doubt that, let me give you an example.

We all know the story of Abraham and Isaac. Abraham is ordered by God to offer up his only son, and without argument, he takes Isaac to the mountaintop, binds him to an altar, and raises his knife, prepared to act as God has commanded.

Of course, in the end God sends down an angel to intercede at the very last minute, and Abraham passes God's test of devotion.

But it's fair to say that if any of us leaving this church saw Abraham on a roof of a building raising his knife, we would, at the very least, call the police and expect the Department of Children and Family Services to take Isaac away from Abraham. We would do so because we do not hear what

Abraham hears, do not see what Abraham sees, true as those experiences may be. So the best we can do is act in accordance with those things that we all see, and that we all hear, be it common laws or basic reason.

Finally, any reconciliation between faith and democratic pluralism requires some sense of proportion.

This goes for both sides.

Even those who claim the Bible's inerrancy makes distinctions between Scriptural edicts, sensing that some passages — the Ten Commandments, say, or a belief in Christ's divinity — are central to Christian faith, while others are more culturally specific and may be modified to accommodate modern life.

The American people intuitively understand this, which is why the majority of Catholics practice birth control and some of those opposed to gay marriage nevertheless are opposed to a Constitutional amendment to ban it. Religious leadership need not accept such wisdom in counseling their flocks, but they should recognize this wisdom in their politics.

But a sense of proportion should also guide those who police the boundaries between church and state. Not every mention of God in public is a breach to the wall of separation — context matters. It is doubtful that children reciting the Pledge of Allegiance feel oppressed or brainwashed as a consequence of muttering the phrase "under God." I didn't. Having voluntary student prayer groups use school property to meet should not be a threat, any more than its use by the High School Republicans should threaten Democrats. And one can envision certain faith-based programs — targeting ex-offenders or substance abusers — that offer a uniquely powerful way of solving problems.

So we all have some work to do here. But I am hopeful that we can bridge the gaps that exist and overcome the prejudices each of us bring to this debate. And I have faith that millions of believing Americans want that to happen. No matter how religious they may or may not be, people are tired of seeing faith used as a tool of attack. They don't want faith used to belittle or to divide. They're tired of hearing folks deliver more screed than sermon. Because in the end, that's not how they think about faith in their own lives.

So let me end with just one other interaction I had during my campaign. A few days after I won the Democratic nomination in my U.S. Senate race, I received an e-mail from a doctor at the University of Chicago Medical School that said the following:

"Congratulations on your overwhelming and inspiring primary win. I was happy to vote for you, and I will tell you that I am seriously considering voting for you in the general election. I write to express my concerns that may, in the end, prevent me from supporting you."

The doctor described himself as a Christian who understood his commitments to be "totalizing." His faith led him to a strong opposition to abortion and gay marriage, although he said that his faith also led him to question the idolatry of the free market and quick resort to militarism that seemed to characterize much of the Republican agenda.

But the reason the doctor was considering not voting for me was not simply my position on abortion. Rather, he had read an entry that my campaign had posted on my website, which suggested that I would fight "right-wing ideologues who want to take away a woman's right to choose." The doctor went on to write:

"I sense that you have a strong sense of justice . . . and I also sense that you are a fair-minded person with a high regard for reason. . . . Whatever your convictions, if you truly believe that those who oppose abortion are all ideologues driven by perverse desires to inflict suffering on women, then you, in my judgment, are not fair-minded. . . . You know that we enter times that are fraught with possibilities for good and for harm, times when we are struggling to make sense of a common polity in the context of plurality, when we are unsure of what grounds we have for making any claims that involve others . . . I do not ask at this point that you oppose abortion, only that you speak about this issue in fair-minded words."

Fair-minded words.

So I looked at my website and found the offending words. In fairness to them, my staff had written them using standard Democratic boilerplate language to summarize my pro-choice position during the Democratic primary, at a time when some of my opponents were questioning my commitment to protect *Roe v. Wade.*[13]

Re-reading the doctor's letter, though, I felt a pang of shame. It is people like him who are looking for a deeper, fuller conversation about religion in this country. They may not change their positions, but they are willing to listen and learn from those who are willing to speak in fair-minded words. Those who know of the central and awesome place that God holds in the lives of so many, and who refuse to treat faith as simply another political issue with which to score points.

So I wrote back to the doctor, and I thanked him for his advice. The next day, I circulated the e-mail to my staff and changed the language on my website to state in clear but simple terms my pro-choice position. And that night, before I went to bed, I said a prayer of my own — a prayer that I might extend the same presumption of good faith to others that the doctor had extended to me.

And that night, before I went to bed, I said a prayer of my own. It's a prayer I think I share with a lot of Americans. A hope that we can live with one another in a way that reconciles the beliefs of each with the good of all. It's a prayer worth praying, and a conversation worth having in this country in the months and years to come.

Thank you.

Notes

1. Jerry Lamon Falwell Sr. (1933–2007), U.S. televangelist and cofounder in 1971 of the Moral Majority, an organization for Christian-based political lobbying that dissolved in 1989. After the terrorist attacks of September 11, 2001, Falwell, a guest on fellow televangelist Pat Robertson's *The 700 Club* TV show, said, "I really believe that the pagans, and the abortionists, and the feminists, and the gays, and the lesbians who are actively trying to make that an alternative lifestyle, the ACLU, People For The American Way, all of them who have tried to secularize America. I point the finger in their face and say, 'You helped make this happen.'" The American Civil Liberties Union is a leading U.S. civil-rights organization. People For The American Way, founded in the 1980s by liberal TV producer Norman Lear (*All In The Family*, *Maude*, et al.), promotes anti-poverty, civil rights, and other progressive causes.
2. Marion Gordon "Pat" Robertson (b. 1930), U.S. televangelist, founder of the Christian Coalition and the Christian Broadcasting Network, candidate for U.S. president in 1988. Robertson has described feminism as a "socialist, anti-family political movement that encourages women to leave their husbands, kill their children, practice witchcraft, destroy capitalism, and become lesbians."
3. Marian Wright Edelman (b. 1939), prominent U.S. children's-rights activist, founder and president of the Children's Defense Fund.
4. William Jennings Bryan (1860–1925), three-time Democratic nominee for U.S. president, best known for his crusade against Darwinism.
5. Dorothy Day (1897–1980), U.S. journalist, social activist, and devout Catholic, leader of social-justice campaigns on behalf of the poor.
6. Rick Warren (b. 1954), founder and senior pastor of the Saddleback Church, largest Christian congregation in California, author of books including the bestselling *The Purpose Driven Life*.

7. Thomas Dexter "T.D." Jakes (b. 1957), U.S. pastor of The Potter's House, a 30,000 member non-denominational, mostly African-American church in Dallas, Texas.
8. Jim Wallis (b. 1948), U.S. liberal evangelical writer and political activist, founder and editor of *Sojourners* magazine and the Washington, DC–based Sojourners community.
9. Tony Campolo (b. 1935), U.S. pastor and author of liberal political and social views.
10. John Leland (1754–1841), Baptist minister, fighter for religious freedom in the U.S.
11. James Clayton "Jim" Dobson (b. 1936), conservative evangelical Christian, founder and chairman of Focus On The Family, which broadcasts radio and TV programs reaching about 220 million people in 164 countries.
12. Alfred Charles "Al" Sharpton (b. 1954), U.S. African-American Baptist minister and civil-rights activist, presidential candidate in 2004.
13. *Roe v. Wade*, landmark 1973 U.S. Supreme Court decision that overturned most state and federal laws prohibiting abortion, finding that they were a violation of the constitutional right to privacy.

STEM CELL RESEARCH

A reminder that science has saved millions of lives

"By expanding scientific access to embryonic stem cells which would be otherwise discarded, this bill will help our nation's scientists and researchers develop treatments and cures to help people who suffer from illnesses and injuries for which there currently are none."

Logic and eloquence don't always carry the day, as Barack Obama anticipated even as he made this cogent case for removing federal impediments to potentially life-saving stem cell research. Despite bipartisan majorities in the Republican-controlled House of Representatives and U.S. Senate in favor of legislation to release the federal funds required for significant, more rapid advancement of stem cell development, President George W. Bush after more than six years in office used his veto power for the first time to thwart the will of Congress and a majority of Americans favoring the initiative, of which Obama was a Senate cosponsor. As Obama later mused, passion without power had been a frustration to him while in the minority in the Illinois Senate and more recently in Washington.

"SENATE REMARKS ON STEM CELL RESEARCH"

July 17, 2006

Washington, DC

Mr. President, a few weeks ago I was visited by two of my constituents, Mary Schneider and her son Ryan.

When Ryan was just two years old, his parents and doctors noted severe delays in his motor and speech development, and he was diagnosed with cerebral palsy. His parents were devastated, as the prognosis for many children with cerebral palsy is quite grim, and given the severity of Ryan's condition, his doctors didn't have much hope for his improvement.

Yet his parents had hope. Because when Ryan was born, his parents had saved his cord blood, a viable but limited source of stem cells. They found a doctor at Duke University who was willing to perform an experimental infusion with these cells to see if they might improve his condition.

They did. In fact, they seem to have cured him.

Within months of the transfusion, Ryan was able to speak, use his arms, and eat normally, just like any other child — a miracle his family had once only dreamed of.

Ryan's story exemplifies the power and the promise of stem cells to treat and cure the millions of Americans who are suffering from catastrophic, debilitating, and life-threatening diseases and health conditions.

Each year, 100,000 Americans will develop Alzheimer's disease. Over one million adults will be diagnosed with diabetes this year, which can lead to complications such as blindness, damaged nerves, and loss of kidney function. And there are far too many individuals with spinal cord injuries who are struggling to maintain mobility and independence.

For most of our history, medicine has offered little hope of recovery to individuals affected by these and other devastating illnesses and injuries.

Until now.

Recent developments in stem cell research may hold the key to improved treatments, if not cures, for those affected by Alzheimer's disease, diabetes, spinal cord injury, and countless other conditions.

Many men, women, and children who are cancer survivors are already familiar with the life-saving applications of adult stem cell research. Patients with leukemia or lymphoma often undergo bone marrow transplants, a type of stem cell transplant, which can significantly prolong life, or permanently get rid of the cancer. This therapy has been used successfully for decades, and is saving lives every day.

Yet this breakthrough has serious limitations. Adult stem cells, such as those used in bone marrow transplants, can only be collected in small quantities, may not be a match for the patient, and have limited ability to transform into specialized cells.

Cord blood, like the kind Ryan used, has limitations as well. If, for example, young Ryan's condition should deteriorate or he should develop another illness, there simply are not enough cord blood cells left for a second use.

His mother has told us that the few remaining cells would have to be cloned to get enough cells for future use, or they would have to obtain stem cells from another source.

These and other difficulties are the reasons why scientists have started to explore other types and other sources for stem cells, including embryonic stem cell research.

Embryonic stem cells can be obtained from a number of sources, including in vitro fertilization. At this very moment, there are over 400,000 embryos being stored in over 400 facilities throughout the United States. The majority of them are reserved for infertile couples. However, many of these embryos will go unused, destined for permanent storage in a freezer or disposal. We should expand and accelerate research using these embryos, just as we should continue to explore the viability of adult stem cell use and cord cell use.

All over the country, exciting progress is being made in the area of embryonic stem cell research. At the University of Illinois, they're finding that stem cells have the potential to treat blood disorders, lung diseases, and heart damage.

At Johns Hopkins, researchers were able to use mouse embryonic stem cells to repair damaged nerves and restore mobility in paralyzed rats. One can't help but think that it's a matter of when, not if, this research will be able to one day help those who have lost the ability to walk.

For these reasons, I'm proud to be a long-term supporter of greater stem cell research. While I was a member of the Illinois Senate, I was the chief cosponsor of the Ronald Reagan Biomedical Research Act, which would specifically permit embryonic stem cell research in Illinois, and establish review of this research by the Illinois Department of Public Health.

And I'm proud to be a cosponsor of the stem cell bill before us today. This bill embodies the innovative thinking that we as a society demand and medical advancement requires. By expanding scientific access to embryonic stem cells which would be otherwise discarded, this bill will help our nation's scientists and researchers develop treatments and cures to help people who suffer from illnesses and injuries for which there currently are none. But the bill is not without limits; it requires that scientific research also be subject to rigorous oversight.

I realize there are moral and ethical issues surrounding this debate. But I also realize that we're not talking about harvesting cells that would've been used to create life and we're not talking about cloning humans. We're talking about using stem cells that would have otherwise been discarded and lost forever — and we're talking about using those stem cells to possibly save the lives of millions of Americans.

Democrats want this bill to pass. Conservative, pro-life Republicans want this bill to pass. By large margins, the American people want this bill to pass. It is only the White House standing in the way of progress — standing in the way of so many potential cures.

I would only ask that the President thinks about this before he picks up his pen to deliver his first veto in six years. I would ask that he thinks about Ryan Schneider and his parents, and all the other families who are sitting and waiting and praying for a cure, hoping that somewhere a researcher or scientist will find the answer.

There was a time in the middle of the last century when America watched helplessly as a mysterious disease left thousands — especially children — disabled for life. The medical community worked tirelessly to try and find a cure, but they needed help — they needed funding to make their research possible.

With a world war raging and the country still emerging from depression, the federal government could have ignored their plight or told them to find a cure on their own.

But that didn't happen. Instead, Franklin Delano Roosevelt helped galvanize a community of compassion and organize the March of Dimes to find the cure for polio. And while Roosevelt knew that his own polio would never be cured by the discovery of a vaccine, he also knew that, at its best, government can be used as a force to accomplish together what we cannot achieve on our own.

And so the people began to care and the dimes piled up and the funding started to flow, and fifty years ago, Jonas Salk discovered the polio vaccine.

Americans are looking for that kind of leadership today. All over the country, patients and their families are waiting today for Congress and the President to open the door to the cures of tomorrow. At the dawn of the 21st century, we should approach this research with the same passion and commitment that have led to so many cures and saved so many lives throughout our history.

I urge my colleagues to support this bill. Thank you.

COMPASSION

The role of Dr. King's example in everyday American life

"By erecting this monument, we are reminded that this different, better place beckons us, and that we will find it not across distant hills or within some hidden valley, but rather we will find it somewhere in our hearts."

In this unusual address, on the occasion of the groundbreaking for a King memorial in Washington, DC, Obama dwells on the prosaic aspects of Dr. King's character, as if to say it is not beyond the reach of everyday Americans to engage in the same noble work as the Nobel Peace Prize–winning civil-rights champion.

"REMARKS AT DR. MARTIN LUTHER KING JR. NATIONAL MEMORIAL GROUNDBREAKING CEREMONY"

November 13, 2006

Washington, DC

I want to thank first of all the King family; we would not be here without them. I want to thank Mr. Johnson and the foundation for allowing me to share this day with all of you. I wish to recognize as well my colleagues in the United States Senate who have helped make today possible. Senators Paul Sarbanes and John Warner, who wrote the bill for this memorial. Senators Thad Cochran and Robert Byrd, who appropriated the money to help build it. Thank you all.

I have two daughters, ages five and eight. And when I see the plans for this memorial, I think about what it will be like when I first bring them here upon the memorial's completion. I imagine us walking down to this tidal basin, between one memorial dedicated to the man who helped give birth to a nation, and another dedicated to the man who preserved it. I picture us walking beneath the shadows cast by the Mountain of Despair, and gazing up the Stone of Hope, and reading the quotes on the wall together as the water falls like rain.

And at some point, I know that one of my daughters, perhaps my youngest, will ask, "Daddy, why is this monument here? What did this man do?"

How might I answer them? Unlike the others commemorated in this place, Dr. Martin Luther King Jr. was not a president of the United States — at no time in his life did he hold public office. He was not a hero of foreign wars. He never had much money, and while he lived he was reviled at least as much as he was celebrated. By his own accounts, he was a man frequently racked with doubt, a man not without flaws, a man who, like Moses before him, more than once questioned why he had been chosen for so arduous a task — the task of leading a people to freedom, the task of healing the festering wounds of a nation's original sin.

And yet lead a nation he did. Through words he gave voice to the voiceless. Through deeds he gave courage to the faint of heart. By dint of vision, and determination, and most of all faith in the redeeming power of love, he endured the humiliation of arrest, the loneliness of a prison cell, the constant threats to his life, until he finally inspired a nation to transform itself, and begin to live up to the meaning of its creed.

Like Moses before him, he would never live to see the Promised Land. But from the mountain top, he pointed the way for us — a land no longer torn asunder with racial hatred and ethnic strife, a land that measured itself by how it treats the least of these, a land in which strength is defined not simply by the capacity to wage war but by the determination to forge peace — a land in which all of God's children might come together in a spirit of brotherhood.

We have not yet arrived at this longed for place. For all the progress we have made, there are times when the land of our dreams recedes before us — when we are lost, wandering spirits, content with our suspicions and our angers, our long-held grudges and petty disputes, our frantic diversions and tribal allegiances.

And yet, by erecting this monument, we are reminded

that this different, better place beckons us, and that we will find it not across distant hills or within some hidden valley, but rather we will find it somewhere in our hearts.

In the Book of Micah, chapter six, verse eight, the prophet says that God has already told us what is good. "What doth the Lord require of thee," the verse tells us, "but to do justly, and to love mercy, and to walk humbly with thy God?"

The man we honor today did what God required. In the end, that is what I will tell my daughters — I will leave it to their teachers and their history books to tell them the rest. As Dr. King asked to be remembered, I will tell them that this man gave his life serving others. I will tell them that this man tried to love somebody. I will tell them that because he did these things, they live today with the freedom God intended, their citizenship unquestioned, their dreams unbounded. And I will tell them that they too can love. That they too can serve. And that each generation is beckoned anew — to fight for what is right, and strive for what is just, and to find within itself the spirit, the sense of purpose, that can remake a nation and transform a world. Thank you very much.

RESOLVING IRAQ

A blueprint for Iraq withdrawal and restoring Mideast stability

"It is time to give Iraqis their country back. And it is time to refocus America's efforts on the wider struggle yet to be won."

Not yet a presidential candidate, Barack Obama describes an ambitious plan for extracting America from the Iraq quagmire while stabilizing the Middle East and redoubling U.S. efforts to destroy al Qaeda. In other speeches on Iraq, Obama has dealt at length with the mendacity by which the war was "sold" to the American people, and enumerated the blunders of the U.S. occupation and their cost — in lives, treasure, and American global esteem. This speech differs: it was delivered two weeks after Americans, in a de facto referendum of the Bush administration's "progress" in Iraq, stripped his Republican party of control of both the U.S. Senate and House of Representatives. Thus in this address to the Chicago Council on Global Affairs, Obama focuses on solutions in an Iraq where there are only bad and worse options. Many were adopted by the Baker-Hamilton Commission on Iraq, whose report in late 2006 for a phased military withdrawal from Iraq was rejected by U.S. President George W. Bush. Instead, Bush installed yet another set of U.S. commanders in Iraq and deployed still more troops to that country. Obama's blueprint expressed here differs little from the proposed approach he would take to voters in the presidential campaign commencing in 2007.

"A WAY FORWARD IN IRAQ"

November 20, 2006

Chicago, IL

Throughout American history, there have been moments that call on us to meet the challenges of an uncertain world, and pay whatever price is required to secure our freedom. They are the soul-trying times our forebears spoke of, when the ease of complacency and self-interest must give way to the more difficult task of rendering judgment on what is best for the nation and for posterity, and then acting on that judgment — making the hard choices and sacrifices necessary to uphold our most deeply held values and ideals.

This was true for those who went to Lexington and Concord. It was true for those who lie buried at Gettysburg. It was true for those who built democracy's arsenal to vanquish fascism, and who then built a series of alliances and a world order that would ultimately defeat communism.

And this has been true for those of us who looked on the rubble and ashes of 9/11, and made a solemn pledge that such an atrocity would never again happen on United States soil; that we would do whatever it took to hunt down those responsible, and use every tool at our disposal — diplomatic, economic, and military — to root out both the agents of terrorism and the conditions that helped breed it.

In each case, what has been required to meet the challenges we face has been good judgment and clear vision from our leaders, and a fundamental seriousness and engagement on the part of the American people — a willingness on the part of each of us to look past what is petty and small and sensational, and look ahead to what is necessary and purposeful.

A few Tuesdays ago, the American people embraced this seriousness with regards to America's policy in Iraq. Americans were originally persuaded by the President to go to war in part because of the threat of weapons of mass destruction, and in part because they were told that it would help reduce the threat of international terrorism.

Neither turned out to be true. And now, after three long years of watching the same back and forth in Washington, the American people have sent a clear message that the days of using the war on terror as a political football are over. That policy-by-slogan will no longer pass as an acceptable form of debate in this country. "Mission Accomplished," "cut and run," "stay the course" — the American people have determined that all these phrases have become meaningless in the face of a conflict that grows more deadly and chaotic with each passing day — a conflict that has only increased the terrorist threat it was supposed to help contain.

Two thousand, eight hundred and sixty-seven Americans have now died in this war. Thousands more have suffered wounds that will last a lifetime. Iraq is descending into chaos based on ethnic divisions that were around long before American troops arrived. The conflict has left us distracted from containing the world's growing threats — in North Korea, in Iran, and in Afghanistan. And a report by our own intelligence agencies has concluded that al Qaeda is successfully using the war in Iraq to recruit a new generation of terrorists for its war on America.

These are serious times for our country, and with their votes two weeks ago, Americans demanded a feasible strategy with defined goals in Iraq — a strategy no longer driven by ideology and politics, but one that is based on a realistic assessment of the sobering facts on the ground and our interests in the region.

This kind of realism has been missing since the very conception of this war, and it is what led me to publicly oppose it in 2002. The notion that Iraq would quickly and easily become a bulwark of flourishing democracy in the Middle East was not a plan for victory, but an ideological fantasy. I said then and believe now that Saddam Hussein was a ruthless dictator who craved weapons of mass destruction but posed no imminent threat to the United States; that a war in Iraq would harm, not help, our efforts to defeat al Qaeda and finish the job in Afghanistan; and that an invasion would require an occupation of undetermined length, at undetermined cost, with undetermined consequences.

Month after month, and then year after year, I've watched with a heavy heart as my deepest suspicions about this war's conception have been confirmed and exacerbated in its disastrous implementation. No matter how bad it gets, we are told to wait, and not ask questions. We have been assured that the insurgency is in its last throes. We have been told that progress is just around the corner, and that when the Iraqis stand up, we will be able to stand down. Last week, without a trace of irony, the President even chose Vietnam as the backdrop for remarks counseling "patience" with his policies in Iraq.

When I came here and gave a speech on this war a year ago, I suggested that we begin to move towards a phased redeployment of American troops from Iraqi soil. At that point, seventy-five U.S. Senators, Republican and Democrat, including myself, had also voted in favor of a resolution demanding that 2006 be a year of significant transition in Iraq.

What we have seen instead is a year of significant deterioration. A year in which well-respected Republicans like John Warner, former administration officials like Colin Powell, generals who have served in Iraq, and intelligence experts have all said that what we are doing is not working. A year that is ending with an attempt by the bipartisan Iraq Study Group to determine what can be done about a country that is quickly spiraling out of control.

According to our own Pentagon, the situation on the ground is now pointing towards chaos. Sectarian violence has reached an all-time high, and 365,000 Iraqis have fled their homes since the bombing of a Shia mosque in Samarra last February. Three hundred thousand Iraqi security forces have supposedly been recruited and trained over the last two years, and yet American troop levels have not been reduced by a single soldier. The addition of 4,000 American troops in Baghdad has not succeeded in securing that increasingly perilous city. And polls show that almost two-thirds of all Iraqis now sympathize with attacks on American soldiers.

Prime Minister Maliki is not making our job easier. In just the past three weeks, he has — and I'm quoting from a *New York Times* article here — "rejected the notion of an

American 'timeline' for action on urgent Iraqi political issues; ordered American commanders to lift checkpoints they had set up around the Shiite district of Sadr City to hunt for a kidnapped American soldier and a fugitive Shiite death squad leader; and blamed the Americans for the deteriorating security situation in Iraq."

This is now the reality of Iraq.

Now, I am hopeful that the Iraq Study Group emerges next month with a series of proposals around which we can begin to build a bipartisan consensus. I am committed to working with this White House and any of my colleagues in the months to come to craft such a consensus. And I believe that it remains possible to salvage an acceptable outcome to this long and misguided war.

But it will not be easy. For the fact is that there are no good options left in this war. There are no options that do not carry significant risks. And so the question is not whether there is some magic formula for success, or guarantee against failure, in Iraq. Rather, the question is what strategies, imperfect though they may be, are most likely to achieve the best outcome in Iraq, one that will ultimately put us on a more effective course to deal with international terrorism, nuclear proliferation, and other critical threats to our security.

What is absolutely clear is that it is not enough for the President to respond to Iraq's reality by saying that he is "open to" or "interested in" new ideas while acting as if all that's required is doing more of the same. It is not enough for him to simply lay out benchmarks for progress with no consequences attached for failing to meet them. And it is not enough for the President to tell us that victory in this war is simply a matter of American resolve. The American people have been extraordinarily resolved. They have seen their sons and daughters killed or wounded in the streets of Fallujah. They have spent hundreds of billions of their hard-earned dollars on this effort — money that could have been devoted to strengthening our homeland security and our competitive standing as a nation. No, it has not been a failure of resolve that has led us to this chaos, but a failure of strategy — and that strategy must change.

It may be politically advantageous for the President to simply define victory as staying and defeat as leaving, but it prevents a serious conversation about the realistic objectives we can still achieve in Iraq. Dreams of democracy and hopes for a perfect government are now just that — dreams and hopes. We must instead turn our focus to those concrete objectives that are possible to attain — namely, preventing Iraq from becoming what Afghanistan once was, maintaining our influence in the Middle East, and forging a political settlement to stop the sectarian violence so that our troops can come home.

There is no reason to believe that more of the same will achieve these objectives in Iraq. And, while some have proposed escalating this war by adding thousands of more troops, there is little reason to believe that this will achieve these results either. It's not clear that these troop levels are sustainable for a significant period of time, and according to our commanders on the ground, adding American forces will only relieve the Iraqis from doing more on their own. Moreover, without a coherent strategy or better cooperation from the Iraqis, we would only be putting more of our soldiers in the crossfire of a civil war.

Let me underscore this point. The American soldiers I met when I traveled to Iraq this year were performing their duties with bravery, with brilliance, and without question. They are doing so today. They have battled insurgents, secured cities, and maintained some semblance of order in Iraq. But even as they have carried out their responsibilities with excellence and valor, they have also told me that there is no military solution to this war. Our troops can help suppress the violence, but they cannot solve its root causes. And all the troops in the world won't be able to force Shia, Sunni, and Kurd to sit down at a table, resolve their differences, and forge a lasting peace.

I have long said that the only solution in Iraq is a political one. To reach such a solution, we must communicate clearly and effectively to the factions in Iraq that the days of asking, urging, and waiting for them to take control of their own country are coming to an end. No more coddling, no more equivocation. Our best hope for success is to use the tools we have — military, financial, diplomatic — to pressure the Iraqi leadership to finally come to a political agreement between the warring factions that can create some sense of stability in the country and bring this conflict under control.

The first part of this strategy begins by exerting the greatest leverage we have on the Iraqi government — a phased redeployment of U.S. troops from Iraq on a timetable that would begin in four to six months.

When I first advocated steps along these lines over a year ago, I had hoped that this phased redeployment could begin by the end of 2006. Such a timetable may now need to begin in 2007, but begin it must. For only through this phased redeployment can we send a clear message to the Iraqi factions that the U.S. is not going to hold together this country indefinitely — that it will be up to them to form a viable government that can effectively run and secure Iraq.

Let me be more specific. The President should announce to the Iraqi people that our policy will include a gradual and substantial reduction in U.S. forces. He should then work with our military commanders to map out the best plan for such a redeployment and determine precise levels and dates. When possible, this should be done in consultation with the Iraqi government — but it should not depend on Iraqi approval.

I am not suggesting that this timetable be overly rigid. We cannot compromise the safety of our troops, and we should be willing to adjust to realities on the ground. The redeployment could be temporarily suspended if the parties in Iraq reach an effective political arrangement that stabilizes the situation and they offer us a clear and compelling rationale for maintaining certain troop levels. Moreover, it could be suspended if at any point U.S. commanders believe that a further reduction would put American troops in danger.

Drawing down our troops in Iraq will allow us to redeploy additional troops to Northern Iraq and elsewhere in the region as an over-the-horizon force. This force could help prevent the conflict in Iraq from becoming a wider war, consolidate gains in Northern Iraq, reassure allies in the Gulf, allow our troops to strike directly at al Qaeda wherever it may exist, and demonstrate to international terrorist organizations that they have not driven us from the region.

Perhaps most importantly, some of these troops could be redeployed to Afghanistan, where our lack of focus and commitment of resources has led to an increasing deterioration of the security situation there. The President's decision to go to war in Iraq has had disastrous consequences for Afghanistan — we have seen a fierce Taliban offensive, a spike in terrorist attacks, and a narcotrafficking problem spiral out of control. Instead of consolidating the gains made by the Karzai government, we are backsliding towards chaos. By redeploying from Iraq to Afghanistan, we will answer NATO's call for more troops and provide a much-needed boost to this critical fight against terrorism.

As a phased redeployment is executed, the majority of the U.S. troops remaining in Iraq should be dedicated to the critical, but less visible roles, of protecting logistics supply points, critical infrastructure, and American enclaves like the Green Zone, as well as acting as a rapid reaction force to respond to emergencies and go after terrorists.

In such a scenario, it is conceivable that a significantly reduced U.S. force might remain in Iraq for a more extended period of time. But only if U.S. commanders think such a force would be effective; if there is substantial movement towards a political solution among Iraqi factions; if the Iraqi government showed a serious commitment to disbanding the militias; and if the Iraqi government asked us — in a public and unambiguous way — for such continued support. We would make clear in such a scenario that the United States would not be maintaining permanent military bases in Iraq, but would do what was necessary to help prevent a total collapse of the Iraqi state and further polarization of Iraqi society. Such a reduced but active presence will also send a clear message to hostile countries like Iran and Syria that we intend to remain a key player in this region.

The second part of our strategy should be to couple this phased redeployment with a more effective plan that puts the Iraqi security forces in the lead, intensifies and focuses our efforts to train those forces, and expands the numbers of our personnel — especially special forces — who are deployed with Iraqi units as advisers.

An increase in the quality and quantity of U.S. personnel in training and advisory roles can guard against militia infiltration of Iraqi units; develop the trust and goodwill of Iraqi soldiers and the local populace; and lead to better intelligence while undercutting grassroots support for the insurgents.

Let me emphasize one vital point — any U.S. strategy must address the problem of sectarian militias in Iraq. In the absence of a genuine commitment on the part of all of the factions in Iraq to deal with this issue, it is doubtful that a unified Iraqi government can function for long, and it is doubtful that U.S. forces, no matter how large, can prevent an escalation of widespread sectarian killing.

Of course, in order to convince the various factions to embark on the admittedly difficult task of disarming their militias, the Iraqi government must also make headway on reforming the institutions that support the military and the police. We can teach the soldiers to fight and police to patrol, but if the Iraqi government will not properly feed, adequately pay, or provide them with the equipment they need, they will continue to desert in large numbers, or maintain fealty only to their religious group rather than the national government. The security forces have to be far more inclusive — standing up an army composed mainly of Shiites and Kurds will only cause the Sunnis to feel more threatened and fight even harder.

The third part of our strategy should be to link continued economic aid in Iraq with the existence of tangible progress toward a political settlement.

So far, Congress has given the Administration unprecedented flexibility in determining how to spend more than twenty billion dollars in Iraq. But instead of effectively targeting this aid, we have seen some of the largest waste, fraud, and abuse of foreign aid in American history. Today, the Iraqi landscape is littered with ill-conceived, half-finished projects that have done almost nothing to help the Iraqi people or stabilize the country.

This must end in the next session of Congress, when we reassert our authority to oversee the management of this war. This means no more bloated no-bid contracts that cost the taxpayers millions in overhead and administrative expenses.

We need to continue to provide some basic reconstruction funding that will be used to put Iraqis to work and help our troops stabilize key areas. But we need to also move towards more condition-based aid packages where economic assistance is contingent upon the ability of Iraqis to make measurable progress on reducing sectarian violence and forging a lasting political settlement.

Finally, we have to realize that the entire Middle East has an enormous stake in the outcome of Iraq, and we must engage neighboring countries in finding a solution.

This includes opening dialogue with both Syria and Iran, an idea supported by both James Baker and Robert Gates. We know these countries want us to fail, and we should remain steadfast in our opposition to their support of terrorism and Iran's nuclear ambitions. But neither Iran nor Syria want to see a security vacuum in Iraq filled with chaos, terrorism, refugees, and violence, as it could have a destabilizing effect throughout the entire region — and within their own countries.

And so I firmly believe that we should convene a regional conference with the Iraqis, Saudis, Iranians, Syrians, the Turks, Jordanians, the British, and others. The goal of this conference should be to get foreign fighters out of Iraq, prevent a further descent into civil war, and push the various Iraqi factions towards a political solution.

Make no mistake — if the Iranians and Syrians think they can use Iraq as another Afghanistan or a staging area from which to attack Israel or other countries, they are badly mistaken. It is in our national interest to prevent this from happening. We should also make it clear that, even after we begin to draw down forces, we will still work with our allies in the region to combat international terrorism and prevent the spread of weapons of mass destruction. It is simply not productive for us not to engage in discussions with Iran and Syria on an issue of such fundamental importance to all of us.

This brings me to a set of broader points. As we change strategy in Iraq, we should also think about what Iraq has taught us about America's strategy in the wider struggle against rogue threats and international terrorism.

Many who supported the original decision to go to war in Iraq have argued that it has been a failure of implementation. But I have long believed it has also been a failure of conception — that the rationale behind the war itself was misguided. And so going forward, I believe there are strategic lessons to be learned from this as we continue to confront the new threats of this new century.

The first is that we should be more modest in our belief that we can impose democracy on a country through military force. In the past, it has been movements for freedom from within tyrannical regimes that have led to flourishing democracies; movements that continue today. This doesn't mean abandoning our values and ideals; wherever we can, it's in our interest to help foster democracy through the diplomatic and economic resources at our disposal. But even as we provide such help, we should be clear that the institutions of democracy — free markets, a free press, a strong civil society — cannot be built overnight, and they cannot be built at the end of a barrel of a gun. And so we must realize that the freedoms FDR once spoke of — especially freedom from want and freedom from fear — do not just come from deposing a tyrant and handing out ballots; they are only realized once the personal and material security of a people is ensured as well.

The second lesson is that in any conflict, it is not enough to simply plan for war; you must also plan for success. Much has been written about how the military invasion of Iraq was planned without any thought to what political situation we would find after Baghdad fell. Such lack of foresight is simply inexcusable. If we commit our troops anywhere in the world, it is our solemn responsibility to define their mission and formulate a viable plan to fulfill that mission and bring our troops home.

The final lesson is that in an interconnected world, the defeat of international terrorism — and most importantly, the prevention of these terrorist organizations from obtaining weapons of mass destruction — will require the cooperation of many nations. We must always reserve the right to strike unilaterally at terrorists wherever they may exist. But we should know that our success in doing so is enhanced by engaging our allies so that we receive the crucial diplomatic, military, intelligence, and financial support that can lighten our load and add legitimacy to our actions. This means talking to our friends and, at times, even our enemies.

We need to keep these lessons in mind as we think about the broader threats America now faces — threats we haven't paid nearly enough attention to because we have been distracted in Iraq.

The National Intelligence Estimate, which details how we're creating more terrorists in Iraq than we're defeating, is the most obvious example of how the war is hurting our efforts in the larger battle against terrorism. But there are many others.

The overwhelming presence of our troops, our intelligence, and our resources in Iraq has stretched our military to the breaking point and distracted us from the growing threats of a dangerous world. The Chairman of the Joint Chiefs recently said that if a conflict arose in North Korea, we'd have to largely rely on the Navy and Air Force to take care of it, since the Army and Marines are engaged elsewhere. In my travels to Africa, I have seen weak governments and broken societies that can be exploited by al Qaeda. And on a trip to the former Soviet Union, I have seen the biological and nuclear weapons terrorists could easily steal while the world looks the other way.

There is one other place where our mistakes in Iraq have cost us dearly — and that is the loss of our government's credibility with the American people. According to a Pew survey, 42 percent of Americans now agree with the statement that the U.S. should "mind its own business internationally and let other countries get along the best they can on their own."

We cannot afford to be a country of isolationists right now. 9/11 showed us that try as we might to ignore the rest of the world, our enemies will no longer ignore us. And so we need to maintain a strong foreign policy, relentless in pursuing our enemies and hopeful in promoting our values around the world.

But to guard against isolationist sentiments in this country, we must change conditions in Iraq and the policy that has characterized our time there — a policy based on blind hope and ideology instead of fact and reality.

Americans called for this more serious policy a few Tuesdays ago. It's time that we listen to their concerns and win back their trust. I spoke here a year ago and delivered a message about Iraq that was similar to the one I did today. I refuse to accept the possibility that I will have to come back a year from now and say the same thing.

There have been too many speeches. There have been too many excuses. There have been too many flag-draped coffins, and there have been too many heartbroken families.

The time for waiting in Iraq is over. It is time to change our policy. It is time to give Iraqis their country back. And it is time to refocus America's efforts on the wider struggle yet to be won.

Thank you.

HEALTH CARE

Universal coverage as an American competitive advantage

"It's wrong when businesses have to lay off one employee because they can't afford health care of another. Wrong when a parent cannot take a sick child to the doctor because they cannot afford the bill that comes with it. Wrong when forty-six million Americans have no health care at all. In a country that spends more on health care than any other nation on earth, it's just wrong."

On announcing his presidential candidacy in early 2007, Obama wasn't ready to outline the detailed health-care reforms that would emerge later in the contest. But in this speech Obama hastened to prepare the ground for acceptance of sweeping health-care reform. He did so by reframing the decades-old debate, from whether all Americans deserved health-care coverage as a right, to whether Americans would tolerate the growing harm to the nation's global competitiveness in the absence of a more efficient and affordable means of delivering quality health care to everyone.

"THE TIME HAS COME FOR UNIVERSAL HEALTH CARE IN AMERICA"

January 25, 2007
Washington, DC

Thank you Ron Pollack and thank you Families USA for inviting me to speak here this morning.

On this January morning of 2007, more than sixty years after President Truman first issued the call for national health insurance, we find ourselves in the midst of an historic moment on health care. From Maine to California, from business to labor, from Democrats to Republicans, the emergence of new and bold proposals from across the spectrum has effectively ended the debate over whether or not we should have universal health care in this country.

Plans that tinker and halfway measures now belong to yesterday. The President's latest proposal that does little to bring down cost or guarantee coverage falls into this category. There will be many others offered in the coming campaign, and I am working with experts to develop my own plan as we speak, but let's make one thing clear right here, right now:

In the 2008 campaign, affordable, universal health care for every single American must not be a question of whether, it must be a question of how. We have the ideas, we have the resources, and we must find the will to pass a plan by the end of the next president's first term.

I know there's a cynicism out there about whether this can happen, and there's reason for it. Every four years, health-care plans are offered up in campaigns with great fanfare and promise. But once those campaigns end, the plans collapse under the weight of Washington politics, leaving the rest of America to struggle with skyrocketing costs.

For too long, this debate has been stunted by what I call the smallness of our politics — the idea that there isn't much we can agree on or do about the major challenges facing our country. And when some try to propose something bold, the interest groups and the partisans treat it like a sporting event, with each side keeping score of who's up and who's down, using fear and divisiveness and other cheap tricks to win their argument, even if we lose our solution in the process.[1]

Well we can't afford another disappointing charade in 2008. It's not only tiresome, it's wrong. It's wrong when businesses have to lay off one employee because they can't afford health care of another. Wrong when a parent cannot take a sick child to the doctor because they cannot afford the bill that comes with it. Wrong when forty-six million Americans have no health care at all. In a country that spends more on health care than any other nation on earth, it's just wrong.[2]

And yet, in recent years, what's caught the attention of those who haven't always been in favor of reform is the realization that this crisis isn't just morally offensive, it's economically untenable. For years, the can't-do crowd has scared the American people into believing that universal health care would mean socialized medicine and burdensome taxes — that we should just stay out of the way and tinker at the margins.

You know the statistics. Family premiums are up by nearly 87 percent over the last five years, growing five times faster than workers' wages. Deductibles are up 50 percent. Co-payments for care and prescriptions are through the roof.

Nearly eleven million Americans who are already insured spent more than a quarter of their salary on health care last year. And over half of all family bankruptcies today are caused by medical bills.

But they say it's too costly to act.

Almost half of all small businesses no longer offer health care to their workers, and so many others have responded to rising costs by laying off workers or shutting their doors for good. Some of the biggest corporations in America, giants of industry like GM and Ford, are watching foreign competitors based in countries with universal health care run circles around them, with a GM car containing twice as much health-care cost as a Japanese car.

But they say it's too risky to act.

They tell us it's too expensive to cover the uninsured, but they don't bother to mention that every time an American without health insurance walks into an emergency room, we pay even more. Our family's premiums are $922 higher because of the cost of care for the uninsured.

We pay fifteen billion dollars more in taxes because of the cost of care for the uninsured. And it's trapped us in a vicious cycle. As the uninsured cause premiums to rise, more employers drop coverage. As more employers drop coverage, more people become uninsured, and premiums rise even further.

But the skeptics tell us that reform is too costly, too risky, too impossible for America.

Well the skeptics must be living somewhere else. Because when you see what the health-care crisis is doing to our families, to our economy, to our country, you realize that caution is what's costly. Inaction is what's risky.

Doing nothing is what's impossible when it comes to health care in America.

It's time to act. This isn't a problem of money, this is a problem of will. A failure of leadership. We already spend $2.2 trillion a year on health care in this country. My colleague Senator Ron Wyden, who's recently developed a bold new health plan of his own, tells it this way:

For the money Americans spent on health care last year, we could have hired a group of skilled physicians, paid each one of them $200,000 to care for just seven families, and guaranteed every single American quality, affordable health care.

So where's all that money going? We know that a quarter of it — one out of every four health-care dollars — is spent on non-medical costs; mostly bills and paperwork. And we also know that this is completely unnecessary. Almost every other industry in the world has saved billions on these administrative costs by doing it all online. Every transaction you make at a bank now costs them less than a penny. Even at the Veterans Administration, where it used to cost nine dollars to pull up your medical record, new technology means you can call up the same record on the Internet for next to nothing.

But because we haven't updated technology in the rest of the health-care industry, a single transaction still costs up to twenty-five dollars — not one dime of which goes toward improving the quality of our health care.

This is simply inexcusable, and if we brought our entire health-care system online, something everyone from Ted Kennedy to Newt Gingrich believes we should do, we'd already be saving over six hundred million dollars a year on health care costs.

The federal government should be leading the way here. If you do business with the federal employee health benefits program, you should move to an electronic claims system. If you are a provider who works with Medicare, you should have to report your patient's health outcomes so that we can figure out, on a national level, how to improve health-care quality. These are all things experts tell us must be done but aren't being done. And the federal government should lead.

Another, more controversial area we need to look at is how much of our health-care spending is going toward the record-breaking profits earned by the drug and health-care industry. It's perfectly understandable for a corporation to try to make a profit, but when those profits are soaring higher and higher each year while millions lose their coverage and premiums skyrocket, we have a responsibility to ask why.

At a time when businesses are facing increased competition and workers rarely stay with one company throughout their lives, we also have to ask if the employer-based system of health care itself is still the best for providing insurance to all Americans. We have to ask what we can do to provide more Americans with preventative care, which would mean fewer doctor's visits and less cost down the road. We should make sure that every single child who's eligible is signed up for the children's health insurance program, and the federal government should make sure that our states have the money to make that happen. And we have to start looking at some of the interesting ideas on comprehensive reform that are coming out of states like Maine and Illinois and California, to see what we can replicate on a national scale and what will move us toward that goal of universal coverage for all.

But regardless of what combination of policies and proposals get us to this goal, we must reach it. We must act. And we must act boldly. As one health-care advocate recently said, "The most expensive course is to do nothing." But it wasn't a liberal Democrat or union leader who said this.

It was the president of the very health industry association that funded the "Harry and Louise" ads designed to kill the Clinton health-care plan in the early 1990s.

The debate in this country over health care has shifted . . . and so Washington no longer has an excuse for caution.

Leaders no longer have a reason to be timid. And America can no longer afford inaction. That's not who we are — and that's not the story of our nation's improbable progress.

Half a century ago, America found itself in the midst of another health-care crisis. For millions of elderly Americans, the single greatest cause of poverty and hardship was the crippling cost of health care and the lack of affordable insurance. Two out of every three elderly Americans had annual incomes of less than $1,000, and only one in eight had health insurance.

As health care and hospital costs continued to rise, more and more private insurers simply refused to insure our elderly, believing they were too great of a risk to care for.

The resistance to action was fierce. Proponents of health-care reform were opposed by well-financed, well-connected interest groups who spared no expense in telling the American people that these efforts were "dangerous" and "un-American," "revolutionary," and even "deadly."

And yet the reformers marched on. They testified before Congress and they took their case to the country and they introduced dozens of different proposals but always, always they stood firm on their goal to provide health care for every American senior. And finally, after years of advocacy and negotiation and plenty of setbacks, President Lyndon Johnson signed the Medicare bill into law on July 30, 1965.

The signing ceremony was held in Missouri, in a town called Independence, with the first man who was bold enough to issue the call for universal health care — President Harry Truman.

And as he stood with Truman by his side and signed what would become the most successful government program in history — a program that had seemed impossible for so long — President Johnson looked out at the crowd and said, "History shapes men, but it is a necessary faith of leadership that men can help shape history."

Never forget that we have it within our power to shape history in this country. It is not in our character to sit idly by as victims of fate or circumstance, for we are a people of action and innovation, forever pushing the boundaries of what's possible.

Now is the time to push those boundaries once more. We have come so far in the debate on health care in this country, but now we must finally answer the call first issued by Truman, advanced by Johnson, and fought for by so many leaders and Americans throughout the last century. The time has come for universal health care in America. And I look forward to working with all of you to meet this challenge in the weeks and months to come.

Notes

1. The Clinton initiative failed in large part due to its complexity and Hillary Clinton's fatal miscalculation in not bringing Congressional Democrats and Republicans into the secretive process by which her advisers developed their plan. Yet it also suffered from a successful effort by William Kristol, recently chief of staff for defeated vice-president Dan Quayle, to alert the Republican Congressional leadership to the long-term damage to the GOP should the Clintons succeed, just as the enduring popularity of the Democrats in mid-20th-century America derived in no small part from Franklin Roosevelt's introduction of Social Security. Kristol would re-emerge as the media leader of a group of "neo-conservatives" advocating President George W. Bush's war in Iraq.
2. When Bill Clinton defeated incumbent president George H.W. Bush in 1992 with the internal campaign slogan, "It's the economy, stupid — and don't forget about health care," it was widely regarded as a disgrace that an estimated thirty-four million Americans lacked health-care coverage. By 2008, that number had increased by almost 40 percent, or thirteen million people.

TERRORISM

A long-delayed plan for crushing global terrorism

"We did not finish the job against al Qaeda in Afghanistan. We did not develop new capabilities to defeat a new enemy, or launch a comprehensive strategy to dry up the terrorists' base of support."

Distraction with the Iraq quagmire, Obama argues, has kept the U.S. from fighting terrorism effectively. Obama proposes a multifaceted plan for doing so: better securing the homeland; rebuilding the trust of allies in helping track terrorist networks now operating in scores of countries; reforming America's twenty-two intelligence agencies to better understand the "intel" they gather, and to share it with state and local counterparts who may hold missing pieces of the puzzle; and coupling military and intelligence-gathering operations abroad with humanitarian works that truly win local hearts and minds, leading to more "actionable" intelligence and a reduction in anti-American sentiment.

"THE WAR WE NEED TO WIN"

August 1, 2007

Washington, DC

Thank you Lee, for hosting me here at the Wilson Center, and for your leadership of both the 9/11 Commission and the Iraq Study Group. You have been a steady voice of reason in an unsteady time.

Let me also say that my thoughts and prayers are with your colleague Haleh Esfandiari,[1] and her family. I have made my position known to the Iranian government. It is time for Haleh to be released. It is time for Haleh to come home.

Thanks to the 9/11 Commission, we know that six years ago this week President Bush received a briefing with the headline: "Bin Laden determined to strike in U.S."

It came during what the Commission called the "summer of threat," when the "system was blinking red" about an impending attack. But despite the briefing, many felt the danger was overseas, a threat to embassies and military installations. The extremism, the resentment, the terrorist training camps, and the killers were in the dark corners of the world, far away from the American homeland.

Then, one bright and beautiful Tuesday morning, they were here.

I was driving to a state legislative hearing in downtown Chicago when I heard the news on my car radio: a plane had hit the World Trade Center. By the time I got to my meeting, the second plane had hit, and we were told to evacuate.

People gathered in the streets and looked up at the sky and the Sears Tower, transformed from a workplace to a target. We feared for our families and our country. We mourned the terrible loss suffered by our fellow citizens. Back at my law office, I watched the images from New York: a plane vanishing into glass and steel; men and women clinging to windowsills, then letting go; tall towers crumbling to dust. It seemed all of the misery and all of the evil in the world were in that rolling black cloud, blocking out the September sun.

What we saw that morning forced us to recognize that in a new world of threats, we are no longer protected by our own power. And what we saw that morning was a challenge to a new generation.

The history of America is one of tragedy turned into triumph. And so a war over secession became an opportunity to set the captives free. An attack on Pearl Harbor led to a wave of freedom rolling across the Atlantic and Pacific. An Iron Curtain was punctured by democratic values, new institutions at home, and strong international partnerships abroad.

After 9/11, our calling was to write a new chapter in the American story. To devise new strategies and build new alliances, to secure our homeland and safeguard our values, and to serve a just cause abroad. We were ready. Americans were united. Friends around the world stood shoulder to shoulder with us. We had the might and moralsuasion that was the legacy of generations of Americans. The tide of history seemed poised to turn, once again, toward hope.

But then everything changed.

We did not finish the job against al Qaeda in Afghanistan. We did not develop new capabilities to defeat a new enemy, or launch a comprehensive strategy to dry up the terrorists' base of support. We did not reaffirm our basic values, or secure our homeland.

Instead, we got a color-coded politics of fear. Patriotism as the possession of one political party. The diplomacy of refusing to talk to other countries. A rigid 20th-century ideology that insisted that the 21st century's stateless terrorism could be defeated through the invasion and occupation of a state. A deliberate strategy to misrepresent 9/11 to sell a war against a country that had nothing to do with 9/11.

And so, a little more than a year after that bright September day, I was in the streets of Chicago again, this time speaking at a rally in opposition to war in Iraq. I did not oppose all wars, I said. I was a strong supporter of the war in Afghanistan. But I said I could not support "a dumb war, a rash war" in Iraq. I worried about a "U.S. occupation of undetermined length, at undetermined cost, with undetermined consequences" in the heart of the Muslim world. I pleaded that we "finish the fight with bin Laden and al Qaeda."

The political winds were blowing in a different direction. The President was determined to go to war. There was just one obstacle: the U.S. Congress. Nine days after I spoke, that obstacle was removed. Congress rubber-stamped the rush to war, giving the President the broad and open-ended authority he uses to this day. With that vote, Congress became co-author of a catastrophic war. And we went off to fight on the wrong battlefield, with no appreciation of how many enemies we would create, and no plan for how to get out.

Because of a war in Iraq that should never have been authorized and should never have been waged, we are now less safe than we were before 9/11.

According to the National Intelligence Estimate, the

threat to our homeland from al Qaeda is "persistent and evolving." Iraq is a training ground for terror, torn apart by civil war. Afghanistan is more violent than it has been since 2001. Al Qaeda has a sanctuary in Pakistan. Israel is besieged by emboldened enemies, talking openly of its destruction. Iran is now presenting the broadest strategic challenge to the United States in the Middle East in a generation. Groups affiliated with or inspired by al Qaeda operate worldwide. Six years after 9/11, we are again in the midst of a "summer of threat," with bin Laden and many more terrorists determined to strike in the United States.

What's more, in the dark halls of Abu Ghraib[2] and the detention cells of Guantanamo,[3] we have compromised our most precious values. What could have been a call to a generation has become an excuse for unchecked presidential power. A tragedy that united us was turned into a political wedge issue used to divide us.

It is time to turn the page. It is time to write a new chapter in our response to 9/11.

Just because the President misrepresents our enemies does not mean we do not have them. The terrorists are at war with us. The threat is from violent extremists who are a small minority of the world's 1.3 billion Muslims, but the threat is real. They distort Islam. They kill man, woman, and child; Christian and Hindu, Jew and Muslim. They seek to create a repressive caliphate. To defeat this enemy, we must understand who we are fighting against, and what we are fighting for.

The President would have us believe that every bomb in Baghdad is part of al Qaeda's war against us, not an Iraqi civil war. He elevates al Qaeda in Iraq — which didn't exist before our invasion — and overlooks the people who hit us on 9/11, who are training new recruits in Pakistan. He lumps together groups with very different goals: al Qaeda and Iran, Shiite militias and Sunni insurgents. He confuses our mission.

And worse — he is fighting the war the terrorists want us to fight. Bin Laden and his allies know they cannot defeat us on the field of battle or in a genuine battle of ideas. But they can provoke the reaction we've seen in Iraq: a misguided invasion of a Muslim country that sparks new insurgencies, ties down our military, busts our budgets, increases the pool of terrorist recruits, alienates America, gives democracy a bad name, and prompts the American people to question our engagement in the world.

By refusing to end the war in Iraq, President Bush is giving the terrorists what they really want, and what the Congress voted to give them in 2002: a U.S. occupation of undetermined length, at undetermined cost, with undetermined consequences.

It is time to turn the page. When I am President, we will wage the war that has to be won, with a comprehensive strategy with five elements: getting out of Iraq and on to the right battlefield in Afghanistan and Pakistan; developing the capabilities and partnerships we need to take out the terrorists and the world's most deadly weapons; engaging the world to dry up support for terror and extremism; restoring our values; and securing a more resilient homeland.

The first step must be getting off the wrong battlefield in Iraq, and taking the fight to the terrorists in Afghanistan and Pakistan.

I introduced a plan in January that would have already started bringing our troops out of Iraq, with a goal of removing all combat brigades by March 31, 2008. If the President continues to veto this plan, then ending this war will be my first priority when I take office.

There is no military solution in Iraq. Only Iraq's leaders can settle the grievances at the heart of Iraq's civil war. We must apply pressure on them to act, and our best leverage is reducing our troop presence. And we must also do the hard and sustained diplomatic work in the region on behalf of peace and stability.

In ending the war, we must act with more wisdom than we started it. That is why my plan would maintain sufficient forces in the region to target al Qaeda within Iraq. But we must recognize that al Qaeda is not the primary source of violence in Iraq, and has little support — not from Shia and Kurds who al Qaeda has targeted, or Sunni tribes hostile to foreigners. On the contrary, al Qaeda's appeal within Iraq is enhanced by our troop presence.

Ending the war will help isolate al Qaeda and give Iraqis the incentive and opportunity to take them out. It will also allow us to direct badly needed resources to Afghanistan. Our troops have fought valiantly there, but Iraq has deprived them of the support they need — and deserve. As a result, parts of Afghanistan are falling into the hands of the Taliban, and a mix of terrorism, drugs, and corruption threatens to overwhelm the country.

As President, I would deploy at least two additional brigades to Afghanistan to re-enforce our counter-terrorism operations and support NATO's efforts against the Taliban. As we step up our commitment, our European friends must do the same, and without the burdensome restrictions that have hampered NATO's efforts. We must also put more of an Afghan face on security by improving the training and equipping of the Afghan Army and Police, and including Afghan soldiers in U.S. and NATO operations.

We must not, however, repeat the mistakes of Iraq. The solution in Afghanistan is not just military — it is political and economic. As President, I would increase our non-military aid by $1 billion. These resources should fund projects at the local level to impact ordinary Afghans, including the development of alternative livelihoods for poppy farmers.[4] And we must seek better performance from the Afghan government, and support that performance through tough anti-corruption safeguards on aid, and increased international support to develop the rule of law across the country.

Above all, I will send a clear message: we will not repeat

the mistake of the past, when we turned our back on Afghanistan following Soviet withdrawal. As 9/11 showed us, the security of Afghanistan and America is shared. And today, that security is most threatened by the al Qaeda and Taliban sanctuary in the tribal regions of northwest Pakistan.

Al Qaeda terrorists train, travel, and maintain global communications in this safe haven. The Taliban pursues a hit and run strategy, striking in Afghanistan, then skulking across the border to safety.

This is the wild frontier of our globalized world. There are wind-swept deserts and cave-dotted mountains. There are tribes that see borders as nothing more than lines on a map, and governments as forces that come and go. There are blood ties deeper than alliances of convenience, and pockets of extremism that follow religion to violence. It's a tough place.

But that is no excuse. There must be no safe haven for terrorists who threaten America. We cannot fail to act because action is hard.

As President, I would make the hundreds of millions of dollars in U.S. military aid to Pakistan conditional, and I would make our conditions clear: Pakistan must make substantial progress in closing down the training camps, evicting foreign fighters, and preventing the Taliban from using Pakistan as a staging area for attacks in Afghanistan.

I understand that President Musharraf has his own challenges. But let me make this clear. There are terrorists holed up in those mountains who murdered 3,000 Americans. They are plotting to strike again. It was a terrible mistake to fail to act when we had a chance to take out an al Qaeda leadership meeting in 2005. If we have actionable intelligence about high-value terrorist targets and President Musharraf won't act, we will.

And Pakistan needs more than F-16s to combat extremism. As the Pakistani government increases investment in secular education to counter radical madrasas, my Administration will increase America's commitment. We must help Pakistan invest in the provinces along the Afghan border, so that the extremists' program of hate is met with one of hope. And we must not turn a blind eye to elections that are neither free nor fair — our goal is not simply an ally in Pakistan, it is a democratic ally.

Beyond Pakistan, there is a core of terrorists — probably in the tens of thousands — who have made their choice to attack America. So the second step in my strategy will be to build our capacity and our partnerships to track down, capture, or kill terrorists around the world, and to deny them the world's most dangerous weapons.

I will not hesitate to use military force to take out terrorists who pose a direct threat to America. This requires a broader set of capabilities, as outlined in the Army and Marine Corps's new counter-insurgency manual. I will ensure that our military becomes more stealth, agile, and lethal in its ability to capture or kill terrorists. We need to recruit, train, and equip our armed forces to better target terrorists, and to help foreign militaries to do the same. This must include a program to bolster our ability to speak different languages, understand different cultures, and coordinate complex missions with our civilian agencies.

To succeed, we must improve our civilian capacity. The finest military in the world is adapting to the challenges of the 21st century. But it cannot counter insurgent and terrorist threats without civilian counterparts who can carry out economic and political reconstruction missions — sometimes in dangerous places. As President, I will strengthen these civilian capacities, recruiting our best and brightest to take on this challenge. I will increase both the numbers and capabilities of our diplomats, development experts, and other civilians who can work alongside our military. We can't just say there is no military solution to these problems. We need to integrate all aspects of American might.

I will also strengthen our intelligence. This is about more

than an organizational chart. We need leadership that forces our agencies to share information, and leadership that never — ever — twists the facts to support bad policies. But we must also build our capacity to better collect and analyze information, and to carry out operations to disrupt terrorist plots and break up terrorist networks.

This cannot just be an American mission. Al Qaeda and its allies operate in nearly 100 countries. The United States cannot steal every secret, penetrate every cell, act on every tip, or track down every terrorist — nor should we have to do this alone. This is not just about our security. It is about the common security of all the world.

As President, I will create a Shared Security Partnership Program to forge an international intelligence and law enforcement infrastructure to take down terrorist networks from the remote islands of Indonesia to the sprawling cities of Africa. This program will provide five billion dollars over three years for counter-terrorism cooperation with countries around the world, including information sharing, funding for training, operations, border security, anti-corruption programs, technology, and targeting terrorist financing. And this effort will focus on helping our partners succeed without repressive tactics, because brutality breeds terror, it does not defeat it.

We must also do more to safeguard the world's most dangerous weapons. We know al Qaeda seeks a nuclear weapon. We know they would not hesitate to use one. Yet there is still about fifty tons of highly enriched uranium, some of it poorly secured, at civilian nuclear facilities in over forty countries. There are still about 15,000 to 16,000 nuclear weapons and stockpiles of uranium and plutonium scattered across eleven time zones in the former Soviet Union.

That is why I worked in the Senate with Dick Lugar[5] to pass a law that would help the United States and our allies detect and stop the smuggling of weapons of mass destruction. That is why I am introducing a bill with Chuck Hagel[6] that seeks to prevent nuclear terrorism, reduce global nuclear arsenals, and stop the spread of nuclear weapons. And that is why, as President, I will lead a global effort to secure all nuclear weapons and material at vulnerable sites within four years. While we work to secure existing stockpiles, we should also negotiate a verifiable global ban on the production of new nuclear weapons material.

And I won't hesitate to use the power of American diplomacy to stop countries from obtaining these weapons or sponsoring terror. The lesson of the Bush years is that not talking does not work. Go down the list of countries we've ignored and see how successful that strategy has been. We haven't talked to Iran, and they continue to build their nuclear program. We haven't talked to Syria, and they continue support for terror. We tried not talking to North Korea, and they now have enough material for six to eight more nuclear weapons.

It's time to turn the page on the diplomacy of tough talk and no action. It's time to turn the page on Washington's conventional wisdom that agreement must be reached before you meet, that talking to other countries is some kind of reward, and that presidents can only meet with people who will tell them what they want to hear.

President Kennedy said it best: "Let us never negotiate out of fear, but let us never fear to negotiate." Only by knowing your adversary can you defeat them or drive wedges between them. As President, I will work with our friends and allies, but I won't outsource our diplomacy in Tehran to the Europeans, or our diplomacy in Pyongyang to the Chinese. I will do the careful preparation needed, and let these countries know where America stands. They will no longer have the excuse of American intransigence. They will have our terms: no support for terror and no nuclear weapons.

But America must be about more than taking out terrorists and locking up weapons, or else new terrorists will rise up to take the place of every one we capture or kill. That is why the third step in my strategy will be drying up the rising well of support for extremism.

When you travel to the world's trouble spots as a United States Senator, much of what you see is from a helicopter. So you look out, with the buzz of the rotor in your ear, maybe a door gunner nearby, and you see the refugee camp in Darfur, the flood near Djibouti, the bombed out block in Baghdad. You see thousands of desperate faces.

Al Qaeda's new recruits come from Africa and Asia, the Middle East, and Europe. Many come from disaffected communities and disconnected corners of our interconnected world. And it makes you stop and wonder: when those faces look up at an American helicopter, do they feel hope, or do they feel hate?

We know where extremists thrive. In conflict zones that are incubators of resentment and anarchy. In weak states that cannot control their borders or territory, or meet the basic needs of their people. From Africa to central Asia to the Pacific Rim — nearly sixty countries stand on the brink of conflict or collapse. The extremists encourage the exploitation of these hopeless places on their hate-filled websites.

And we know what the extremists say about us. America is just an occupying army in Muslim lands, the shadow of a shrouded figure standing on a box at Abu Ghraib, the power behind the throne of a repressive leader. They say we are at war with Islam. That is the whispered line of the extremist who has nothing to offer in this battle of ideas but blame — blame America, blame progress, blame Jews. And often he offers something along with the hate. A sense of empowerment. Maybe an education at a madrasa, some charity for your family, some basic services in the neighborhood. And then: a mission and a gun.

We know we are not who they say we are. America is at war with terrorists who killed on our soil. We are not at war with Islam. America is a compassionate nation that wants a better future for all people. The vast majority of the world's

1.3 billion Muslims have no use for bin Ladin or his bankrupt ideas. But too often since 9/11, the extremists have defined us, not the other way around.

When I am President, that will change. We will author our own story.

We do need to stand for democracy. And I will. But democracy is about more than a ballot box. America must show — through deeds as well as words — that we stand with those who seek a better life. That child looking up at the helicopter must see America and feel hope.

As President, I will make it a focus of my foreign policy to roll back the tide of hopelessness that gives rise to hate. Freedom must mean freedom from fear, not the freedom of anarchy. I will never shrug my shoulders and say — as Secretary Rumsfeld[7] did — "Freedom is untidy." I will focus our support on helping nations build independent judicial systems, honest police forces, and financial systems that are transparent and accountable. Freedom must also mean freedom from want, not freedom lost to an empty stomach. So I will make poverty reduction a key part of helping other nations reduce anarchy.

I will double our annual investments to meet these challenges to fifty billion dollars by 2012. And I will support a two billion dollar Global Education Fund to counter the radical madrasas — often funded by money from within Saudi Arabia — that have filled young minds with messages of hate. We must work for a world where every child, everywhere, is taught to build and not to destroy. And as we lead we will ask for more from our friends in Europe and Asia as well — more support for our diplomacy, more support for multilateral peacekeeping, and more support to rebuild societies ravaged by conflict.

I will also launch a program of public diplomacy that is a coordinated effort across my Administration, not a small group of political officials at the State Department explaining a misguided war. We will open "America Houses"[8] in cities across the Islamic world, with Internet, libraries, English lessons, stories of America's Muslims and the strength they add to our country, and vocational programs. Through a new "America's Voice Corps" we will recruit, train, and send out into the field talented young Americans who can speak with — and listen to — the people who today hear about us only from our enemies.

As President, I will lead this effort. In the first one hundred days of my Administration, I will travel to a major Islamic forum and deliver an address to redefine our struggle. I will make clear that we are not at war with Islam, that we will stand with those who are willing to stand up for their future, and that we need their effort to defeat the prophets of hate and violence. I will speak directly to that child who looks up at that helicopter, and my message will be clear: "You matter to us. Your future is our future. And our moment is now."

This brings me to the fourth step in my strategy: I will make clear that the days of compromising our values are over.

Major General Paul Eaton had a long and distinguished career serving this country. It included training the Iraqi Army. After Abu Ghraib, his senior Iraqi advisor came into his office and said: "You have no idea how this will play out on the streets of Baghdad and the rest of the Arab world. How can this be?" This was not the America he had looked up to.

As the counter-insurgency manual reminds us, we cannot win a war unless we maintain the high ground and keep the people on our side. But because the Administration decided to take the low road, our troops have more enemies. Because the Administration cast aside international norms that reflect American values, we are less able to promote our values. When I am President, America will reject torture without exception. America is the country that stood against that kind of behavior, and we will do so again.

I also will reject a legal framework that does not work. There has been only one conviction at Guantanamo. It was for a guilty plea on material support for terrorism. The sentence was nine months. There has not been one conviction of a terrorist act. I have faith in America's courts, and I have faith in our JAGs.[9] As President, I will close Guantanamo, reject the Military Commissions Act, and adhere to the Geneva Conventions. Our Constitution and our Uniform Code of Military Justice provide a framework for dealing with the terrorists.

This Administration also puts forward a false choice between the liberties we cherish and the security we demand. I will provide our intelligence and law enforcement agencies with the tools they need to track and take out the terrorists without undermining our Constitution and our freedom.

That means no more illegal wire-tapping of American citizens. No more national security letters to spy on citizens who are not suspected of a crime. No more tracking citizens who do nothing more than protest a misguided war. No more ignoring the law when it is inconvenient. That is not who we are. And it is not what is necessary to defeat the terrorists. The FISA[10] court works. The separation of powers works. Our Constitution works. We will again set an example for the world that the law is not subject to the whims of stubborn rulers, and that justice is not arbitrary.

This Administration acts like violating civil liberties is the way to enhance our security. It is not. There are no shortcuts to protecting America, and that is why the fifth part of my strategy is doing the hard and patient work to secure a more resilient homeland.

Too often this Administration's approach to homeland security has been to scatter money around and avoid hard choices, or to scare Americans without telling them what to be scared of, or what to do. A department set up to make Americans feel safer didn't even show up when bodies drifted through the streets in New Orleans. That's not acceptable.

My Administration will take an approach to homeland security guided by risk. I will establish a Quadrennial

Review at the Department of Homeland Security — just like at the Pentagon — to undertake a top to bottom review of the threats we face and our ability to confront them. And I will develop a comprehensive National Infrastructure Protection Plan that draws on both local know-how and national priorities.

We have to put resources where our infrastructure is most vulnerable. That means tough and permanent standards for securing our chemical plants. Improving our capability to screen cargo and investing in safeguards that will prevent the disruption of our ports. And making sure our energy sector — our refineries and pipelines and power grids — is protected so that terrorists cannot cripple our economy.

We also have to get past a top-down approach. Folks across America are the ones on the front lines. On 9/11, it was citizens — empowered by their knowledge of the World Trade Center attacks — who protected our government by heroically taking action on Flight 93 to keep it from reaching our nation's capital. When I have information that can empower Americans, I will share it with them.

Information sharing with state and local governments must be a two-way street, because we never know where the two pieces of the puzzle are that might fit together — the tip from Afghanistan, and the cop who sees something suspicious on Michigan Avenue. I will increase funding to help train police to gather information and connect it to the intelligence they receive from the federal government. I will address the problem in our prisons, where the most disaffected and disconnected Americans are being explicitly targeted for conversion by al Qaeda and its ideological allies.

And my Administration will not permit more lives to be lost because emergency responders are not outfitted with the communications capability and protective equipment their job requires, or because the federal government is too slow to respond when disaster strikes. We've been through that on 9/11. We've been through it during Katrina.[11] I will ensure that we have the resources and competent federal leadership we need to support our communities when American lives are at stake.

But this effort can't just be about what we ask of our men and women in uniform. It can't just be about how we spend our time or our money.

It's about the kind of country we are.

We are in the early stages of a long struggle. Yet since 9/11, we've heard a lot about what America can't do or shouldn't do or won't even try. We can't vote against a misguided war in Iraq because that would make us look weak, or talk to other countries because that would be a reward. We can't reach out to the hundreds of millions of Muslims who reject terror because we worry they hate us. We can't protect the homeland because there are too many targets, or secure our people while staying true to our values. We can't get past the America of Red and Blue, the politics of who's up and who's down.

That is not the America that I know.

The America I know is the last, best hope for that child looking up at a helicopter. It's the country that put a man on the moon; that defeated fascism and helped rebuild Europe. It's a country whose strength abroad is measured not just by armies, but rather by the power of our ideals, and by our purpose to forge an ever more perfect union at home.

That's the America I know. We just have to act like it again to write that next chapter in the American story. If we do, we can keep America safe while extending security and opportunity around the world. We can hold true to our values, and in doing so advance those values abroad. And we can be what that child looking up at a helicopter needs us to be: the relentless opponent of terror and tyranny, and the light of hope to the world.

To make this story reality, it's going to take Americans coming together and changing the fundamental direction of this country. It's going to take the service of a new generation of young people. It's going to take facing tragedy head-on and turning it into the next generation's triumph. That is a challenge that I welcome. Because when we do make that change, we'll do more than win a war — we'll live up to that calling to make America, and the world, safer, freer, and more hopeful than we found it.

Notes

1. Iran-American scholar Dr. Haleh Esfandiari was charged in May 2007 by the Iranian government with "allegedly" plotting against the sovereignty of the country as part of a spy ring.
2. In 2004, reports of U.S. Army and Central Intelligence Agency (CIA) abuse of prisoners held at Baghdad's Abu Ghraib prison, the most notorious of toppled leader Saddam Hussein's prisons, first came to light. Seven U.S. soldiers were convicted in courts-martial of abusive and humiliating treatment of prisoners, photographs of which circulated worldwide.
3. The Guantanamo Bay detention center set up at the U.S.'s Guantanamo Bay Naval Base in Cuba, often referred to as "Gitmo," was initially created to house "enemy combatants" captured during the U.S. invasion of Afghanistan in 2001–02. Very few of the 775 detainees shipped to Guantanamo, all denied habeas corpus and other legal rights, turned out to be enemies by any definition of the term.
4. Subsequent to the U.S. invasion of Iraq in March 2003, the Taliban, ousted from power in Afghanistan by the U.S. in 2001–02, began returning to Afghanistan from sanctuaries in bordering Pakistan, and offered protection to Afghan poppy farmers. By 2005, Afghanistan was once again the world's leading poppy producer, the source of about 80 percent of European heroin supplies.
5. Richard Lugar (b. 1932), Republican U.S. senator from Indiana since 1977, former chairman of the U.S. Senate Committee on Foreign Relations, ranking member of that committee following the Democrats' 2006 recapture of control of the Senate.

6. Charles Timothy "Chuck" Hagel (b. 1946), Republican U.S. senator from Nebraska since 1997, a Vietnam combat veteran and critic of the Iraq war.
7. Donald Henry Rumsfeld (b. 1932), U.S. defense secretary for most of the first six years of the Bush administration, 2001 to 2006, a leading advocate of the Iraq invasion of 2003 and chiefly responsible for overseeing its execution, was fired by U.S. President George W. Bush in 2006 the day after elections in which Democrats recaptured control of both the U.S. Senate and House of Representatives largely due to popular antipathy toward the lack of success in the Iraq occupation. Rumsfeld notably said, in response to a reporter's 2003 Pentagon press-conference question about rampant looting soon after the invasion signaling full-blown chaos to come: "Stuff happens."
8. This is a proposed revival of the Amerika Haus experiment in post–World War II Germany. The Amerika Haus facilities throughout Germany organized free concerts and lectures, often conducted by visiting U.S. experts in German and American music, literature, scientific and other fields, and were a cultural exchange by which Germans and Americans learned about each other. Such was their success that there still remains one Amerika Haus in operation in western Germany. The flagship Amerika Haus Berlin wasn't closed until 2008.
9. Judge Advocate General's Corp, the judicial arm of the U.S. Armed Forces. U.S. military law is separate from civilian law, and in many respects is more harsh in its prosecution and punishment of U.S. military personnel found guilty of offenses. Military litigators are known as JAGS.
10. The FISA court, created by the Foreign Intelligence Surveillance Act of 1978, is a secret court that approves or rejects requests for search warrants. Throughout its history the FISA court has very seldom denied such requests. Yet the Bush administration circumvented it in illegally wiretapping U.S. citizens suspected of terrorist activities.
11. Hurricane Katrina, striking the U.S. Gulf of Mexico coast in August 2005, was one of the five deadliest hurricanes in U.S.

history, killing at least 1,836 people, chiefly in New Orleans, where levees designed to protect the below-sea-level portions of the city broke, flooding the city's poorest districts. Washington's slow response to the crisis established a Bush administration reputation for incompetence from which it did not recover, doing more damage to its public-approval ratings even than the repeated U.S. setbacks in Iraq.

THE GOLDEN RULE

Only with mutual respect can Americans move forward

"What Dr. King understood is that . . . if enough Americans were awakened to the injustice; if they joined together, North and South, rich and poor, Christian and Jew, then perhaps that wall would come tumbling down, and justice would flow like water, and righteousness like a mighty stream."

The African-American community is not monolithic, and can be as fractious as any other. In this remarkable address at Martin Luther King's own Ebenezer Baptist Church commemorating the birthday of the great civil-rights leader, Obama wonders if the African-American congregation adheres faithfully to the message of brotherhood, personal responsibility, and peaceful advocacy for social justice that Dr. King preached.

"THE GREAT NEED OF THE HOUR"

January 20, 2008

Atlanta, GA

The Scripture tells us that when Joshua and the Israelites arrived at the gates of Jericho, they could not enter. The walls of the city were too steep for any one person to climb; too strong to be taken down with brute force. And so they sat for days, unable to pass on through.

But God had a plan for his people. He told them to stand together and march together around the city, and on the seventh day he told them that when they heard the sound of the ram's horn, they should speak with one voice. And at the chosen hour, when the horn sounded and a chorus of voices cried out together, the mighty walls of Jericho came tumbling down.

There are many lessons to take from this passage, just as there are many lessons to take from this day, just as there are many memories that fill the space of this church. As I was thinking about which ones we need to remember at this hour, my mind went back to the very beginning of the modern civil rights era.

Because before Memphis and the mountaintop; before

the bridge in Selma and the march on Washington; before Birmingham and the beatings; the fire hoses and the loss of those four little girls; before there was King the icon and his magnificent dream, there was King the young preacher and a people who found themselves suffering under the yoke of oppression.

And on the eve of the bus boycotts in Montgomery, at a time when many were still doubtful about the possibilities of change, a time when those in the black community mistrusted themselves, and at times mistrusted each other, King inspired with words not of anger, but of an urgency that still speaks to us today:

"Unity is the great need of the hour" is what King said. Unity is how we shall overcome.

What Dr. King understood is that if just one person chose to walk instead of ride the bus, those walls of oppression would not be moved. But maybe if a few more walked, the foundation might start to shake. If a few more women were willing to do what Rosa Parks had done, maybe the cracks would start to show. If teenagers took freedom rides from North to South, maybe a few bricks would come loose. Maybe if white folks marched because they had come to understand that their freedom too was at stake in the impending battle, the wall would begin to sway. And if enough Americans were awakened to the injustice; if they joined together, North and South, rich and poor, Christian and Jew, then perhaps that wall would come tumbling down, and justice would flow like water, and righteousness like a mighty stream.

Unity is the great need of the hour — the great need of this hour. Not because it sounds pleasant or because it makes us feel good, but because it's the only way we can overcome the essential deficit that exists in this country.

I'm not talking about a budget deficit. I'm not talking about a trade deficit. I'm not talking about a deficit of good ideas or new plans.

I'm talking about a moral deficit. I'm talking about an empathy deficit. I'm taking about an inability to recognize ourselves in one another; to understand that we are our brother's keeper; we are our sister's keeper; that, in the words of Dr. King, we are all tied together in a single garment of destiny.

We have an empathy deficit when we're still sending our children down corridors of shame — schools in the forgotten corners of America where the color of your skin still affects the content of your education.

We have a deficit when CEOs are making more in ten minutes than some workers make in ten months; when families lose their homes so that lenders make a profit; when mothers can't afford a doctor when their children get sick.

We have a deficit in this country when there is Scooter Libby justice for some and Jena justice for others; when our children see nooses hanging from a schoolyard tree today, in the present, in the 21st century.

We have a deficit when homeless veterans sleep on the streets of our cities; when innocents are slaughtered in the deserts of Darfur; when young Americans serve tour after tour of duty in a war that should've never been authorized and never been waged.

And we have a deficit when it takes a breach in our levees to reveal a breach in our compassion; when it takes a terrible storm to reveal the hungry that God calls on us to feed; the sick He calls on us to care for; the least of these He commands that we treat as our own.

So we have a deficit to close. We have walls — barriers to justice and equality — that must come down. And to do this, we know that unity is the great need of this hour.

Unfortunately, all too often when we talk about unity in this country, we've come to believe that it can be purchased on the cheap. We've come to believe that racial reconciliation can come easily — that it's just a matter of a few ignorant people trapped in the prejudices of the past, and that if the demagogues and those who exploit our racial divisions will simply go away, then all our problems would be solved.

All too often, we seek to ignore the profound institutional barriers that stand in the way of ensuring opportunity for all children, or decent jobs for all people, or health care for those who are sick. We long for unity, but are unwilling to pay the price.

But of course, true unity cannot be so easily won. It starts with a change in attitudes — a broadening of our minds, and a broadening of our hearts.

It's not easy to stand in somebody else's shoes. It's not easy to see past our differences. We've all encountered this in our own lives. But what makes it even more difficult is that we have a politics in this country that seeks to drive us apart — that puts up walls between us.

We are told that those who differ from us on a few things are different from us on all things; that our problems are the fault of those who don't think like us or look like us or come from where we do. The welfare queen is taking our tax money. The immigrant is taking our jobs. The believer condemns the non-believer as immoral, and the non-believer chides the believer as intolerant.

For most of this country's history, we in the African-American community have been at the receiving end of man's inhumanity to man. And all of us understand intimately the insidious role that race still sometimes plays — on the job, in the schools, in our health care system, and in our criminal justice system.

And yet, if we are honest with ourselves, we must admit that none of our hands are entirely clean. If we're honest with ourselves, we'll acknowledge that our own community has not always been true to King's vision of a beloved community.

We have scorned our gay brothers and sisters instead of embracing them. The scourge of anti-Semitism has, at times, revealed itself in our community. For too long, some of us have seen immigrants as competitors for jobs instead of companions in the fight for opportunity.

Every day, our politics fuels and exploits this kind of division across all races and regions; across gender and party. It is played out on television. It is sensationalized by the media. And last week, it even crept into the campaign for President, with charges and counter-charges that served to obscure the issues instead of illuminating the critical choices we face as a nation.

So let us say that on this day of all days, each of us carries with us the task of changing our hearts and minds. The division, the stereotypes, the scape-goating, the ease with which we blame our plight on others — all of this distracts us from the common challenges we face — war and poverty; injustice and inequality. We can no longer afford to build ourselves up by tearing someone else down. We can no longer afford to traffic in lies or fear or hate. It is the poison that we must purge from our politics; the wall that we must tear down before the hour grows too late.

Because if Dr. King could love his jailor; if he could call on the faithful who once sat where you do to forgive those who set dogs and fire hoses upon them, then surely we can look past what divides us in our time, and bind up our wounds, and erase the empathy deficit that exists in our hearts.

But if changing our hearts and minds is the first critical step, we cannot stop there. It is not enough to bemoan the plight of poor children in this country and remain unwilling to push our elected officials to provide the resources to fix our schools. It is not enough to decry the disparities of health care and yet allow the insurance companies and the drug companies to block much-needed reforms. It is not enough for us to abhor the costs of a misguided war, and yet allow ourselves to be driven by a politics of fear that sees the threat of attack as way to scare up votes instead of a call to come together around a common effort.

The Scripture tells us that we are judged not just by word,

but by deed. And if we are to truly bring about the unity that is so crucial in this time, we must find it within ourselves to act on what we know; to understand that living up to this country's ideals and its possibilities will require great effort and resources; sacrifice and stamina.

And that is what is at stake in the great political debate we are having today. The changes that are needed are not just a matter of tinkering at the edges, and they will not come if politicians simply tell us what we want to hear. All of us will be called upon to make some sacrifice. None of us will be exempt from responsibility. We will have to fight to fix our schools, but we will also have to challenge ourselves to be better parents. We will have to confront the biases in our criminal justice system, but we will also have to acknowledge the deep-seated violence that still resides in our own communities and marshal the will to break its grip.

That is how we will bring about the change we seek. That is how Dr. King led this country through the wilderness. He did it with words — words that he spoke not just to the children of slaves, but the children of slave owners. Words that inspired not just black but also white; not just the Christian but the Jew; not just the Southerner but also the Northerner.

He led with words, but he also led with deeds. He also led by example. He led by marching and going to jail and suffering threats and being away from his family. He led by taking a stand against a war, knowing full well that it would diminish his popularity. He led by challenging our economic structures, understanding that it would cause discomfort. Dr. King understood that unity cannot be won on the cheap; that we would have to earn it through great effort and determination.

That is the unity — the hard-earned unity — that we need right now. It is that effort, and that determination, that can transform blind optimism into hope — the hope to imagine, and work for, and fight for what seemed impossible before . . .

It is where we begin. It is why the walls begin to crack and shake.

And if they can shake in Atlanta, they can shake in Georgia.

And if they can shake in Georgia, they can shake all across America. And if enough of our voices join together, we can bring those walls tumbling down. The walls of Jericho can finally come tumbling down. That is our hope — but only if we pray together, and work together, and march together.

Brothers and sisters, we cannot walk alone.

In the struggle for peace and justice, we cannot walk alone.

In the struggle for opportunity and equality, we cannot walk alone.

In the struggle to heal this nation and repair this world, we cannot walk alone.

So I ask you to walk with me, and march with me, and join your voice with mine, and together we will sing the song that tears down the walls that divide us, and lift up an America that is truly indivisible, with liberty, and justice, for all. May God bless the memory of the great pastor of this church, and may God bless the United States of America.

POLITICAL REFORM

It's time the American public, not lobbyists, ran Washington

"Our time has come, our movement is real, and change is coming to America."

In this typical Obama "stump" speech, Obama congratulates adulatory supporters for holding Democratic presidential rival Hillary Rodham Clinton to a draw in the twenty-two state and territorial contests of "Super Tuesday." As recently as the previous fall, Clinton was outpolling the upstart Obama by a margin of two-to-one. Whether Obama can break through to voters beyond his base of youth, African-Americans, and above-average income and education whites wouldn't be known until the general election in November 2008.

What is evident from speeches like this one is that he has a capacity for inspiring others to do the heavy lifting required to confront the slew of challenges facing his country. Adlai Stevenson, the Illinois governor who lost two presidential contests with Dwight Eisenhower in the 1950s, was asked to compare his own speaking style with the up-and-coming Jack Kennedy. The proud Stevenson, identifying himself with Cicero, said: "When Cicero spoke, the crowds declared, 'How well he spoke.' But when Demosthenes spoke, the crowds exclaimed, 'Let us march!'"

"REMARKS ON SUPER TUESDAY"

February 5, 2008

Chicago, IL

Before I begin, I just want to send my condolences to the victims of the storms that hit Tennessee and Arkansas. They are in our thoughts and in our prayers.

Well, the polls are just closing in California and the votes are still being counted in cities and towns across the country. But there is one thing on this February night that we do not need the final results to know — our time has come, our movement is real, and change is coming to America.

Only a few hundred miles from here, almost one year ago to the day, we stood on the steps of the Old State Capitol to reaffirm a truth that was spoken there so many generations ago — that a house divided cannot stand; that we are more than a collection of Red States and Blue States; we are, and always will be, the *United* States of America.

What began as a whisper in Springfield soon carried across the cornfields of Iowa, where farmers and factory workers, students and seniors stood up in numbers we've never seen. They stood up to say that maybe this year, we don't have to settle for a politics where scoring points is more important than solving problems. This time we can finally do something about health care we can't afford or mortgages we can't pay. This time can be different.

Their voices echoed from the hills of New Hampshire to the deserts of Nevada, where teachers and cooks and kitchen workers stood up to say that maybe Washington doesn't have to be run by lobbyists anymore. They reached the coast of South Carolina when people said that maybe we don't have to be divided by race and region and gender; that crumbling schools are stealing the future of black children and white children; that we can come together and build an America that gives every child, everywhere, the opportunity to live their dreams. This time can be different.

And today, on this Tuesday in February, in states north and south, east and west, what began as a whisper in Springfield has swelled to a chorus of millions calling for change. A chorus that cannot be ignored. That cannot be deterred. This time can be different because this campaign for the presidency is different.

It's different not because of me, but because of you. Because you are tired of being disappointed and tired of being let down. You're tired of hearing promises made and plans proposed in the heat of a campaign only to have nothing change when everyone goes back to Washington. Because the lobbyists just write another check. Or because politicians start worrying about how they'll win the next election instead of why they should. Or because they focus on who's up and who's down instead of who matters.

And while Washington is consumed with the same drama and division and distraction, another family puts up a For Sale sign in the front yard. Another factory shuts its doors. Another soldier waves goodbye as he leaves on another tour of duty in a war that should've never been authorized and never been waged. It goes on and on and on.

But in this election — at this moment — you are standing up all across this country to say, not this time. Not this year. The stakes are too high and the challenges too great to play the same Washington game with the same Washington players and expect a different result. This time must be different.

Now, this isn't about me and it's not about Senator Clinton. As I've said before, she was a friend before this campaign and she'll be a friend after it's over. I respect her as a colleague, and I congratulate her on her victories tonight.

But this fall we owe the American people a real choice. It's change versus more of the same. It's the future versus the past.

It's a choice between going into this election with Republicans and Independents already united against us, or going against their nominee with a campaign that has united Americans of all parties around a common purpose.

It's a choice between having a debate with the other party about who has the most experience in Washington, or having one about who's most likely to change Washington. Because that's a debate we can win.

It's a choice between a candidate who's taken more money from Washington lobbyists than either Republican in this race, and a campaign that hasn't taken a dime of their money because we've been funded by you.

And if I am your nominee, my opponent will not be able to say that I voted for the war in Iraq; or that I gave George

Bush the benefit of the doubt on Iran; or that I support the Bush-Cheney policy of not talking to leaders we don't like. And he will not be able to say that I wavered on something as fundamental as whether or not it's okay for America to use torture — because it is never okay. That is the choice in this election.

The Republicans running for President have already tied themselves to the past. They speak of a hundred-year war in Iraq and billions more on tax breaks for the wealthiest few who don't need them and didn't ask for them — tax breaks that mortgage our children's future on a mountain of debt at a time when there are families who can't pay their medical bills and students who can't pay their tuition.

They are running on the politics of yesterday, and that is why our party must be the party of tomorrow. And that is the party I will lead as President.

I'll be the President who ends the tax breaks to companies that ship our jobs overseas and start putting them in the pockets of working Americans who deserve it. And struggling homeowners. And seniors who should retire with dignity and respect.

I'll be the President who finally brings Democrats and Republicans together to make health care affordable and available for every single American. We will put a college education within reach of anyone who wants to go, and instead of just talking about how great our teachers are, we will reward them for their greatness, with more pay and better support. And we will harness the ingenuity of farmers and scientists and entrepreneurs to free this nation from the tyranny of oil once and for all.

And when I am President, we will put an end to a politics that uses 9/11 as a way to scare up votes, and start seeing it as a challenge that should unite America and the world against the common threats of the 21st century: terrorism and nuclear weapons; climate change and poverty; genocide and disease.

We can do this. It will not be easy. It will require struggle and sacrifice. There will setbacks and we will make mistakes. And that is why we need all the help we can get. So tonight I want to speak directly to all those Americans who have yet to join this movement but still hunger for change — we need you. We need you to stand with us, and work with us, and help us prove that together, ordinary people can still do extraordinary things.

I am blessed to be standing in the city where my own extraordinary journey began. A few miles from here, in the shadow of a shuttered steel plant, is where I learned what it takes to make change happen.

I was a young organizer then, intent on fighting joblessness and poverty on the South Side, and I still remember one of the very first meetings I put together. We had worked on it for days, but no one showed up. Our volunteers felt so defeated, they wanted to quit. And to be honest, so did I.

But at that moment, I looked outside and saw some young boys tossing stones at a boarded-up apartment building across the street. They were like boys in so many cities across the country — boys without prospects, without guidance, without hope. And I turned to the volunteers, and I asked them, "Before you quit, I want you to answer one question. What will happen to those boys?" And the volunteers looked out that window, and they decided that night to keep going — to keep organizing, keep fighting for better schools, and better jobs, and better health care. And so did I. And slowly, but surely, in the weeks and months to come, the community began to change.

You see, the challenges we face will not be solved with one meeting in one night. Change will not come if we wait for some other person or some other time.

We are the ones we've been waiting for. We are the change that we seek. We are the hope of those boys who have little; who've been told that they cannot have what they dream; that they cannot be what they imagine.

Yes they can.

We are the hope of the father who goes to work before dawn and lies awake with doubts that tell him he cannot give his children the same opportunities that someone gave him.

Yes he can.

We are the hope of the woman who hears that her city will not be rebuilt; that she cannot reclaim the life that was swept away in a terrible storm.

Yes she can.

We are the hope of the future; the answer to the cynics who tell us our house must stand divided; that we cannot come together; that we cannot remake this world as it should be.

Because we know what we have seen and what we believe — that what began as a whisper has now swelled to a chorus that cannot be ignored; that will not be deterred; that will ring out across this land as a hymn that will heal this nation, repair this world, and make this time different than all the rest — Yes. We. Can.

RACE IN AMERICA

The real grievances of both blacks and whites can no longer be ignored

"The anger [of African-Americans] is real; it is powerful; and to simply wish it away, to condemn it without understanding its roots, only serves to widen the chasm of misunderstanding that exists between the races. . . . To wish away the resentments of white Americans, to label them as misguided or even racist, without recognizing they are grounded in legitimate concerns — this too widens the racial divide, and blocks the path to understanding."

On March 18, 2008, Barack Obama confronted an issue he had hoped would play, at most, a minimal role in the 2008 presidential campaign — America's continuing racial divide.

While Obama was well on his way to becoming the first African-American to secure the presidential nomination of either of America's two major political parties, his campaign suddenly was dogged in early March by allegations that he shared the intemperate views of his pastor of some twenty years, the Reverend Jeremiah Wright, Jr. Obama already had condemned selective sound bites from Wright's more fiery sermons — in which he faulted American foreign policy for the September 11, 2001, attacks, "damned" America for the plight of disadvantaged blacks, and expressed a belief long held among black militants but rarely spoken of publicly that the U.S. government used the AIDS virus to kill African-Americans. But their constant repetition on the Internet made them fodder for mainstream-media questions about the degree to which Obama shared Wright's views.

Rather than douse the controversy with a fresh round of denunciations of Wright's more strident views, Obama put race front and center in the election debate with a speech that acknowledged the "racial stalemate" that continues to divide America 145 years after Lincoln's Emancipation Proclamation. Yet Obama also sought to bind disadvantaged whites and blacks by finding legitimacy in their common economic grievances.

Editorialists in every region of the country praised the speech, lauded in the next day's *New York Times* in a lead editorial titled "Mr. Obama's Profile in Courage." Obama's address set a new record for most-viewed content on YouTube.

"A MORE PEFECT UNION"

March 18, 2008

Philadelphia, PA

"We the people, in order to form a more perfect union."

Two hundred and twenty-one years ago, in a hall that still stands across the street, a group of men gathered and, with these simple words, launched America's improbable experiment in democracy. Farmers and scholars; statesmen and patriots who had traveled across an ocean to escape tyranny and persecution finally made real their declaration of independence at a Philadelphia convention that lasted through the spring of 1787.

The document they produced was eventually signed but ultimately unfinished. It was stained by this nation's original sin of slavery, a question that divided the colonies and brought the convention to a stalemate until the founders chose to allow the slave trade to continue for at least twenty more years, and to leave any final resolution to future generations.

Of course, the answer to the slavery question was already embedded within our Constitution — a Constitution that had at is very core the ideal of equal citizenship under the law; a Constitution that promised its people liberty, and justice, and a union that could be and should be perfected over time.

And yet words on a parchment would not be enough to deliver slaves from bondage, or provide men and women of every color and creed their full rights and obligations as citizens of the United States. What would be needed were Americans in successive generations who were willing to do their part — through protests and struggle, on the streets and in the courts, through a civil war and civil disobedience and always at great risk — to narrow that gap between the promise of our ideals and the reality of their time.

This was one of the tasks we set forth at the beginning of this campaign — to continue the long march of those who came before us, a march for a more just, more equal, more free, more caring, and more prosperous America. I chose to run for the presidency at this moment in history because I believe deeply that we cannot solve the challenges of our time unless we solve them together — unless we perfect our union by understanding that we may have different stories, but we hold common hopes; that we may not look the same and we may not have come from the same place, but we all want to move in the same direction — towards a better future for our children and our grandchildren.

This belief comes from my unyielding faith in the decency and generosity of the American people. But it also comes from my own American story.

I am the son of a black man from Kenya and a white woman from Kansas. I was raised with the help of a white grandfather who survived a Depression to serve in Patton's army during World War II and a white grandmother who worked on a bomber assembly line at Fort Leavenworth while he was overseas. I've gone to some of the best schools in America and lived in one of the world's poorest nations. I am married to a black American who carries within her the blood of slaves and slaveowners — an inheritance we pass on to our two precious daughters. I have brothers, sisters, nieces, nephews, uncles, and cousins, of every race and every hue, scattered across three continents, and for as long as I live, I will never forget that in no other country on earth is my story even possible.

It's a story that hasn't made me the most conventional candidate. But it is a story that has seared into my genetic makeup the idea that this nation is more than the sum of its parts — that out of many, we are truly one.

Throughout the first year of this campaign, against all predictions to the contrary, we saw how hungry the American people were for this message of unity. Despite the temptation to view my candidacy through a purely racial lens, we won commanding victories in states with some of the whitest populations in the country. In South Carolina, where the Confederate Flag still flies, we built a powerful coalition of African-Americans and white Americans.

This is not to say that race has not been an issue in the campaign. At various stages in the campaign, some commentators have deemed me either "too black" or "not black enough." We saw racial tensions bubble to the surface during the week before the South Carolina primary. The press has scoured every exit poll for the latest evidence of racial polarization, not just in terms of white and black, but black and brown as well.

And yet, it has only been in the last couple of weeks that the discussion of race in this campaign has taken a particularly divisive turn.

On one end of the spectrum, we've heard the implication that my candidacy is somehow an exercise in affirmative action; that it's based solely on the desire of wide-eyed liberals to purchase racial reconciliation on the cheap. On the other end, we've heard my former pastor, Reverend Jeremiah Wright, use incendiary language to express views that have the potential not only to widen the racial divide, but views that denigrate both the greatness and the goodness of our nation; that rightly offend white and black alike.

I have already condemned, in unequivocal terms, the statements of Reverend Wright that have caused such controversy. For some, nagging questions remain. Did I know him to be an occasionally fierce critic of American domestic and foreign policy? Of course. Did I ever hear him make remarks that could be considered controversial while I sat in church? Yes. Did I strongly disagree with many of his political views? Absolutely — just as I'm sure many of you have heard remarks from your pastors, priests, or rabbis with which you strongly disagreed.

But the remarks that have caused this recent firestorm

weren't simply controversial. They weren't simply a religious leader's effort to speak out against perceived injustice. Instead, they expressed a profoundly distorted view of this country — a view that sees white racism as endemic, and that elevates what is wrong with America above all that we know is right with America; a view that sees the conflicts in the Middle East as rooted primarily in the actions of stalwart allies like Israel, instead of emanating from the perverse and hateful ideologies of radical Islam.

As such, Reverend Wright's comments were not only wrong but divisive, divisive at a time when we need unity; racially charged at a time when we need to come together to solve a set of monumental problems — two wars, a terrorist threat, a falling economy, a chronic health-care crisis, and potentially devastating climate change; problems that are neither black or white or Latino or Asian, but rather problems that confront us all.

Given my background, my politics, and my professed values and ideals, there will no doubt be those for whom my statements of condemnation are not enough. Why associate myself with Reverend Wright in the first place, they may ask? Why not join another church? And I confess that if all that I knew of Reverend Wright were the snippets of those sermons that have run in an endless loop on the television and YouTube, or if Trinity United Church of Christ conformed to the caricatures being peddled by some commentators, there is no doubt that I would react in much the same way.

But the truth is, that isn't all that I know of the man. The man I met more than twenty years ago is a man who helped introduce me to my Christian faith, a man who spoke to me about our obligations to love one another; to care for the sick and lift up the poor. He is a man who served his country as a U.S. Marine; who has studied and lectured at some of the finest universities and seminaries in the country and who for over thirty years led a church that serves the community by doing God's work here on earth — by housing the homeless, ministering to the needy, providing day care services and scholarships and prison ministries, and reaching out to those suffering from HIV/AIDS.

In my first book, *Dreams from My Father*, I described the experience of my first service at Trinity:

"People began to shout, to rise from their seats and clap and cry out, a forceful wind carrying the reverend's voice up into the rafters. . . . And in that single note — hope! — I heard something else; at the foot of that cross, inside the thousands of churches across the city, I imagined the stories of ordinary black people merging with the stories of David and Goliath, Moses and Pharaoh, the Christians in the lion's den, Ezekiel's field of dry bones. Those stories — of survival, and freedom, and hope — became our story, my story; the blood that had spilled was our blood, the tears our tears; until this black church, on this bright day, seemed once more a vessel carrying the story of a people into future generations and into a larger world. Our trials and triumphs became at once unique and universal, black and more than black; in chronicling our journey, the stories and songs gave us a means to reclaim memories that we didn't need to feel shame about . . . memories that all people might study and cherish — and with which we could start to rebuild."

That has been my experience at Trinity. Like other predominantly black churches across the country, Trinity embodies the black community in its entirety — the doctor and the welfare mom, the model student and the former gang-banger. Like other black churches, Trinity's services are full of raucous laughter and sometimes bawdy humor. They are full of dancing, clapping, screaming, and shouting that may seem jarring to the untrained ear. The church contains in full the kindness and cruelty, the fierce intelligence and the shocking ignorance, the struggles and successes, the love and yes, the bitterness and bias that make up the black experience in America.

And this helps explain, perhaps, my relationship with Reverend Wright. As imperfect as he may be, he has been like family to me. He strengthened my faith, officiated my wedding, and baptized my children. Not once in my conversations with him have I heard him talk about any ethnic group in derogatory terms, or treat whites with whom he interacted with anything but courtesy and respect. He contains within him the contradictions — the good and the bad — of the community that he has served diligently for so many years.

I can no more disown him than I can disown the black community. I can no more disown him than I can my white grandmother — a woman who helped raise me, a woman who sacrificed again and again for me, a woman who loves me as much as she loves anything in this world, but a woman who once confessed her fear of black men who passed by her on the street, and who on more than one occasion has uttered racial or ethnic stereotypes that made me cringe.

These people are a part of me. And they are a part of America, this country that I love.

Some will see this as an attempt to justify or excuse comments that are simply inexcusable. I can assure you it is not. I suppose the politically safe thing would be to move on from this episode and just hope that it fades into the woodwork. We can dismiss Reverend Wright as a crank or a demagogue, just as some have dismissed Geraldine Ferraro,[1] in the aftermath of her recent statements, as harboring some deep-seated racial bias.

But race is an issue that I believe this nation cannot afford to ignore right now. We would be making the same mistake that Reverend Wright made in his offending sermons about America — to simplify and stereotype and amplify the negative to the point that it distorts reality.

The fact is that the comments that have been made and the issues that have surfaced over the last few weeks reflect the complexities of race in this country that we've never really worked through — a part of our union that we have yet to perfect. And if we walk away now, if we simply retreat into our respective corners, we will never be able to come together and solve challenges like health care, or education, or the need to find good jobs for every American.

Understanding this reality requires a reminder of how we arrived at this point. As William Faulkner once wrote, "The past isn't dead and buried. In fact, it isn't even past." We do not need to recite here the history of racial injustice in this country. But we do need to remind ourselves that so many of the disparities that exist in the African-American community today can be directly traced to inequalities passed on from an earlier generation that suffered under the brutal legacy of slavery and Jim Crow.

Segregated schools were, and are, inferior schools; we still haven't fixed them, fifty years after *Brown v. Board of Education*, and the inferior education they provided, then and now, helps explain the pervasive achievement gap between today's black and white students.

Legalized discrimination — where blacks were prevented, often through violence, from owning property, or loans were not granted to African-American business owners, or black homeowners could not access FHA[2] mortgages, or blacks were excluded from unions, or the police force, or fire departments — meant that black families could not amass any meaningful wealth to bequeath to future generations. That history helps explain the wealth and income gap between black and white, and the concentrated pockets of poverty that persist in so many of today's urban and rural communities.

A lack of economic opportunity among black men, and the shame and frustration that came from not being able to provide for one's family, contributed to the erosion of black families — a problem that welfare policies for many years may have worsened. And the lack of basic services in so many urban black neighborhoods — parks for kids to play in, police walking the beat, regular garbage pick-up, and building code enforcement — all helped create a cycle of violence, blight, and neglect that continues to haunt us.

This is the reality in which Reverend Wright and other African-Americans of his generation grew up. They came of age in the late fifties and early sixties, a time when segregation was still the law of the land and opportunity was systematically constricted. What's remarkable is not how many failed in the face of discrimination, but rather how many men and women overcame the odds; how many were able to make a way out for those like me who would come after them.

But for all those who scratched and clawed their way to get a piece of the American Dream, there were many who didn't make it — those who were ultimately defeated, in one way or another, by discrimination. That legacy of defeat was passed on to future generations — those young men and increasingly young women who we see standing on street corners or languishing in our prisons, without hope or prospects for the future. Even for those blacks who did make it, questions of race, and racism, continue to define their worldview in fundamental ways. For the men and women of Reverend Wright's generation, the memories of humiliation and doubt and fear have not gone away; nor has the anger and the bitterness of those years. That anger may not get expressed in public, in front of white co-workers or white friends. But it does find voice in the barbershop or around the kitchen table. At times, that anger is exploited by politicians, to gin up votes along racial lines, or to make up for a politician's own failings.

And occasionally it finds voice in the church on Sunday morning, in the pulpit and in the pews. The fact that so many people are surprised to hear that anger in some of Reverend Wright's sermons simply reminds us of the old truism that the most segregated hour in American life occurs on Sunday morning. That anger is not always productive; indeed, all too often it distracts attention from solving real problems; it keeps us from squarely facing our own complicity in our condition, and prevents the African-American community from forging the alliances it needs to bring about real change. But the anger is real; it is powerful; and to simply wish it away, to condemn it without understanding its roots, only serves to widen the chasm of misunderstanding that exists between the races.

In fact, a similar anger exists within segments of the white community. Most working- and middle-class white Americans don't feel that they have been particularly privileged by their race. Their experience is the immigrant experience — as far as they're concerned, no one's handed them anything, they've built it from scratch. They've worked hard all their lives, many times only to see their jobs shipped overseas or their pension dumped after a lifetime of labor. They are anxious about their futures, and feel their dreams slipping away; in an era of stagnant wages and global competition, opportunity comes to be seen as a zero sum game, in which your dreams come at my expense. So when they are told to bus their children to a school across town; when they hear that an African-American is getting an advantage in landing a good job or a spot in a good college because of an injustice that they themselves never committed; when they're told that their fears about crime in urban neighborhoods are somehow prejudiced, resentment builds over time.

Like the anger within the black community, these resentments aren't always expressed in polite company. But they have helped shape the political landscape for at least a generation. Anger over welfare and affirmative action helped forge the Reagan Coalition. Politicians routinely exploited fears of crime for their own electoral ends. Talk show hosts and conservative commentators built entire careers unmasking bogus claims of racism while dismissing legitimate discussions of racial injustice and inequality as mere political correctness or reverse racism.

Just as black anger often proved counterproductive, so

have these white resentments distracted attention from the real culprits of the middle class squeeze — a corporate culture rife with inside dealing, questionable accounting practices, and short-term greed; a Washington dominated by lobbyists and special interests; economic policies that favor the few over the many. And yet, to wish away the resentments of white Americans, to label them as misguided or even racist, without recognizing they are grounded in legitimate concerns — this too widens the racial divide, and blocks the path to understanding.

This is where we are right now. It's a racial stalemate we've been stuck in for years. Contrary to the claims of some of my critics, black and white, I have never been so naïve as to believe that we can get beyond our racial divisions in a single election cycle, or with a single candidacy — particularly a candidacy as imperfect as my own.

But I have asserted a firm conviction — a conviction rooted in my faith in God and my faith in the American people — that working together we can move beyond some of our old racial wounds, and that in fact we have no choice if we are to continue on the path of a more perfect union.

For the African-American community, that path means embracing the burdens of our past without becoming victims of our past. It means continuing to insist on a full measure of justice in every aspect of American life. But it also means binding our particular grievances — for better health care, and better schools, and better jobs — to the larger aspirations of all Americans — the white woman struggling to break the glass ceiling, the white man who's been laid off, the immigrant trying to feed his family. And it means taking full responsibility for our own lives — by demanding more from our fathers, and spending more time with our children, and reading to them, and teaching them that while they may face challenges and discrimination in their own lives, they must never succumb to despair or cynicism; they must always believe that they can write their own destiny.

Ironically, this quintessentially American — and yes, conservative — notion of self-help found frequent expression in Reverend Wright's sermons. But what my former pastor too often failed to understand is that embarking on a program of self-help also requires a belief that society can change.

The profound mistake of Reverend Wright's sermons is not that he spoke about racism in our society. It's that he spoke as if our society was static; as if no progress has been made; as if this country — a country that has made it possible for one of his own members to run for the highest office in the land and build a coalition of white and black, Latino and Asian, rich and poor, young and old — is still irrevocably bound to a tragic past. But what we know — what we have seen — is that America can change. That is the true genius of this nation. What we have already achieved gives us hope — the audacity to hope — for what we can and must achieve tomorrow.

In the white community, the path to a more perfect union means acknowledging that what ails the African-American community does not just exist in the minds of black people; that the legacy of discrimination — and current incidents of discrimination, while less overt than in the past — are real and must be addressed. Not just with words, but with deeds — by investing in our schools and our communities; by enforcing our civil-rights laws and ensuring fairness in our criminal justice system; by providing this generation with ladders of opportunity that were unavailable for previous generations. It requires all Americans to realize that your dreams do not have to come at the expense of my dreams; that investing in the health, welfare, and education of black and brown and white children will ultimately help all of America prosper.

In the end, then, what is called for is nothing more, and nothing less, than what all the world's great religions demand — that we do unto others as we would have them do unto us. Let us be our brother's keeper, Scripture tells us.

Let us be our sister's keeper. Let us find that common stake we all have in one another, and let our politics reflect that spirit as well.

For we have a choice in this country. We can accept a politics that breeds division, and conflict, and cynicism. We can tackle race only as spectacle — as we did in the O.J. trial[3] — or in the wake of tragedy, as we did in the aftermath of Katrina[4] — or as fodder for the nightly news. We can play Reverend Wright's sermons on every channel, every day and talk about them from now until the election, and make the only question in this campaign whether or not the American people think that I somehow believe or sympathize with his most offensive words. We can pounce on some gaffe by a Hillary supporter as evidence that she's playing the race card, or we can speculate on whether white men will all flock to John McCain in the general election regardless of his policies.

We can do that.

But if we do, I can tell you that in the next election, we'll be talking about some other distraction. And then another one. And then another one. And nothing will change.

That is one option. Or, at this moment, in this election, we can come together and say, "Not this time." This time we want to talk about the crumbling schools that are stealing the future of black children and white children and Asian children and Hispanic children and Native American children. This time we want to reject the cynicism that tells us that these kids can't learn; that those kids who don't look like us are somebody else's problem. The children of America are not those kids, they are our kids, and we will not let them fall behind in a 21st-century economy. Not this time.

This time we want to talk about how the lines in the Emergency Room are filled with whites and blacks and Hispanics who do not have health care; who don't have the power on their own to overcome the special interests in Washington, but who can take them on if we do it together.

This time we want to talk about the shuttered mills that once provided a decent life for men and women of every race, and the homes for sale that once belonged to Americans from every religion, every region, every walk of life. This time we want to talk about the fact that the real problem is not that someone who doesn't look like you might take your job; it's that the corporation you work for will ship it overseas for nothing more than a profit.

This time we want to talk about the men and women of every color and creed who serve together, and fight together, and bleed together under the same proud flag. We want to talk about how to bring them home from a war that never should've been authorized and never should've been waged, and we want to talk about how we'll show our patriotism by caring for them, and their families, and giving them the benefits they have earned.

I would not be running for President if I didn't believe with all my heart that this is what the vast majority of Americans want for this country. This union may never be perfect, but generation after generation has shown that it can always be perfected. And today, whenever I find myself feeling doubtful or cynical about this possibility, what gives me the most hope is the next generation — the young people whose attitudes and beliefs and openness to change have already made history in this election.

There is one story in particularly that I'd like to leave you with today — a story I told when I had the great honor of speaking on Dr. King's birthday at his home church, Ebenezer Baptist, in Atlanta.

There is a young, twenty-three-year-old white woman named Ashley Baia who organized for our campaign in Florence, South Carolina. She had been working to organize a mostly African-American community since the beginning of this campaign, and one day she was at a roundtable discussion where everyone went around telling their story and why they were there.

And Ashley said that when she was nine years old, her mother got cancer. And because she had to miss days of work, she was let go and lost her health care. They had to file for bankruptcy, and that's when Ashley decided that she had to do something to help her mom.

She knew that food was one of their most expensive costs, and so Ashley convinced her mother that what she really liked and really wanted to eat more than anything else was mustard and relish sandwiches. Because that was the cheapest way to eat.

She did this for a year until her mom got better, and she told everyone at the roundtable that the reason she joined our campaign was so that she could help the millions of other children in the country who want and need to help their parents too.

Now Ashley might have made a different choice. Perhaps somebody told her along the way that the source of her mother's problems were blacks who were on welfare and too lazy to work, or Hispanics who were coming into the country illegally. But she didn't. She sought out allies in her fight against injustice.

Anyway, Ashley finishes her story and then goes around the room and asks everyone else why they're supporting the campaign. They all have different stories and reasons. Many bring up a specific issue. And finally they come to this elderly black man who's been sitting there quietly the entire time. And Ashley asks him why he's there. And he does not bring up a specific issue. He does not say health care or the economy. He does not say education or the war. He does not say that he was there because of Barack Obama. He simply says to everyone in the room, "I am here because of Ashley."

"I'm here because of Ashley." By itself, that single moment of recognition between that young white girl and that old black man is not enough. It is not enough to give health care to the sick, or jobs to the jobless, or education to our children.

But it is where we start. It is where our union grows

stronger. And as so many generations have come to realize over the course of the 221 years since a band of patriots signed that document in Philadelphia, that is where the perfection begins.

Notes

1. Geraldine Anne Ferraro (b. 1935), former Democratic member of the U.S. Congress from New York, 1984 running mate of unsuccessful Democratic presidential candidate Walter Mondale, and supporter of Hillary Clinton's 2008 presidential bid. In a March 7, 2008, interview with a California newspaper, the *Daily Breeze*, Ferraro said: If Obama was a white man, he would not be in this position. And if he was a woman (of any color) he would not be in this position. He happens to be very lucky to be who he is. And the country is caught up in the concept." It was Ferraro's view that the lead Obama had gained on Clinton in the presidential primaries that winter derived largely from the novelty of his race — an observation she had earlier made about the 1980s African-American Democratic presidential candidate Jesse Jackson — and that Clinton, by contrast, was a victim of sexism. Indeed, Ferraro later labeled Obama a sexist, and said she might not vote for him if he emerged as the Democratic presidential nominee.
2. Federal Housing Administration, established in 1934 to ease access to home-mortgage financing for aspiring homeowners of limited means.
3. Possibly the major U.S. popular-cultural event of the 1990s, the protracted, nationally televised trial of former professional football player and actor O.J. Simpson on charges of murdering his estranged wife, Nicole Brown Simpson, and her friend Ronald Goldman ended with an acquittal in October 1995. A majority of white Americans were convinced the trial was botched and that Simpson was, in fact, guilty; while a majority of African-Americans felt Simpson had been wrongly

accused and celebrated his acquittal.

4. Hurricane Katrina, which struck the U.S. coast of the Gulf of Mexico at New Orleans and other Gulf communities in August 2005, was one of the five deadliest hurricanes in U.S. history, killing at least 1,836 people in the storm and subsequent flooding. Because much of New Orleans' large African-American population lived in substandard housing in neighborhoods below sea level, blacks were disproportionately among the victims when levees designed to protect the city gave way, flooding the poorest neighborhoods. Some prominent American blacks, including filmmaker Spike Lee, took from Washington's slow and ineffectual response to the devastation that a national government dominated by white decision-makers simply didn't care about the fate of African-Americans.

FOREIGN POLICY

A new American worldview both hard-line and humanitarian

"When America leads with principle and pragmatism, hope can triumph over fear. It is time, once again, for America to lead."

In this flagship foreign-policy speech, Obama reveals a holistic approach of contemplating the consequences of U.S. actions — diplomatic, military, and humanitarian — within a reassuring framework of continued, indeed more comprehensive and multidimensional, U.S. leadership beyond its borders.

"THE WORLD BEYOND IRAQ"

March 19, 2008

Fayetteville, NC

Just before America's entry into World War I, President Woodrow Wilson addressed Congress. "It is a fearful thing to lead this great peaceful people into war," he said, ". . . but the right is more precious than peace." Wilson's words captured two awesome responsibilities that test any Commander-in-Chief — to never hesitate to defend America, but to never go to war unless you must. War is sometimes necessary, but it has grave consequences, and the judgment to go to war can never be undone.

Five years ago today, President George W. Bush addressed the nation. Bombs had started to rain down on Baghdad. War was necessary, the President said, because the United States could not "live at the mercy of an outlaw regime that threatens the peace with weapons of mass murder." Recalling the pain of 9/11, he said the price of inaction in Iraq was to meet the threat with "armies of fire fighters and police and doctors on the streets of our cities."

At the time the President uttered those words, there was no hard evidence that Iraq had those stockpiles of weapons of mass destruction. There was not any evidence that Iraq was responsible for the attacks of September 11, or that Iraq had operational ties to the al Qaeda terrorists who carried them out. By launching a war based on faulty premises and bad intelligence, President Bush failed Wilson's test. So did Congress when it voted to give him the authority to wage war.

Five years have gone by since that fateful decision. This war has now lasted longer than World War I, World War II, or the Civil War. Nearly four thousand Americans have given their lives. Thousands more have been wounded. Even under the best case scenarios, this war will cost American taxpayers well over a trillion dollars. And where are we for all of this sacrifice? We are less safe and less able to shape events abroad. We are divided at home, and our alliances around the world have been strained. The threats of a new century have roiled the waters of peace and stability, and yet America remains anchored in Iraq.

History will catalog the reasons why we waged a war that didn't need to be fought, but two stand out. In 2002, when the fateful decisions about Iraq were made, there was a President for whom ideology overrode pragmatism, and there were too many politicians in Washington who spent too little time reading the intelligence reports, and too much time reading public opinion. The lesson of Iraq is that when we are making decisions about matters as grave as war, we need a policy rooted in reason and facts, not ideology and politics.

Now we are debating who should be our next Commander-in-Chief. And I am running for President because it's time to turn the page on a failed ideology and a fundamentally flawed political strategy, so that we can make pragmatic judgments to keep our country safe. That's what I did when I stood up and opposed this war from the start, and said that we needed to finish the fight against al Qaeda. And that's what I'll do as President of the United States.

Senator Clinton says that she and Senator McCain have passed a "Commander-in-Chief test" — not because of the judgments they've made, but because of the years they've spent in Washington. She made a similar argument when she said her vote for war was based on her experience at both ends of Pennsylvania Avenue. But here is the stark reality: there is a security gap in this country — a gap between the rhetoric of those who claim to be tough on national security, and the reality of growing insecurity caused by their decisions. A gap between Washington experience, and the wisdom of Washington's judgments. A gap between the rhetoric of those who tout their support for our troops, and the overburdened state of our military.

It is time to have a debate with John McCain about the future of our national security. And the way to win that debate is not to compete with John McCain over who has more experience in Washington, because that's a contest that he'll win. The way to win a debate with John McCain is not to talk, and act, and vote like him on national security, because then we all lose. The way to win that debate and to keep America safe is to offer a clear contrast, and that's what I will do when I am the nominee of the Democratic Party — because since before this war in Iraq began, I have made different judgments, I have a different vision, and I will offer a clean break from the failed policies and politics of the past.

Nowhere is that break more badly needed than in Iraq.

In the year since President Bush announced the surge — the bloodiest year of the war for America — the level of violence in Iraq has been reduced. Our troops — including so many from Fort Bragg and Pope Air Force Base — have done a brilliant job under difficult circumstances. Yet while we have a General who has used improved tactics to reduce violence, we still have the wrong strategy. As General [David] Petraeus [U.S. commander in Iraq at the time] has himself acknowledged, the Iraqis are not achieving the political progress needed to end their civil war. Beyond Iraq, our military is badly overstretched, and we have neither the strategy nor resources to deal with nearly every other national security challenge we face.

This is why the judgment that matters most on Iraq —

and on any decision to deploy military force — is the judgment made first. If you believe we are fighting the right war, then the problems we face are purely tactical in nature. That is what Senator McCain wants to discuss — tactics. What he and the Administration have failed to present is an overarching strategy: how the war in Iraq enhances our long-term security, or will in the future. That's why this Administration cannot answer the simple question posed by Senator John Warner in hearings last year: are we safer because of this war? And that is why Senator McCain can argue — as he did last year — that we couldn't leave Iraq because violence was up, and then argue this year that we can't leave Iraq because violence is down.

When you have no overarching strategy, there is no clear definition of success. Success comes to be defined as the ability to maintain a flawed policy indefinitely. Here is the truth: fighting a war without end will not force the Iraqis to take responsibility for their own future. And fighting in a war without end will not make the American people safer.

So when I am Commander-in-Chief, I will set a new goal on Day One: I will end this war. Not because politics compels it. Not because our troops cannot bear the burden — as heavy as it is. But because it is the right thing to do for our national security, and it will ultimately make us safer.

In order to end this war responsibly, I will immediately begin to remove our troops from Iraq. We can responsibly remove one to two combat brigades each month. If we start with the number of brigades we have in Iraq today, we can remove all of them in sixteen months. After this redeployment, we will leave enough troops in Iraq to guard our embassy and diplomats, and a counter-terrorism force to strike al Qaeda if it forms a base that the Iraqis cannot destroy. What I propose is not — and never has been — a precipitous drawdown. It is instead a detailed and prudent plan that will end a war nearly seven years after it started.

My plan to end this war will finally put pressure on Iraq's

leaders to take responsibility for their future. Because we've learned that when we tell Iraq's leaders that we'll stay as long as it takes, they take as long as they want. We need to send a different message. We will help Iraq reach a meaningful accord on national reconciliation. We will engage with every country in the region — and the UN — to support the stability and territorial integrity of Iraq. And we will launch a major humanitarian initiative to support Iraq's refugees and people. But Iraqis must take responsibility for their country. It is precisely this kind of approach — an approach that puts the onus on the Iraqis, and that relies on more than just military power — that is needed to stabilize Iraq.

Let me be clear: ending this war is not going to be easy. There will be dangers involved. We will have to make tactical adjustments, listening to our commanders on the ground, to ensure that our interests in a stable Iraq are met, and to make sure that our troops are secure. Senator Clinton has tried to use my position to score political points, suggesting that I am somehow less committed to ending the war. She makes this argument despite the fact that she has taken the same position in the past. So ask yourself: who do you trust to end a war — someone who opposed the war from the beginning, or someone who started opposing it when they started preparing a run for President?

Now we know what we'll hear from those like John McCain who support open-ended war. They will argue that leaving Iraq is surrender. That we are emboldening the enemy. These are the mistaken and misleading arguments we hear from those who have failed to demonstrate how the war in Iraq has made us safer. Just yesterday, we heard Senator McCain confuse Sunni and Shiite, Iran and al Qaeda. Maybe that is why he voted to go to war with a country that had no al Qaeda ties. Maybe that is why he completely fails to understand that the war in Iraq has done more to embolden America's enemies than any strategic choice that we have made in decades.

The war in Iraq has emboldened Iran, which poses the greatest challenge to American interests in the Middle East in a generation, continuing its nuclear program and threatening our ally, Israel. Instead of the new Middle East we were promised, Hamas runs Gaza, Hezbollah flags fly from the rooftops in Sadr City, and Iran is handing out money left and right in southern Lebanon.

The war in Iraq has emboldened North Korea, which built new nuclear weapons and even tested one before the Administration finally went against its own rhetoric, and pursued diplomacy.

The war in Iraq has emboldened the Taliban, which has rebuilt its strength since we took our eye off of Afghanistan.

Above all, the war in Iraq has emboldened al Qaeda, whose recruitment has jumped and whose leadership enjoys a safe haven in Pakistan — a thousand miles from Iraq.

The central front in the war against terror is not Iraq, and it never was. What more could America's enemies ask for than an endless war where they recruit new followers and try out new tactics on a battlefield so far from their base of operations? That is why my presidency will shift our focus. Rather than fight a war that does not need to be fought, we need to start fighting the battles that need to be won on the central front of the war against al Qaeda in Afghanistan and Pakistan.

This is the area where the 9/11 attacks were planned. This is where Osama bin Laden and his top lieutenants still hide. This is where extremism poses its greatest threat. Yet in both Afghanistan and Pakistan, we have pursued flawed strategies that are too distant from the needs of the people, and too timid in pursuit of our common enemies.

It may not dominate the evening news, but in Afghanistan, last year was the most deadly since 2001. Suicide attacks are up. Casualties are up. Corruption and drug trafficking are rampant. Neither the government nor the legal economy can meet the needs of the Afghan people.

It is not too late to prevail in Afghanistan. But we cannot prevail until we reduce our commitment in Iraq, which will allow us to do what I called for last August — providing at least two additional combat brigades to support our efforts in Afghanistan. This increased commitment in turn can be used to leverage greater assistance — with fewer restrictions — from our NATO allies. It will also allow us to invest more in training Afghan security forces, including more joint NATO operations with the Afghan Army, and a national police training plan that is effectively coordinated and resourced.

A stepped up military commitment must be backed by a long-term investment in the Afghan people. We will start with an additional one billion dollars in non-military assistance each year — aid that is focused on reaching ordinary Afghans. We need to improve daily life by supporting education, basic infrastructure, and human services. We have to counter the opium trade by supporting alternative livelihoods for Afghan farmers. And we must call on more support from friends and allies, and better coordination under a strong international coordinator.

To succeed in Afghanistan, we also need to fundamentally rethink our Pakistan policy. For years, we have supported stability over democracy in Pakistan, and gotten neither. The core leadership of al Qaeda has a safe haven in Pakistan. The Taliban are able to strike inside Afghanistan and then return to the mountains of the Pakistani border. Throughout Pakistan, domestic unrest has been rising. The full democratic aspirations of the Pakistani people have been too long denied. A child growing up in Pakistan, more often than not, is taught to see America as a source of hate — not hope.

This is why I stood up last summer and said we cannot base our entire Pakistan policy on President Musharraf. Pakistan is our ally, but we do our own security and our ally no favors by supporting its President while we are seen to be ignoring the interests of the people. Our counter-terrorism assistance must be conditioned on Pakistani action to root out the al Qaeda sanctuary. And any U.S. aid not directly needed for the fight against al Qaeda or to invest in the Pakistani people should be conditioned on the full restoration of Pakistan's democracy and rule of law.

The choice is not between Musharraf and Islamic extremists. As the recent legislative elections showed, there is a moderate majority of Pakistanis, and they are the people we need on our side to win the war against al Qaeda. That is why we should dramatically increase our support for the Pakistani people — for education, economic development, and democratic institutions. That child in Pakistan must know that we want a better life for him, that America is on his side, and that his interest in opportunity is our interest as well. That's the promise that America must stand for.

And for his sake and ours, we cannot tolerate a sanctuary for terrorists who threaten America's homeland and Pakistan's stability. If we have actionable intelligence about high-level al Qaeda targets in Pakistan's border region, we must act if Pakistan will not or cannot. Senator Clinton, Senator McCain, and President Bush have all distorted and derided this position, suggesting that I would invade or bomb Pakistan. This is politics, pure and simple. My position, in fact, is the same pragmatic policy that all three of them have belatedly — if tacitly — acknowledged is one we should pursue. Indeed, it was months after I called for this policy that a top al Qaeda leader was taken out in Pakistan by an American aircraft. And remember that the same three individuals who now criticize me for supporting a targeted strike on the terrorists who carried out the 9/11 attacks, are the same three individuals that supported an invasion of Iraq — a country that had nothing to do with 9/11.

It is precisely this kind of political point-scoring that has opened up the security gap in this country. We have a security gap when candidates say they will follow Osama bin Laden to the gates of hell, but refuse to follow him where he actually goes. What we need in our next Commander-in-Chief is not a stubborn refusal to acknowledge reality or empty rhetoric about 3 a.m. phone calls.[1] What we need is a pragmatic strategy that focuses on fighting our real enemies, rebuilding alliances, and renewing our engagement with the world's people.

In addition to freeing up resources to take the fight to al Qaeda, ending the war in Iraq will allow us to more effectively confront other threats in the world — threats that cannot be conquered with an occupying army or dispatched with a single decision in the middle of the night. What lies in the heart of a child in Pakistan matters as much as the airplanes we sell her government. What's in the head of a scientist from Russia can be as lethal as a plutonium reactor in Yongbyon. What's whispered in refugee camps in Chad can be as dangerous as a dictator's bluster. These are the neglected landscapes of the 21st century, where technology and extremism empower individuals just as they give governments the ability to repress them; where the ancient divides of region and religion wash into the swift currents of globalization.

Without American leadership, these threats will fester. With strong American leadership, we can shape them into opportunities to protect our common security and advance our common humanity — for it has always been the genius of American leadership to find opportunity embedded in adversity; to focus on a source of fear, and confront it with hope.

Here are just five ways in which a shift in strategy away from Iraq will help us address the critical challenges of the 21st century.

First, in addressing global terror and violent extremism, we need the kind of comprehensive counter-terrorism strategy I called for last August. We need to strengthen security partnerships to take out terrorist networks, while investing in education and opportunity. We need to give our national security agencies the tools they need, while restoring the adherence to rule of law that helps us win the battle for hearts and minds. This means closing Guantanamo, restoring habeas corpus, and respecting civil liberties. And we need to support the forces of moderation in the Islamic world, so that alliances of convenience mature into friendships of conviction.

Second, the threat of nuclear proliferation must serve as a call to action. I have worked across the aisle with Richard Lugar and Chuck Hagel in the Senate to secure dangerous weapons and loose nuclear materials. And as President, I will secure all loose nuclear materials around the world in my first term, seek deep cuts in global nuclear arsenals, strengthen the Nuclear Non-Proliferation Treaty, and once more seek a world without nuclear weapons.

Third, the danger of weak and failed states risks spreading poverty and refugees; genocide and disease. Now is the time to meet the goal of cutting extreme poverty in half, in part by doubling our foreign assistance while demanding more from those who receive it. And now is the time to build the capacity of regional partners in conflict prevention, peacekeeping, and the reconstruction of ravaged societies.

Fourth, the catastrophic consequences of the global climate crisis are matched by the promise of collective action. Now is the time for America to lead, because if we take action, others will act as well. Through our own cap and trade system and investments in new sources of energy, we can end our dependence on foreign oil and gas, and free ourselves from the tyranny of oil-rich states from Saudi Arabia to Russia to Venezuela. We can create millions of new jobs here in America. And we can secure our planet for our children and grandchildren.

And fifth, America's sluggish economy risks ceding our economic prominence to a rising China. Competition has always been a catalyst for American innovation, and now should be no different. We must invest in the education of our children, renew our leadership in science, and advance trade that is not just free, but fair for our workers. We must ensure that America is the economic engine in the 21st century just as we were in the 20th.

I have no illusions that any of this will be easy. But I do know that we can only begin to make these changes when we end the mindset that focuses on Iraq and ignores the rest of the world.

I also know that meeting these new threats will require a President who deploys the power of tough, principled diplomacy. It is time to present a country like Iran with a clear choice. If it abandons its nuclear program, support for terror, and threats to Israel, then Iran can rejoin the community of nations — with all the benefits that entails. If not, Iran will face deeper isolation and steeper sanctions. When we engage directly, we will be in a stronger position to rally real international support for increased pressure. We will also engender more goodwill from the Iranian people. And make no mistake — if and when we ever have to use military force against any country, we must exert the power of American diplomacy first.

Once again, Senator Clinton, Senator McCain, and President Bush have made the same arguments against my position on diplomacy, as if reading from the same political playbook. They say I'll be penciling the world's dictators on to my social calendar. But just as they are misrepresenting my position, they are mistaken in standing up for a policy of not talking that is not working. What I've said is that we cannot seize opportunities to resolve our problems unless we create them. That is what Kennedy did with Khrushchev;[2] what Nixon did with Mao; what Reagan did with Gorbachev. And that is what I will do as President of the United States.

What I have talked about today is a new strategy, a new set of priorities for pursuing our interests in the 21st century. And as President, I will provide the tools required to implement this strategy. When President Truman put the policy of containment in place, he also invested in and organized our government to carry it out — creating the National Security Council and the CIA, and founding NATO. Now, we must upgrade our tools of power to fit a new strategy.

That starts with enhancing the finest military in the history of the world. As Commander-in-Chief, I will begin by giving a military overstretched by Iraq the support it needs. It is time to reduce the strain on our troops by completing the effort to increase our ground forces by 65,000 soldiers and 27,000 Marines, while ensuring the quality of our troops. In an age marked by technology, it is the people of our military — our Soldiers, Sailors, Airmen, Marines, and Coast Guardsmen — who bear the responsibility for complex missions. That is why we need to ensure adequate training and time home between deployments. That is why we need to expand our Special Forces. And that is why we must increase investments in capabilities like civil affairs and training foreign militaries.

But we cannot place the burden of a new national security strategy on our military alone. We must integrate our diplomatic, information, economic, and military power. That is why, as soon as I take office, I will call for a National Strategy and Security Review, to help determine a 21st-century inter-agency structure to integrate the elements of our national power.

In addition, I will invest in our civilian capacity to operate alongside our troops in post-conflict zones and on humanitarian and stabilization missions. Instead of shuttering consulates in tough corners of the world, it's time to grow our Foreign Service and to expand USAID. Instead of giving up on the determination of young people to serve, it's time to double the size of our Peace Corps. Instead of letting people learn about America from enemy propaganda, it's time to recruit, train, and send out into the world an America's Voice Corps.

And while we strengthen our own capacity, we must

strengthen the capability of the international community. We honor NATO's sacrifice in Afghanistan, but we must strive to make it a larger and more nimble alliance. We must work with powers like Russia and China, but we must also speak up for human rights and democracy — and we can start now by speaking out for the human rights and religious freedom of the people of Tibet. And while we are frustrated by the UN, we must invest in its capability to keep the peace, resolve disputes, monitor disarmament, and support good governance around the world — and that depends on a more engaged United States.

We are at a defining moment in our history.

We can choose the path of unending war and unilateral action, and sap our strength and standing. We can choose the path of disengagement, and cede our leadership. Or, we can meet fear and danger head-on with hope and strength; with common purpose as a united America; and with common cause with old allies and new partners.

What we've seen these last few years is what happens when the rigid ideology and dysfunctional politics of Washington is projected abroad. An ideology that does not fit the shape of the times cannot shape events in foreign countries. A politics that is based on fear and division does not allow us to call on the world to hope, and keeps us from coming together as one people, as one nation, to write the next great chapter in the American story.

We also know that there is another face of America that we have seen these last five years. From down the road at Fort Bragg, our soldiers have gone abroad with a greater sense of common purpose than their leaders in Washington. They have learned the lessons of the 21st century's wars. And they have shown a sense of service and selflessness that represents the very best of the American character.

This must be the election when we stand up and say that we will serve them as well as they have served us. This must be the election when America comes together behind a common purpose on behalf of our security and our values. That is what we do as Americans. It's how we founded a republic based on freedom, and faced down fascism. It's how we defended democracy through a Cold War, and shined a light of hope bright enough to be seen in the darkest corners of the world.

When America leads with principle and pragmatism, hope can triumph over fear. It is time, once again, for America to lead.

Notes

1. During the Democratic primary contests, the Clinton campaign ran a TV advertisement depicting a unrecognizable figure answering the phone at 3 a.m. as a child sleeps safely in bed, suggesting Clinton would be more prepared than Obama to deal with sudden emergencies. As it happens, the sleeping girl in the dated stock footage used by the campaign, now an adult, declared herself an Obama supporter.
2. Obama could have chosen a better example, such as Nixon's early 1970s meetings with Soviet leader Leonid Brezhnev, launching an era of "détente." Kennedy's 1961 Vienna summit with Nikita Khrushchev was a disaster in which the then-Soviet leader browbeat the recently elected U.S. president, came away convinced JFK was weak, and shortly after erected the Berlin Wall and triggered the Cuban missile crisis.

ECONOMIC RENEWAL

The Iraq conflict distracts us from crises at home and abroad

"This war has diverted us from fighting al Qaeda in Afghanistan and Pakistan, and from addressing the other challenges of the 21st century: violent extremism and nuclear weapons; climate change and poverty; genocide and disease."

Economists use the term "opportunity cost" to describe activities forsaken in order to pursue a particular goal. In this address, Obama calculates the less obvious Iraq-war costs of postponing action on the crises of poverty, crumbling schools, forty-seven million Americans without health-care coverage, genocide in Darfur, global warming, and an energy crisis manifested in four dollar–a–gallon gasoline prices.

"THE COST OF WAR"

March 20, 2008

Charleston, WV

Five years ago, the war in Iraq began. And on this fifth anniversary, we honor the brave men and women who are serving this nation in Iraq, Afghanistan, and around the world. We pay tribute to the sacrifices of their families back home. And a grateful nation mourns the loss of our fallen heroes.

I understand that the first serviceman killed in Iraq was a native West Virginian, Marine 1st Lieutenant Shane Childers, who died five years ago tomorrow. And so on this anniversary, my thoughts and prayers go out to Lieutenant Childers' family, and to all who've lost loved ones in Iraq and Afghanistan.

The costs of war are greatest for the troops and those who love them, but we know that war has other costs as well. Yesterday, I addressed some of these other costs in a speech on the strategic consequences of the Iraq war. I spoke about how this war has diverted us from fighting al Qaeda in Afghanistan and Pakistan, and from addressing the other challenges of the 21st century: violent extremism and nuclear weapons; climate change and poverty; genocide and disease.

And today, I want to talk about another cost of this war — the toll it has taken on our economy. Because at a time when we're on the brink of recession — when neighborhoods have For Sale signs outside every home, and working families are struggling to keep up with rising costs — ordinary Americans are paying a price for this war.

When you're spending over fifty dollars to fill up your car because the price of oil is four times what it was before Iraq, you're paying a price for this war.

When Iraq is costing each household about one hundred dollars a month, you're paying a price for this war.

When a National Guard unit is over in Iraq and can't help out during a hurricane in Louisiana or with floods here in West Virginia, our communities are paying a price for this war.

And the price our families and communities are paying reflects the price America is paying. The most conservative estimates say that Iraq has now cost more than half a trillion dollars, more than any other war in our history besides World War II. Some say the true cost is even higher and that by the time it's over, this could be a three trillion dollar war.

But what no one disputes is that the cost of this war is far higher than what we were told it would be. We were told this war would cost fifty to sixty billion dollars, and that reconstruction would pay for itself out of Iraqi oil profits. We were told higher estimates were nothing but "baloney." Like so much else about this war, we were not told the truth.

What no one disputes is that the costs of this war have been compounded by its careless and incompetent execution — from the billions that have vanished in Iraq to the billions more in no-bid contracts for reckless contractors like Halliburton.

What no one disputes is that five years into this war, soldiers up at Fort Drum are having to wait more than a month to get their first mental health screening — even though we know that incidences of PTSD [post-traumatic stress disorder] skyrocket between the second, third, and fourth tours of duty. We have a sacred trust to our troops and our veterans, and we have to live up to it.

What no one disputes is that President Bush has done what no other President has ever done, and given tax cuts to the rich in a time of war. John McCain once opposed these tax cuts — he rightly called them unfair and fiscally irresponsible. But now he has done an about face and wants to make them permanent, just like he wants a permanent occupation in Iraq. No matter what the costs, no matter what the consequences, John McCain seems determined to carry out a third Bush term.

That's an outcome America can't afford. Because of the Bush-McCain policies, our debt has ballooned. This is creating problems in our fragile economy. And that kind of debt also places an unfair burden on our children and grandchildren, who will have to repay it.

It also means we're having to pay for this war with loans from China. Having China as our banker isn't good for our economy, it isn't good for our global leadership, and it isn't good for our national security. History teaches us that for a nation to remain a preeminent military power, it must remain a preeminent economic power. That is why it is so important to manage the costs of war wisely.

This is a lesson that the first President Bush understood. The conduct of the Gulf War cost America less than twenty billion dollars — what we pay in two months in Iraq today. That's because that war was prosecuted on solid grounds, and in a responsible way, and with the support of allies, who paid most of the costs. None of this has been the case in the way George W. Bush and John McCain have waged the current Iraq war.

Now, at that debate in Texas several weeks ago, Senator Clinton attacked John McCain for supporting the policies that have led to our enormous war costs. But her point would have been more compelling had she not joined

Senator McCain in making the tragically ill-considered decision to vote for the Iraq war in the first place.

The truth is, this is all part of the reason I opposed this war from the start. It's why I said back in 2002 that it could lead to an occupation not just of undetermined length or undetermined consequences, but of undetermined costs. It's why I've said this war should have never been authorized and never been waged.

Now, let me be clear: when I am President, I will spare no expense to ensure that our troops have the equipment and support they need. There is no higher obligation for a Commander-in-Chief. But we also have to understand that the more than ten billion dollars we're spending each month in Iraq is money we could be investing here at home. Just think about what battles we could be fighting instead of fighting this misguided war.

Instead of fighting this war, we could be fighting the terrorists who attacked us on 9/11 and who are plotting against us in Afghanistan and Pakistan. We could be securing our homeland and stopping the world's most dangerous weapons from falling into terrorist hands.

Instead of fighting this war, we could be fighting for the people of West Virginia. For what folks in this state have been spending on the Iraq war, we could be giving health care to nearly 450,000 of your neighbors, hiring nearly 30,000 new elementary school teachers, and making college more affordable for over 300,000 students.

We could be fighting to put the American dream within reach for every American — by giving tax breaks to working families, offering relief to struggling homeowners, reversing President Bush's cuts to the Manufacturing Extension Partnership, and protecting Social Security today, tomorrow, and forever. That's what we could be doing instead of fighting this war.

Instead of fighting this war, we could be fighting to make universal health care a reality in this country. We could be fighting for the young woman who works the night shift after a full day of college and still can't afford medicine for a sister who's ill. For what we spend in several months in Iraq, we could be providing them with the quality, affordable health care that every American deserves.

Instead of fighting this war, we could be fighting to give every American a quality education. We could be fighting for the young men and women all across this country who dream big dreams but aren't getting the kind of education they need to reach for those dreams. For a fraction of what we're spending each year in Iraq, we could be giving our teachers more pay and more support, rebuilding our crumbling schools, and offering a tax credit to put a college degree within reach for anyone who wants one.

Instead of fighting this war, we could be fighting to rebuild our roads and bridges. I've proposed a fund that would do just that and generate nearly two million new jobs — many in the construction industry that's been hard hit by our housing crisis. And it would cost just 6 percent of what we spend each year in Iraq.

Instead of fighting this war, we could be freeing ourselves from the tyranny of oil, and saving this planet for our children. We could be investing in renewable sources of energy, and in clean coal technology, and creating up to five million new green jobs in the bargain, including new clean coal jobs. And we could be doing it all for the cost of less than a year and a half in Iraq.

These are the investments we could be making, all within the parameters of a more responsible and disciplined budget. This is the future we could be building. And that is why I will bring this war to an end when I'm President of the United States of America.

But we also know that even after this war comes to an end, the costs of this war will not. We'll have to keep our sacred trust with our veterans and fully fund the VA. We'll have to look after our wounded warriors — whether they're suffering from wounds seen or unseen. That must include the signature injuries of the wars in Iraq and Afghanistan — not just PTSD, but Traumatic Brain Injury. We'll have to give veterans the health care and disability benefits they deserve, the support they need, and the respect they've earned. This is an obligation I have fought to uphold on the Senate Veterans' Affairs Committee by joining Jay Rockefeller to expand educational opportunities for our veterans. It's an obligation I will uphold as President, and it's an obligation that will endure long after this war is over.

And our obligation to rebuild our military will endure as well. This war has stretched our military to its limits, wearing down troops and equipment as a result of tour after tour after tour of duty. The Army has said it will need thirteen billion dollars a year just to replace and repair all the equipment that's been broken or lost. So in the coming years we won't just have to restore our military to its peak level of readiness, and we won't just have to make sure our National Guard is back to being fully prepared to handle a domestic crisis, we'll also have to ensure that our soldiers are trained and equipped to confront the new threats of the 21st century and that our military can meet any challenge around the world. And that is a responsibility I intend to meet as Commander-in-Chief.

So we know what this war has cost us — in blood and in treasure. But in the words of Robert Kennedy, "past error is no excuse for its own perpetuation." And yet, John McCain refuses to learn from the failures of the Bush years. Instead of offering an exit strategy for Iraq, he's offering us a one hundred-year occupation. Instead of offering an economic plan that works for working Americans, he's supporting tax cuts for the wealthiest among us who don't need them and aren't asking for them. Senator McCain is embracing the failed policies of the past, but America is ready to embrace the future.

When I am your nominee, the American people will have

a real choice in November — between change and more of the same, between giving the Bush policies another four years, or bringing them to an end. And that is the choice the American people deserve.

Somewhere in Baghdad today, a soldier is stepping into his Humvee and heading out on a patrol. That soldier knows the cost of war. He's been bearing it for five years. It's the cost of being kept awake at night by the whistle of falling mortars. It's the cost of a heart that aches for a loved one back home, and a family that's counting the days until the next R&R. It's the cost of losing a friend, who asked for nothing but to serve his country.

How much longer are we going to ask our troops to bear the cost of this war?

How much longer are we going to ask our families and our communities to bear the cost of this war?

When are we going to stop mortgaging our children's future for Washington's mistake?

This election is our chance to reclaim our future — to end the fight in Iraq and take up the fight for good jobs and universal health care. To end the fight in Iraq and take up the fight for a world-class education and retirement security. To end the fight in Iraq and take up the fight for opportunity, and equality, and prosperity here at home.

Those are the battles we need to fight. That is the leadership I want to offer. And that is the future we can build together when I'm President of the United States. Thank you.

NOBILITY OF PUBLIC SERVICE

America needs your service to community, country, and the world

"I began to realize that I wasn't just helping other people. Through service, I found a community that embraced me; citizenship that was meaningful; the direction I'd been seeking."

Subbing for U.S Senator Edward Kennedy, recently diagnosed with a cancerous brain tumor, Obama at Kennedy's request uses this commencement address at Wesleyan University to dwell on the nobility of public service, citing a Kennedy career whose extraordinary accomplishments have touched almost every American life. And to invite Wesleyan graduates to make community service part of their lives.

"WESLEYAN UNIVERSITY COMMENCEMENT"

May 25, 2008

Middletown, CT

Thank you, President Roth, for that generous introduction, and congratulations on your first year at the helm of Wesleyan. Congratulations also to the class of 2008, and thank you for allowing me to be a part of your graduation.

I have the distinct honor today of pinch-hitting for one of my personal heroes and a hero to this country, Senator Edward Kennedy. Teddy wanted to be here very much, but as you know, he's had a very long week and is taking some much-needed rest. He called me up a few days ago and I said that I'd be happy to be his stand-in, even if there was no way I could fill his shoes.

I did, however, get the chance to glance at the speech he planned on delivering today, and I'd like to start by passing along a message from him: "To all those praying for my return to good health, I offer my heartfelt thanks. And to any who'd rather have a different result, I say, don't get your hopes up just yet!"

So we know that Ted Kennedy's legendary sense of humor is as strong as ever, and I have no doubt that his equally legendary fighting spirit will carry him through this latest challenge. He is our friend, he is our champion, and we hope and pray for his return to good health.

The topic of his speech today was common for a commencement, but one that nobody could discuss with more authority or inspiration than Ted Kennedy. And that is the topic of service to one's country — a cause that is synonymous with his family's name and their legacy.

I was born the year that his brother John called a generation of Americans to ask their country what they could do. And I came of age at a time when they did it. They were the Peace Corps volunteers who won a generation of goodwill toward America at a time when America's ideals were challenged. They were the teenagers and college students, not much older than you, who watched the civil rights movement unfold on their television sets; who saw the dogs and the fire hoses and the footage of marchers beaten within an inch or their lives; who knew it was probably smarter and safer to stay at home, but still decided to take those Freedom Rides down south — who still decided to march. And because they did, they changed the world.

I bring this up because today, you are about to enter a world that makes it easy to get caught up in the notion that there are actually two different stories at work in our lives.

The first is the story of our everyday cares and concerns — the responsibilities we have to our jobs and our families — the bustle and busyness of what happens in our own life. And the second is the story of what happens in the life of our country — of what happens in the wider world. It's the story you see when you catch a glimpse of the day's headlines or turn on the news at night — a story of big challenges like war and recession; hunger and climate change; injustice and inequality. It's a story that can sometimes seem distant and separate from our own — a destiny to be shaped by forces beyond our control.

And yet, the history of this nation tells us this isn't so. It tells us that we are a people whose destiny has never been written for us, but by us — by generations of men and women, young and old, who have always believed that their story and the American story are not separate, but shared. And for more than two centuries, they have served this country in ways that have forever enriched both.

I say this to you as someone who couldn't be standing here today if not for the service of others, and wouldn't be standing here today if not for the purpose that service gave my own life.

You see, I spent much of my childhood adrift. My father left my mother and I when I was two. When my mother remarried, I lived in Indonesia for a time, but was mostly raised in Hawaii by her and my grandparents from Kansas. My teenage years were filled with more than the usual dose of adolescent rebellion, and I'll admit that I didn't always take myself or my studies very seriously. I realize that none of you can probably relate to this, but there were many times when I wasn't sure where I was going, or what I would do.

But during my first two years of college, perhaps because the values my mother had taught me — hard work, honesty, empathy — had resurfaced after a long hibernation; or perhaps because of the example of wonderful teachers and lasting friends, I began to notice a world beyond myself. I became active in the movement to oppose the apartheid regime of South Africa. I began following the debates in this country about poverty and health care. So that by the time I graduated from college, I was possessed with a crazy idea — that I would work at a grassroots level to bring about change.

I wrote letters to every organization in the country I could think of. And one day, a small group of churches on the South Side of Chicago offered me a job to come work as a community organizer in neighborhoods that had been devastated by steel plant closings. My mother and grandparents wanted me to go to law school. My friends were applying to jobs on Wall Street. Meanwhile, this organization offered me $12,000 a year plus $2,000 for an old, beat-up car.

And I said yes.

Now, I didn't know a soul in Chicago, and I wasn't sure what this community organizing business was all about. I had always been inspired by stories of the civil rights movement and JFK's call to service, but when I got to the South Side, there were no marches, and no soaring speeches. In the shadow of an empty steel plant, there were just a lot of folks who were struggling. And we didn't get very far at first.

I still remember one of the very first meetings we put together to discuss gang violence with a group of community leaders. We waited and waited for people to show up, and finally, a group of older people walked into the hall. And they sat down. And a little old lady raised her hand and asked, "Is this where the bingo game is?"

It wasn't easy, but eventually, we made progress. Day by day, block by block, we brought the community together, and registered new voters, and set up after-school programs, and fought for new jobs, and helped people live lives with some measure of dignity.

But I also began to realize that I wasn't just helping other people. Through service, I found a community that embraced me; citizenship that was meaningful; the direction I'd been seeking. Through service, I discovered how my own improbable story fit into the larger story of America.

Each of you will have the chance to make your own discovery in the years to come. And I say "chance" because you won't have to take it. There's no community service requirement in the real world; no one forcing you to care. You can take your diploma, walk off this stage, and chase only after the big house and the nice suits and all the other things that our money culture says you should buy. You can choose to narrow your concerns and live your life in a way that tries to keep your stories separate from America's.

But I hope you don't. Not because you have an obligation to those who are less fortunate, though you do have that obligation. Not because you have a debt to all those who helped you get here, though you do have that debt.

It's because you have an obligation to yourself. Because our individual salvation depends on collective salvation. Because thinking only about yourself, fulfilling your immediate wants and needs, betrays a poverty of ambition. Because it's only when you hitch your wagon to something larger than yourself that you realize your true potential and discover the role you'll play in writing the next great chapter in America's story.

There are so many ways to serve and so much need at this defining moment in our history. You don't have to be a community organizer or do something crazy like run for President. Right here at Wesleyan, many of you have already volunteered at local schools, contributed to United Way, and even started a program that brings fresh produce to needy families in the area. One hundred and sixty-four graduates of this school have joined the Peace Corps since 2001, and I'm especially proud that two of you are about to leave for my father's homeland of Kenya to bring alternative sources of energy to impoverished areas.[1]

I ask you to seek these opportunities when you leave here, because the future of this country — your future — depends on it. At a time when our security and moral standing depend on winning hearts and minds in the forgotten corners of this world, we need more of you to serve abroad. As President, I intend to grow the Foreign Service, double the Peace Corps over the next few years, and engage the young people of other nations in similar programs, so that we work side by side to take on the common challenges that confront all humanity.

At a time when our ice caps are melting and our oceans are rising, we need you to help lead a green revolution. We still have time to avoid the catastrophic consequences of climate change if we get serious about investing in renewable sources of energy, and if we get a generation of volunteers to work on renewable energy projects, and teach folks about conservation, and help clean up polluted areas; if we send talented engineers and scientists abroad to help developing countries promote clean energy.

At a time when a child in Boston must compete with children in Beijing and Bangalore, we need an army of you to become teachers and principals in schools that this nation cannot afford to give up on. I will pay our educators what they deserve, and give them more support, but I will also ask more of them to be mentors to other teachers, and serve in high-need schools and high-need subject areas like math and science.

At a time when there are children in the city of New Orleans who still spend each night in a lonely trailer, we need more of you to take a weekend or a week off from work, and head down South, and help rebuild. If you can't get the time, volunteer at the local homeless shelter or soup kitchen in your own community. Find an organization that's fighting poverty, or a candidate who promotes policies you believe in, and find a way to help them.

At a time of war, we need you to work for peace. At a time of inequality, we need you to work for opportunity. At a time of so much cynicism and so much doubt, we need you to make us believe again.

Now understand this — believing that change is possible is not the same as being naïve. Go into service with your eyes wide open, for change will not come easily. On the big issues that our nation faces, difficult choices await. We'll have to face some hard truths, and some sacrifice will be required — not only from you individually, but from the nation as a whole.

There is no magic bullet to our energy problems, for example; no perfect energy source — so all of us will have to use the energy sources we have more wisely. Deep-rooted poverty will not be reversed overnight, and will require both money and reform at a time when our federal and state budgets are strapped and Washington is skeptical that reform is possible. Transforming our education system will require not only bold government action, but a change in attitudes among parents and students. Bringing an end to the slaughter in Darfur will involve navigating extremely difficult realities on the ground, even for those with the best of intentions.

And so, should you take the path of service, should you choose to take up one of these causes as your own, know that you'll experience frustrations and failures. Even your successes will be marked by imperfections and unintended consequences. I guarantee you, there will certainly be times when friends or family urge you to pursue more sensible endeavors with more tangible rewards. And there will be times when you are tempted to take their advice.

But I hope you'll remember, during those times of doubt and frustration, that there is nothing naïve about your impulse to change this world. Because all it takes is one act of service — one blow against injustice — to send forth that tiny ripple of hope that Robert Kennedy spoke of.

You know, Ted Kennedy often tells a story about the fifth anniversary celebration of the Peace Corps. He was there, and he asked one of the young Americans why he had chosen to volunteer. And the man replied, "Because it was the first time someone asked me to do something for my country."

I don't know how many of you have been asked that question, but after today, you have no excuses. I am asking you, and if I should have the honor of serving this nation as President, I will be asking again in the coming years. We may disagree on certain issues and positions, but I believe we can be unified in service to a greater good. I intend to make it a cause of my presidency, and I believe with all my heart that this generation is ready, and eager, and up to the challenge.

We will face our share of cynics and doubters. But we always have. I can still remember a conversation I had with an older man all those years ago just before I left for Chicago. He said, "Barack, I'll give you a bit of advice.

Forget this community organizing business and do something that's gonna make you some money. You can't change the world, and people won't appreciate you trying. But you've got a nice voice, so you should think about going into television broadcasting. I'm telling you, you've got a future."

Now, he may have been right about the TV thing, but he was wrong about everything else. For that old man has not seen what I have seen. He has not seen the faces of ordinary people the first time they clear a vacant lot or build a new playground or force an unresponsive leader to provide services to their community. He has not seen the face of a child brighten because of an inspiring teacher or mentor. He has not seen scores of young people educate their parents on issues like Darfur, or mobilize the conscience of a nation around the challenge of climate change. He has not seen lines of men and women that wrap around schools and churches, that stretch block after block just so they could make their voices heard, many for the very first time.

And that old man who didn't believe the world could change — who didn't think one person could make a difference — well he certainly didn't know much about the life of Joseph Kennedy's youngest son.

It is rare in this country of ours that a person exists who has touched the lives of nearly every single American without many of us even realizing it. And yet, because of Ted Kennedy, millions of children can see a doctor when they get sick. Mothers and fathers can leave work to spend time with their newborns. Working Americans are paid higher wages, and compensated for overtime, and can keep their health insurance when they change jobs. They are protected from discrimination in the workplace, and those who are born with disabilities can still get an education, and health care, and fair treatment on the job. Our schools are stronger and our colleges are filled with more Americans who can afford it. And I have a feeling that Ted Kennedy is not done just yet.

But surely, if one man can achieve so much and make such

a difference in the lives of so many, then each of us can do our part. Surely, if his service and his story can forever shape America's story, then our collective service can shape the destiny of this generation. At the very least, his living example calls each of us to try. That is all I ask of you on this joyous day of new beginnings; that is what Senator Kennedy asks of you as well, and that is how we will keep so much needed work going, and the cause of justice everlasting, and the dream alive for generations to come. Thank you so much to the class of 2008, and congratulations on your graduation.

Note

1. Class of '08 Wesleyan graduates Robert McCourt and Nyambura Gichohi.

PATRIOTISM

Obama redefines patriotism for the 21st century

"I believe those who attack America's flaws without acknowledging the singular greatness of our ideals, and their proven capacity to inspire a better world, do not truly understand America."

In one of the most interesting explorations of patriotism and its meanings in the annals of the subject, Obama reconciles patriots with opposing views, praises contemporary and historic leaders for unconventional acts he deems patriotic, and finds patriotic meaning in all walks of life.

"THE AMERICA WE LOVE"

June 30, 2008

Independence, MO

On a spring morning in April of 1775, a simple band of colonists — farmers and merchants, blacksmiths and printers, men and boys — left their homes and families in Lexington and Concord to take up arms against the tyranny of an Empire. The odds against them were long and the risks enormous — for even if they survived the battle, any ultimate failure would bring charges of treason, and death by hanging.

And yet they took that chance. They did so not on behalf of a particular tribe or lineage, but on behalf of a larger idea. The idea of liberty. The idea of God-given, inalienable rights. And with the first shot of that fateful day — a shot heard round the world — the American Revolution, and America's experiment with democracy, began.

Those men of Lexington and Concord were among our first patriots. And at the beginning of a week when we celebrate the birth of our nation, I think it is fitting to pause for a moment and reflect on the meaning of patriotism — theirs, and ours. We do so in part because we are in the midst of war — more than one and a half million of our finest young men and women have now fought in Iraq and Afghanistan; over 60,000 have been wounded, and over 4,600 have been laid to rest. The costs of war have been great, and the debate surrounding our mission in Iraq has been fierce. It is natural, in light of such sacrifice by so many, to think more deeply about the commitments that bind us to our nation, and to each other.

We reflect on these questions as well because we are in the midst of a presidential election, perhaps the most consequential in generations; a contest that will determine the course of this nation for years, perhaps decades, to come. Not only is it a debate about big issues — health care, jobs, energy, education, and retirement security — but it is also a debate about values. How do we keep ourselves safe and secure while preserving our liberties? How do we restore trust in a government that seems increasingly removed from its people and dominated by special interests? How do we ensure that in an increasingly global economy, the winners maintain allegiance to the less fortunate? And how do we resolve our differences at a time of increasing diversity?

Finally, it is worth considering the meaning of patriotism because the question of who is — or is not — a patriot all too often poisons our political debates, in ways that divide us rather than bringing us together. I have come to know this from my own experience on the campaign trail. Throughout my life, I have always taken my deep and abiding love for this country as a given. It was how I was raised; it is what propelled me into public service; it is why I am running for President. And yet, at certain times over the last sixteen months, I have found, for the first time, my patriotism challenged — at times as a result of my own carelessness, more often as a result of the desire by some to score political points and raise fears about who I am and what I stand for.

So let me say at this at outset of my remarks. I will never question the patriotism of others in this campaign. And I will not stand idly by when I hear others question mine.

My concerns here aren't simply personal, however. After all, throughout our history, men and women of far greater stature and significance than me have had their patriotism questioned in the midst of momentous debates. Thomas Jefferson was accused by the Federalists of selling out to the French. The anti-Federalists were just as convinced that John Adams was in cahoots with the British and intent on restoring monarchal rule. Likewise, even our wisest Presidents have sought to justify questionable policies on the basis of patriotism. Adams' Alien and Sedition Act, Lincoln's suspension of habeas corpus, Roosevelt's internment of Japanese Americans — all were defended as expressions of patriotism, and those who disagreed with their policies were sometimes labeled as unpatriotic.

In other words, the use of patriotism as a political sword or a political shield is as old as the Republic. Still, what is striking about today's patriotism debate is the degree to which it remains rooted in the culture wars of the 1960s — in arguments that go back forty years or more. In the early years of the civil rights movement and opposition to the Vietnam War, defenders of the status quo often accused anybody who questioned the wisdom of government policies of being unpatriotic. Meanwhile, some of those in the so-called counter-culture of the sixties reacted not merely by criticizing particular government policies, but by attacking the symbols, and in extreme cases, the very idea, of America itself — by burning flags; by blaming America for all that was wrong with the world; and perhaps most tragically, by failing to honor those veterans coming home from Vietnam, something that remains a national shame to this day.

Most Americans never bought into these simplistic worldviews — these caricatures of left and right. Most Americans understood that dissent does not make one unpatriotic, and that there is nothing smart or sophisticated about a cynical disregard for America's traditions and institutions. And yet the anger and turmoil of that period never entirely drained away. All too often our politics still seems trapped in these old, threadbare arguments — a fact most evident during our recent debates about the war in Iraq, when those who opposed administration policy were tagged by some as unpatriotic, and a general providing his best counsel on how to move forward in Iraq was accused of betrayal.

Given the enormous challenges that lie before us, we can no longer afford these sorts of divisions. None of us expect that arguments about patriotism will, or should, vanish entirely; after all, when we argue about patriotism, we are arguing about who we are as a country, and more importantly, who we should be. But surely we can agree that no party or political philosophy has a monopoly on patriotism. And surely we can arrive at a definition of patriotism that, however rough and imperfect, captures the best of America's common spirit.

What would such a definition look like? For me, as for most Americans, patriotism starts as a gut instinct, a loyalty and love for country rooted in my earliest memories. I'm not just talking about the recitations of the Pledge of Allegiance or the Thanksgiving pageants at school or the fireworks on the Fourth of July, as wonderful as those things may be. Rather, I'm referring to the way the American ideal wove its way throughout the lessons my family taught me as a child.

One of my earliest memories is of sitting on my grandfather's shoulders and watching the astronauts come to shore in Hawaii. I remember the cheers and small flags that people waved, and my grandfather explaining how we Americans could do anything we set our minds to do. That's my idea of America.

I remember listening to my grandmother telling stories about her work on a bomber assembly-line during World War II. I remember my grandfather handing me his dog-tags from his time in Patton's army, and understanding that his defense of this country marked one of his greatest sources of pride. That's my idea of America.

I remember, when living for four years in Indonesia as a child, listening to my mother reading me the first lines of the Declaration of Independence — "We hold these truths to be self-evident, that all men are created equal. That they are endowed by their Creator with certain unalienable rights, that among these are Life, Liberty and the pursuit of Happiness." I remember her explaining how this declaration applied to every American, black and white and brown alike; how those words, and words of the United States Constitution, protected us from the injustices that we witnessed other people suffering during those years abroad. That's my idea of America.

As I got older, that gut instinct — that America is the greatest country on earth — would survive my growing awareness of our nation's imperfections: its ongoing racial strife; the perversion of our political system laid bare during the Watergate hearings; the wrenching poverty of the Mississippi Delta and the hills of Appalachia. Not only because, in my mind, the joys of American life and culture, its vitality, its variety, and its freedom, always outweighed its imperfections, but because I learned that what makes America great has never been its perfection but the belief that it can be made better. I came to understand that our revolution was waged for the sake of that belief — that we could be governed by laws, not men; that we could be equal in the eyes of those laws; that we could be free to say what we want and assemble with whomever we want and worship as we please; that we could have the right to pursue our individual dreams but the obligation to help our fellow citizens pursue theirs.

For a young man of mixed race, without firm anchor in any particular community, without even a father's steadying hand, it is this essential American idea — that we are not constrained by the accident of birth but can make of our lives what we will — that has defined my life, just as it has defined the life of so many other Americans.

That is why, for me, patriotism is always more than just loyalty to a place on a map or a certain kind of people. Instead, it is also loyalty to America's ideals — ideals for which anyone can sacrifice, or defend, or give their last full measure of devotion. I believe it is this loyalty that allows a country teeming with different races and ethnicities, religions and customs, to come together as one. It is the application of these ideals that separate us from Zimbabwe, where the opposition party and their supporters have been silently hunted, tortured or killed; or Burma, where tens of thousands continue to struggle for basic food and shelter in the wake of a monstrous storm because a military junta fears opening up the country to outsiders; or Iraq, where despite the heroic efforts of our military, and the courage of many ordinary Iraqis, even limited cooperation between various factions remains far too elusive.

I believe those who attack America's flaws without acknowledging the singular greatness of our ideals, and their proven capacity to inspire a better world, do not truly understand America.

Of course, precisely because America isn't perfect, precisely because our ideals constantly demand more from us, patriotism can never be defined as loyalty to any particular leader or government or policy. As Mark Twain, that greatest of American satirists and proud son of Missouri, once wrote, "Patriotism is supporting your country all the time, and your government when it deserves it." We may hope that our leaders and our government stand up for our ideals, and there are many times in our history when that's occurred. But when our laws, our leaders, or our government are out of alignment with our ideals, then the dissent of ordinary Americans may prove to be one of the truest expression of patriotism.

The young preacher from Georgia, Martin Luther King, Jr., who led a movement to help America confront our tragic history of racial injustice and live up to the meaning of our creed — he was a patriot. The young soldier who first spoke about the prisoner abuse at Abu Ghraib — he is a patriot. Recognizing a wrong being committed in this country's name; insisting that we deliver on the promise of our Constitution — these are the acts of patriots, men and women who are defending that which is best in America. And we should never forget that — especially when we disagree with them; especially when they make us uncomfortable with their words.

Beyond a loyalty to America's ideals, beyond a willingness to dissent on behalf of those ideals, I also believe that patriotism must, if it is to mean anything, involve the willingness to sacrifice — to give up something we value on behalf of a larger cause. For those who have fought under the flag of this nation — for the young veterans I meet when I visit Walter Reed; for those like John McCain who have endured physical torment in service to our country — no further proof of such sacrifice is necessary. And let me also add that no one should ever devalue that service, especially for the sake of a political campaign, and that goes for supporters on both sides.

We must always express our profound gratitude for the service of our men and women in uniform. Period. Indeed, one of the good things to emerge from the current conflict in Iraq has been the widespread recognition that whether you support this war or oppose it, the sacrifice of our troops is always worthy of honor.

For the rest of us — for those of us not in uniform or without loved ones in the military — the call to sacrifice for the country's greater good remains an imperative of citizenship. Sadly, in recent years, in the midst of war on two fronts, this call to service never came. After 9/11, we were asked to shop. The wealthiest among us saw their tax obligations decline, even as the costs of war continued to mount. Rather than work together to reduce our dependence on foreign oil, and thereby lessen our vulnerability to a volatile region, our energy policy remained unchanged, and our oil dependence only grew.

In spite of this absence of leadership from Washington, I have seen a new generation of Americans begin to take up the call. I meet them everywhere I go, young people involved in the project of American renewal; not only those who have signed up to fight for our country in distant lands, but those who are fighting for a better America here at home, by teaching in underserved schools, or caring for the sick in understaffed hospitals, or promoting more sustainable energy policies in their local communities.

I believe one of the tasks of the next Administration is to ensure that this movement towards service grows and sustains itself in the years to come. We should expand AmeriCorps and grow the Peace Corps. We should encourage national service by making it part of the requirement for a new college assistance program, even as we strengthen the benefits for those whose sense of duty has already led them to serve in our military.

We must remember, though, that true patriotism cannot be forced or legislated with a mere set of government programs. Instead, it must reside in the hearts of our people, and cultivated in the heart of our culture, and nurtured in the hearts of our children.

As we begin our fourth century as a nation, it is easy to take the extraordinary nature of America for granted. But it is our responsibility as Americans and as parents to instill that history in our children, both at home and at school. The loss of quality civic education from so many of our classrooms has left too many young Americans without the most basic knowledge of who our forefathers are, or what they did, or the significance of the founding documents that bear their names. Too many children are ignorant of the sheer effort, the risks and sacrifices made by previous generations, to ensure that this country survived war and depression; through the great struggles for civil, and social, and workers' rights.

It is up to us, then, to teach them. It is up to us to teach them that even though we have faced great challenges and made our share of mistakes, we have always been able to come together and make this nation stronger, and more prosperous, and more united, and more just. It is up to us to teach them that America has been a force for good in the world, and that other nations and other people have looked to us as the last, best hope of earth. It is up to us to teach them that it is good to give back to one's community; that it is honorable to serve in the military; that it is vital to participate in our democracy and make our voices heard.

And it is up to us to teach our children a lesson that those of us in politics too often forget: that patriotism involves not only defending this country against external threat, but also working constantly to make America a better place for future generations.

When we pile up mountains of debt for the next generation to absorb, or put off changes to our energy policies, knowing full well the potential consequences of inaction, we are placing our short-term interests ahead of the nation's long-term well-being. When we fail to educate effectively millions of our children so that they might compete in a global economy, or we fail to invest in the basic scientific research that has driven innovation in this country, we risk leaving behind an America that has fallen in the ranks of the world. Just as patriotism involves each of us making a commitment to this nation that extends beyond our own immediate self-interest, so must that commitment extend beyond our own time here on earth.

Our greatest leaders have always understood this. They've defined patriotism with an eye toward posterity. George Washington is rightly revered for his leadership of the Continental Army, but one of his greatest acts of patriotism was his insistence on stepping down after two terms, thereby setting a pattern for those that would follow, reminding future presidents that this is a government of and by and for the people.

Abraham Lincoln did not simply win a war or hold the Union together. In his unwillingness to demonize those against whom he fought; in his refusal to succumb to either the hatred or self-righteousness that war can unleash; in his ultimate insistence that in the aftermath of war the nation would no longer remain half slave and half free; and his trust in the better angels of our nature — he displayed the wisdom and courage that sets a standard for patriotism.

And it was the most famous son of Independence, Harry S. Truman, who sat in the White House during his final days in office and said in his Farewell Address: "When Franklin Roosevelt died, I felt there must be a million men better qualified than I, to take up the Presidential task. . . . But through all of it, through all the years I have worked here in this room, I have been well aware than I did not really work alone — that you were working with me. No President could ever hope to lead our country, or to sustain the burdens of this office, save the people helped with their support."

In the end, it may be this quality that best describes patriotism in my mind — not just a love of America in the abstract, but a very particular love for, and faith in, the American people. That is why our heart swells with pride at the sight of our flag; why we shed a tear as the lonely notes of Taps sound. For we know that the greatness of this country — its victories in war, its enormous wealth, its scientific and cultural achievements — all result from the energy and imagination of the American people; their toil, drive, struggle, restlessness, humor, and quiet heroism.

That is the liberty we defend — the liberty of each of us to pursue our own dreams. That is the equality we seek — not an equality of results, but the chance of every single one of us to make it if we try. That is the community we strive to build — one in which we trust in this sometimes messy democracy of ours, one in which we continue to insist that there is nothing we cannot do when we put our mind to it, one in which we see ourselves as part of a larger story, our own fates wrapped up in the fates of those who share allegiance to America's happy and singular creed.

Thank you, God Bless you, and may God Bless the United States of America.

VICTORY SPEECH

A new beginning for a nation that finally has transcended the ultimate race barrier

---

"[You] proved that more than two centuries later, a government of the people, by the people and for the people has not perished from this earth. This is your victory."

Obama's improbable, twenty-one-month presidential campaign culminated in the election of the first U.S. president raised on food stamps, the first president with a previous career as a community organizer, the first African-American to serve in the White House. Gracious after a sweeping victory for Democrats, who strengthened their control of Congress that night, Obama praised adversaries and supporters alike, seeking already to unite them in the face of hard economic times.

Addressing tens of thousands of supporters at Grant Park in his Chicago hometown, Obama sought to lower the expectations his charismatic persona had raised. "The road will be long," he warned. "There will be setbacks and false starts." But Obama then invoked the unceasing progress that has marked America's history, ending with his uplifting campaign slogan, "Yes we can."

"REMARKS OF PRESIDENT-ELECT BARACK OBAMA: ELECTION NIGHT"

November 4, 2008

Chicago, IL

If there is anyone out there who still doubts that America is a place where all things are possible; who still wonders if the dream of our founders is alive in our time; who still questions the power of our democracy, tonight is your answer.

It's the answer told by lines that stretched around schools and churches in numbers this nation has never seen; by people who waited three hours and four hours, many for the very first time in their lives, because they believed that this time must be different; that their voice could be that difference.

It's the answer spoken by young and old, rich and poor, Democrat and Republican, black, white, Latino, Asian, Native-American, gay, straight, disabled and not disabled — Americans who sent a message to the world that we have never been a collection of Red States and Blue States: we are, and always will be, the United States of America.

It's the answer that led those who have been told for so long by so many to be cynical, and fearful, and doubtful of what we can achieve to put their hands on the arc of history and bend it once more toward the hope of a better day.

It's been a long time coming, but tonight, because of what we did on this day, in this election, at this defining moment, change has come to America.

I just received a very gracious call from Senator McCain. He fought long and hard in this campaign, and he's fought even longer and harder for the country he loves. He has endured sacrifices for America that most of us cannot begin to imagine, and we are better off for the service rendered by this brave and selfless leader. I congratulate him and Governor Palin for all they have achieved, and I look forward to working with them to renew this nation's promise in the months ahead.

I want to thank my partner in this journey, a man who campaigned from his heart and spoke for the men and women he grew up with on the streets of Scranton and rode with on that train home to Delaware, the Vice President-elect of the United States, Joe Biden.

I would not be standing here tonight without the unyielding support of my best friend for the last sixteen years, the rock of our family and the love of my life, our nation's next First Lady, Michelle Obama. Sasha and Malia, I love you both so much, and you have earned the new puppy that's coming with us to the White House. And while she's no longer with us, I know my grandmother is watching, along with the family that made me who I am. I miss them tonight, and know that my debt to them is beyond measure.

To my campaign manager David Plouffe, my chief strategist David Axelrod, and the best campaign team ever assembled in the history of politics — you made this happen, and I am forever grateful for what you've sacrificed to get it done.

But above all, I will never forget who this victory truly belongs to — it belongs to you.

I was never the likeliest candidate for this office. We didn't start with much money or many endorsements. Our campaign was not hatched in the halls of Washington — it began in the backyards of Des Moines and the living rooms of Concord and the front porches of Charleston.

It was built by working men and women who dug into what little savings they had to give five dollars and ten dollars and twenty dollars to this cause. It grew strength from the young people who rejected the myth of their generation's apathy; who left their homes and their families for jobs that offered little pay and less sleep; from the not-so-young people who braved the bitter cold and scorching heat to knock on the doors of perfect strangers; from the millions of Americans who volunteered, and organized, and proved that more than two centuries later, a government of the people, by the people and for the people has not perished from this earth. This is your victory.

I know you didn't do this just to win an election and I know you didn't do it for me. You did it because you understand the enormity of the task that lies ahead. For even as we celebrate tonight, we know the challenges that tomorrow will bring are the greatest of our lifetime — two wars, a planet in peril, the worst financial crisis in a century. Even as we stand here tonight, we know there are brave Americans waking up in the deserts of Iraq and the mountains of Afghanistan to risk their lives for us. There are mothers and fathers who will lie awake after their children fall asleep and wonder how they'll make the mortgage, or pay their doctor's bills, or save enough for college. There is new energy to harness and new jobs to be created; new schools to build and threats to meet and alliances to repair.

The road ahead will be long. Our climb will be steep. We may not get there in one year or even one term, but America — I have never been more hopeful than I am tonight that we will get there. I promise you — we as a people will get there.

There will be setbacks and false starts. There are many who won't agree with every decision or policy I make as President, and we know that government can't solve every problem. But I will always be honest with you about the challenges we face. I will listen to you, especially when we disagree. And above all, I will ask you join in the work of remaking this nation the only way it's been done in America for two-hundred and twenty-one years — block by block, brick by brick, calloused hand by calloused hand.

What began twenty-one months ago in the depths of winter must not end on this autumn night. This victory alone is not the change we seek — it is only the chance for us to make that change. And that cannot happen if we go back to the way things were. It cannot happen without you.

So let us summon a new spirit of patriotism; of service and responsibility where each of us resolves to pitch in and work harder and look after not only ourselves, but each other. Let us remember that if this financial crisis taught us anything, it's that we cannot have a thriving Wall Street while Main Street suffers — in this country, we rise or fall as one nation; as one people.

Let us resist the temptation to fall back on the same partisanship and pettiness and immaturity that has poisoned our politics for so long. Let us remember that it was a man from this state who first carried the banner of the Republican Party to the White House — a party founded on the values of self-reliance, individual liberty, and national unity. Those are values we all share, and while the Democratic Party has won a great victory tonight, we do so with a measure of humility and determination to heal the divides that have held back our progress. As Lincoln said to a nation far more divided than ours, "We are not enemies, but friends . . . though passion may have strained it must not break our bonds of affection." And to those Americans whose support I have yet to earn — I may not have won your vote, but I hear your voices, I need your help, and I will be your President too.

And to all those watching tonight from beyond our shores, from parliaments and palaces to those who are huddled around radios in the forgotten corners of our world — our stories are singular, but our destiny is shared, and a new dawn of American leadership is at hand. To those who would tear this world down — we will defeat you. To those who seek peace and security — we support you. And to all those who have wondered if America's beacon still burns as bright — tonight we proved once more that the true strength of our nation comes not from the might of our arms or the scale of our wealth, but from the enduring power of our ideals: democracy, liberty, opportunity, and unyielding hope.

For that is the true genius of America — that America can change. Our union can be perfected. And what we have already achieved gives us hope for what we can and must achieve tomorrow.

This election had many firsts and many stories that will be told for generations. But one that's on my mind tonight is about a woman who cast her ballot in Atlanta. She's a lot like the millions of others who stood in line to make their voice heard in this election except for one thing — Ann Nixon Cooper is 106 years old.

She was born just a generation past slavery; a time when there were no cars on the road or planes in the sky; when someone like her couldn't vote for two reasons — because she was a woman and because of the color of her skin.

And tonight, I think about all that she's seen throughout her century in America — the heartache and the hope; the struggle and the progress; the times we were told that we can't, and the people who pressed on with that American creed: Yes we can.

At a time when women's voices were silenced and their hopes dismissed, she lived to see them stand up and speak out and reach for the ballot. Yes we can.

When there was despair in the dust bowl and depression across the land, she saw a nation conquer fear itself with a New Deal, new jobs and a new sense of common purpose. Yes we can.

When the bombs fell on our harbor and tyranny threatened the world, she was there to witness a generation rise to greatness and a democracy was saved. Yes we can.

She was there for the buses in Montgomery, the hoses in Birmingham, a bridge in Selma, and a preacher from Atlanta who told a people that "We Shall Overcome." Yes we can.

A man touched down on the moon, a wall came down in Berlin, a world was connected by our own science and imagination. And this year, in this election, she touched her finger to a screen, and cast her vote, because after 106 years in America, through the best of times and the darkest of hours, she knows how America can change. Yes we can.

America, we have come so far. We have seen so much. But there is so much more to do. So tonight, let us ask ourselves — if our children should live to see the next century; if my daughters should be so lucky to live as long as Ann Nixon Cooper, what change will they see? What progress will we have made?

This is our chance to answer that call. This is our moment. This is our time — to put our people back to work and open doors of opportunity for our kids; to restore prosperity and promote the cause of peace; to reclaim the American Dream and reaffirm that fundamental truth — that out of many, we are one; that while we breathe, we hope, and where we are met with cynicism, and doubt, and those who tell us that we can't, we will respond with that timeless creed that sums up the spirit of a people:

Yes We Can. Thank you, God bless you, and may God Bless the United States of America.

INAUGURAL ADDRESS

Confronting econcomic adversity, Obama invokes America's long tradition of triumph in trying times

"Our time of standing pat, of protecting narrow interests and putting off unpleasant decisions — that time has surely passed. Starting today, we must pick ourselves up, dust ourselves off, and begin again the work of remaking America."

Speaking to a record-sized inaugural crowd January 20, 2009, on the Capitol steps facing Washington's Mall, where Dr. King had articulated his dream forty-six years ago, and with Lincoln's Memorial and legacy in the background, Barack Obama was sworn in as forty-fourth president of the United States in an address marked by humility and resolve.

Obama described the American project as a communal one, requiring the sustained faith and effort of every citizen. His administration, Obama vowed, would be open and honest with the people, be guided by facts rather than fixed ideology, and seek the guidance of Americans of all walks of life. The nation might be confronted with brutal economic conditions, Obama allowed, but it had triumphed in even more difficult times in the past, and would do so again — united, confident, and once more widely respected in the world.

"INAUGURAL ADDRESS"

January 20, 2009

Washington, D.C.

My fellow citizens: I stand here today humbled by the task before us, grateful for the trust you have bestowed, mindful of the sacrifices borne by our ancestors. I thank President Bush for his service to our nation, as well as the generosity and cooperation he has shown throughout this transition.

Forty-four Americans have now taken the presidential oath. The words have been spoken during rising tides of prosperity and the still waters of peace. Yet, every so often the oath is taken amidst gathering clouds and raging storms. At these moments, America has carried on not simply because of the skill or vision of those in high office, but because We the People have remained faithful to the ideals of our forbearers, and true to our founding documents.

So it has been. So it must be with this generation of Americans.

That we are in the midst of crisis is now well understood. Our nation is at war, against a far-reaching network of violence and hatred. Our economy is badly weakened, a consequence of greed and irresponsibility on the part of some, but also our collective failure to make hard choices and prepare the nation for a new age. Homes have been lost; jobs shed; businesses shuttered. Our health care is too costly; our schools fail too many; and each day brings further evidence that the ways we use energy strengthen our adversaries and threaten our planet.

These are the indicators of crisis, subject to data and statistics. Less measurable but no less profound is a sapping of confidence across our land — a nagging fear that America's decline is inevitable, and that the next generation must lower its sights.

Today I say to you that the challenges we face are real. They are serious and they are many. They will not be met easily or in a short span of time. But know this, America — they will be met.

On this day, we gather because we have chosen hope over fear, unity of purpose over conflict and discord.

On this day, we come to proclaim an end to the petty grievances and false promises, the recriminations and worn-out dogmas, that for far too long have strangled our politics.

We remain a young nation, but in the words of Scripture, the time has come to set aside childish things. The time has come to reaffirm our enduring spirit; to choose our better history; to carry forward that precious gift, that noble idea, passed on from generation to generation: the God-given promise that all are equal, all are free, and all deserve a chance to pursue their full measure of happiness.

In reaffirming the greatness of our nation, we understand that greatness is never a given. It must be earned. Our journey has never been one of short-cuts or settling for less. It has not been the path for the faint-hearted — for those who prefer leisure over work, or seek only the pleasures of riches and fame. Rather, it has been the risk takers, the doers, the makers of things — some celebrated but more often men and women obscure in their labor, who have carried us up the long, rugged path towards prosperity and freedom.

For us, they packed up their few worldly possessions and traveled across oceans in search of a new life.

For us, they toiled in sweatshops and settled the West; endured the lash of the whip and plowed the hard earth.

For us, they fought and died, in places like Concord and Gettysburg; Normandy and Khe Sanh.

Time and again these men and women struggled and sacrificed and worked till their hands were raw so that we might live a better life. They saw America as bigger than the sum of our individual ambitions; greater than all the differences of birth or wealth or faction.

This is the journey we continue today. We remain the most prosperous, powerful nation on earth. Our workers are no less productive than when this crisis began. Our minds are no less inventive, our goods and services no less needed than they were last week or last month or last year. Our capacity remains undiminished. But our time of standing pat, of protecting narrow interests and putting off unpleasant decisions — that time has surely passed. Starting today, we must pick ourselves up, dust ourselves off, and begin again the work of remaking America.

For everywhere we look, there is work to be done. The state of our economy calls for action, bold and swift, and we will act — not only to create new jobs, but to lay a new foundation for growth. We will build the roads and bridges, the electric grids and digital lines that feed our commerce and bind us together. We will restore science to its rightful place, and wield technology's wonders to raise health care's quality and lower its cost. We will harness the sun and the winds and the soil to fuel our cars and run our factories. And we will transform our schools and colleges and universities to meet the demands of a new age. All this we can do. And all this we will do.

Now, there are some who question the scale of our ambitions — who suggest that our system cannot tolerate too many big plans. Their memories are short. For they have forgotten what this country has already done; what free men and women can achieve when imagination is joined to common purpose, and necessity to courage.

What the cynics fail to understand is that the ground has shifted beneath them — that the stale political arguments that have consumed us for so long no longer apply. The question we ask today is not whether our government is too big or too small, but whether it works — whether it helps families find jobs at a decent wage, care they can afford, a retirement that is dignified. Where the answer is yes, we intend to move forward. Where the answer is no, programs will end. And those of us who manage the public's dollars will be held to account — to spend wisely, reform bad habits, and do our business in the light of day — because only then can we restore the vital trust between a people and their government.

Nor is the question before us whether the market is a force for good or ill. Its power to generate wealth and expand freedom is unmatched, but this crisis has reminded us that without a watchful eye, the market can spin out of control — and that a nation cannot prosper long when it favors only the prosperous. The success of our economy has always depended not just on the size of our Gross Domestic Product, but on the reach of our prosperity; on the ability to extend opportunity to every willing heart — not out of charity, but because it is the surest route to our common good.

As for our common defense, we reject as false the choice between our safety and our ideals. Our Founding Fathers, faced with perils that we can scarcely imagine, drafted a charter to assure the rule of law and the rights of man, a charter expanded by the blood of generations. Those ideals still light the world, and we will not give them up for expedience's sake. And so to all the other peoples and governments who are watching today, from the grandest capitals to the small village where my father was born: know that America is a friend of each nation and every man, woman, and child who seeks a future of peace and dignity, and we are ready to lead once more.

Recall that earlier generations faced down fascism and communism not just with missiles and tanks, but with sturdy alliances and enduring convictions. They understood that our power alone cannot protect us, nor does it entitle us to do as we please. Instead, they knew that our power grows through its prudent use; our security emanates from the justness of our cause, the force of our example, the tempering qualities of humility and restraint.

We are the keepers of this legacy. Guided by these principles once more, we can meet those new threats that demand even greater effort — even greater cooperation and understanding between nations. We will begin to responsibly leave Iraq to its people, and forge a hard-earned peace in Afghanistan. With old friends and former foes, we will work tirelessly to lessen the nuclear threat, and roll back the specter of a warming planet. We will not apologize for our way of life, nor will we waver in its defense, and for those who seek to advance their aims by inducing terror and slaughtering innocents, we say to you now that our spirit is stronger and cannot be broken; you cannot outlast us, and we will defeat you.

For we know that our patchwork heritage is a strength, not a weakness. We are a nation of Christians and Muslims, Jews and Hindus — and nonbelievers. We are shaped by every language and culture, drawn from every end of this earth; and because we have tasted the bitter swill of civil war and segregation, and emerged from that dark chapter stronger and more united, we cannot help but believe that the old hatreds shall someday pass; that the lines of tribe shall soon dissolve; that as the world grows smaller, our common humanity shall reveal itself; and that America must play its role in ushering in a new era of peace.

To the Muslim world, we seek a new way forward, based on mutual interest and mutual respect. To those leaders around the globe who seek to sow conflict, or blame their society's ills on the West — know that your people will judge you on what you can build, not what you destroy. To those who cling to power through corruption and deceit and the silencing of dissent, know that you are on the wrong side of history; but that we will extend a hand if you are willing to unclench your fist.

To the people of poor nations, we pledge to work alongside you to make your farms flourish and let clean waters flow; to nourish starved bodies and feed hungry minds. And to those nations like ours that enjoy relative plenty, we say we can no longer afford indifference to the suffering outside our borders; nor can we consume the world's resources without regard to effect. For the world has changed, and we must change with it.

As we consider the road that unfolds before us, we remember with humble gratitude those brave Americans who, at this very hour, patrol far-off deserts and distant mountains. They have something to tell us, just as the fallen heroes who lie in Arlington whisper through the ages. We honor them not only because they are guardians of our liberty, but because they embody the spirit of service; a willingness to find meaning in something greater than themselves. And yet, at this moment — a moment that will define a generation — it is precisely this spirit that must inhabit us all.

For as much as government can do and must do, it is ultimately the faith and determination of the American people upon which this nation relies. It is the kindness to take in a stranger when the levees break, the selflessness of workers who would rather cut their hours than see a friend lose their job which sees us through our darkest hours. It is the firefighter's courage to storm a stairway filled with smoke, but also a parent's willingness to nurture a child, that finally decides our fate.

Our challenges may be new. The instruments with which we meet them may be new. But those values upon which our success depends — honesty and hard work, courage and fair play, tolerance and curiosity, loyalty and patriotism — these things are old. These things are true. They have been the quiet force of progress throughout our history. What is demanded then is a return to these truths. What is required of us now is a new era of responsibility — a recognition, on the part of every American, that we have duties to ourselves, our nation, and the world, duties that we do not grudgingly accept but rather seize gladly, firm in the knowledge that there is nothing so satisfying to the spirit, so defining of our character, than giving our all to a difficult task.

This is the price and the promise of citizenship.

This is the source of our confidence — the knowledge that God calls on us to shape an uncertain destiny.

This is the meaning of our liberty and our creed — why men and women and children of every race and every faith can join in celebration across this magnificent mall, and why a man whose father less than sixty years ago might not have been served at a local restaurant can now stand before you to take a most sacred oath.

So let us mark this day with remembrance, of who we are and how far we have traveled. In the year of America's birth, in the coldest of months, a small band of patriots huddled by dying campfires on the shores of an icy river. The capital was abandoned. The enemy was advancing. The snow was stained with blood. At a moment when the outcome of our revolution was most in doubt, the father of our nation ordered these words be read to the people: "Let it be told to the future world . . . that in the depth of winter, when nothing but hope and virtue could survive . . . that the city and the country, alarmed at one common danger, came forth to meet [it]."

America. In the face of our common dangers, in this winter of our hardship, let us remember these timeless words. With hope and virtue, let us brave once more the icy currents, and endure what storms may come. Let it be said by our children's children that when we were tested we refused to let this journey end, that we did not turn back nor did we falter; and with eyes fixed on the horizon and God's grace upon us, we carried forth that great gift of freedom and delivered it safely to future generations.

Thank you. God bless you. And God bless the United States of America.

AN OBAMA PRIMER

From birth to 44th US president

EARLY LIFE AND EDUCATION

Barack Hussein Obama Jr. is born on **August 4, 1961**, in Honolulu, Hawaii, son of Ann Dunham, originally of Wichita, Kansas, and Barack Hussein Obama of Nyangoma-Kogelo, Siaya District, Kenya, who met as classmates at the University of Hawaii. Dunham nicknamed her son Barry, but in his adolescence he discarded that name, partly at the encouragement of a female friend who liked "Barack." He also wanted to embrace his African-American status and honor his father, a Kenyan who had herded goats as a youth and gained prominence in his homeland as a Harvard-educated senior public official. "Barack" is Swahili for "blessed."

Obama is abandoned by his natural father at age two, in **1963**, when Obama Sr. chooses to return to Kenya. Barack spends most of his childhood and adolescence in Honolulu, where he is raised by his white mother and her parents, Madelyn and Stanley Armour Dunham. Obama's restless maternal grandfather, a furniture salesman, had relocated the family from Kansas to Hawaii by way of Texas and Washington state.

Once divorced from Barack Obama Sr., Ann Dunham is remarried to Loro Soetoro in **1967**, who works for the Indonesian government and later a U.S. oil company. Soetoro moves the family to his home in Jakarta, where Barack attends Christian and Muslim schools from age six to ten. This is Obama's first experience with wide disparities between rich and poor. Soetoro's Muslim faith, like that of many Indonesians, was an amalgam that embraced Hindu and ancient animist beliefs. "He explained," Obama wrote in his memoir, *Dreams from My Father*, "that a man took on the powers of whatever he ate. One day soon, he promised, he would bring home a piece of tiger meat for us to share." Ann Dunham's second marriage ends in divorce in the 1970s.

Unhappy in Indonesia, Obama returns to Hawaii in **1971** to live with his maternal grandparents. He attends Hawaii's most prestigious academy, Honolulu's Panuhou School, from fifth grade to his graduation in **1979**.

Obama moves to California to attend the upscale Occidental College in Los Angeles from **1979 to 1981**. This is his first experience with the U.S. mainland and with racial prejudice, which was rare in multicultural Hawaii.

Obama moves to New York City in **1981** to attend Columbia University, graduating in **1983** with a bachelor's degree in political science with a specialty in international affairs. In contrast to his active social and athletic life in Hawaii and California (basketball and surfing were preoccupations), Obama's New York life is somewhat solitary, as for the first time he applies himself rigorously to academics and becomes a voracious and eclectic reader. Keen to learn about business, upon his graduation Obama works for two years at Business International Corporation and New York Public Interest Research Group.

COMMUNITY ORGANIZER, LAWYER, PROFESSOR, AND AUTHOR

Turning down social-work opportunities in New York, in 1985 Obama accepts a community-organizer job from a group of black churches in Chicago, a city unfamiliar to him, working with public-housing residents in the city's gritty South Side for three years. With Obama's guidance, residents succeed in pressuring city hall to remove asbestos insulation from their homes and improve policing and other services in the district.

Feeling he still lacks the complete set of skills required to be an effective social worker, Obama moves to Cambridge, Massachusetts, to attend Harvard Law School in 1988.

In 1990, Obama is the first African-American elected president of the *Harvard Law Review*, America's most influential legal publication, where he supervises a staff of about seventy-five law students. Obama distinguishes himself by giving equal prominence to the work of conservative and liberal contributors, initially to the consternation of the latter.

The *Review* election is widely reported, gaining Obama his first, albeit modest, national press exposure. This leads to a publishing contract, to write about current conditions in the African-American community. Obama soon rejects that topic, feeling it presumptuous to write a sweeping account of the history and current status of black America. He instead begins work on a memoir that, incidentally, achieves much the same initial goal, as one person's account of his broken home and youthful struggles with faith, conflicting career ambitions, and the tragic legacy of his absent father, about which he had been misled by well-meaning relatives. As a child, Obama was encouraged to regard his father as an influential figure in post-colonial Kenyan politics. In fact, Obama Sr. soon fell out of favor, and died an alcoholic.

Obama graduates Harvard in **1991** with a Juris Doctor magna cum laude. He returns to Chicago to head a voter-registration drive and complete his memoir, published in **1995** as *Dreams from My Father.* The remarkably candid autobiography sells modestly but is well received by critics.

Obama marries Michelle LaVaughn Robinson of Chicago on **October 3, 1992.** Barack and Michelle have two children, Malia Ann (b. 1998) and Natasha (called Sasha, b. 2001).

From **1993 to 2004,** Obama is an associate attorney at the Chicago law firm of Davis, Miner, Barnhill & Galland, noted for its civil-rights work. He represents clients in discrimination and civil-rights cases and community organizers. To augment his income, he spends this decade teaching constitutional law part time at the University of Chicago Law School, where he repeatedly turns down invitations to join the faculty full time and is accorded the title of full professor.

ILLINOIS SENATE

As a three-term Illinois senator, Obama was frustrated at his limited ability to get things done as a member of the minority Democrats, which drove him to learn how to achieve legislative progress through bipartisanship. During his last two Senate years, when Democrats regained control of the Senate, Obama was one of the chamber's most productive members.

He was also frustrated during this time with accusations in Chicago's African-American community, to which he was a relative newcomer, that he was not "black enough," was too close to the city's white establishment, and that his legislative successes were sometimes compromised in an effort to gain bipartisan support needed for passage. Obama's legislative initiatives during these seven years were geared to increasing state assistance to the disadvantaged, who in his district were disproportionately African-American, making the "not black enough" charge initially difficult for him to grasp.

Obama serves more than seven years in the Illinois Senate (1997–2004), representing the 13th District, which covers the South Side, Hyde Park–Kenwood, and Chicago Lawn neighborhoods. He is reelected in 1998 and 2002. Obama's Democrats are in the minority in all but the last two years of his Illinois Senate tenure.

While in the minority, Obama is able to gain bipartisan support for ethics-reform and health-care legislation. He negotiates welfare reforms, writes legislation that greatly expands the number of poor children covered by Illinois' medical insurance system, and increases tax credits for low-income workers.

Obama's most conspicuous achievement in this period is his success in gaining police and prosecutor support for landmark legislation requiring compulsory videotaping of homicide interrogations, which reduces the incidence of innocent people being condemned to the death penalty. Despite initial opposition from police organizations, a dogged Obama is able to gain passage of the law by bringing criminal-justice-system participants into the process. He makes it clear he shares their frustration that judges are throwing out convictions based on confessions they believe were obtained by inappropriately coercive means. A *Chicago Tribune* investigative series shows that more than a dozen innocent Illinois men, all African-Americans, have been condemned to death row, prompting then-governor George Ryan to commute the sentences of all prisoners in Illinois sentenced to the death penalty. In his 2004 U.S. Senate bid, Obama is credited by police leaders for seeking their input in his legislation.

Obama also leads passage of a law monitoring racial profiling of detained motorists by police, an issue of widespread concern across North America.

Obama's productivity soars after Democrats regain control of the Illinois Senate in **2002**, when he becomes chairman of the Senate Health and Human Services Committee. In his last two years in the Senate, Obama sponsors close to 800 bills, 282 of which are signed into law by new Democratic governor Rod Blagojevich. Most of these laws are designed to enhance the government's ability to improve conditions for the elderly, children, and the poor.

From **1993 to 2002**, Obama serves on the board of Chicago's Woods Fund, a venerable charity providing grants to disadvantaged people and communities in the city. He is joined on the board in **1999** by Bill Ayers, a Chicago professor once associated with the Weather Underground, a militant 1960s-era anti–Vietnam war group (a.k.a. the Weathermen). (The Clinton campaign tried with little success to make Ayers an issue in the 2008 presidential campaign. Ayers, a neighbor of Obama's in Chicago's Hyde Park, had hosted an Obama fundraiser in 1996, but otherwise connections between the two men are tenuous. It was a poorly chosen association, as Ayers remains unrepentant about his activities with the Weathermen and their responsibility for a slain police officer.)

In his only electoral drubbing prior to his bid for the U.S. presidency, Obama challenges popular four-term U.S. Representative Bobby Rush, a former Black Panther, for the Democratic congressional nomination in **2000** and is defeated by a two-to-one margin. It is during this contest that Obama is first accused of not being black enough.

OPPOSITION TO WAR IN IRAQ

In **2002**, Obama speaks out against a possible U.S. invasion of Iraq at Chicago's first high-profile antiwar rally, in Federal Plaza on **October 2** — the day President George W.

Bush and the then-Republican-controlled Congress agree on a joint resolution authorizing U.S. combat in Iraq. On **March 16, 2003**, when the president gives Iraqi leader Saddam Hussein a forty-eight-hour ultimatum to leave Iraq with his sons, Obama tells the largest Chicago antiwar rally to date, in Daley Plaza, that it is not too late to prevent war.

While a majority of U.S. Senate Democrats vote in support of the Iraq-war resolution, Obama is not the only early opponent. There are higher-profile early critics, including U.S. senators Ted Kennedy (D-Mass.), Robert Byrd (D-W.Va.), former Vice President Al Gore, and future U.S. Senator Jim Webb (D-Va.). (This fact was somewhat lost in the 2008 presidential campaign in which, among the Democratic candidates from the Senate, only Obama had warned of dire consequences of an Iraq invasion.) As a state senator, Obama's opposition gains little attention outside of Chicago. While seeking to use his early position on the war, vindicated by events, to his advantage in the 2008 presidential contest, Obama acknowledges more than once that, since he only entered the U.S. Senate in 2005, he did not vote on the issue, and that he could not be sure how he would have voted if he had been given the same intelligence and administration briefings afforded to senators and members of Congress.

As a senator, Obama supports efforts by the Democratic leadership to pressure Bush into changing direction in Iraq and introduces at least one proposed bill of his own that would remove U.S. combat brigades from Iraq by April 2008.

At the same time, however, Obama consistently supports additional appropriations for continued funding of the war effort. While some of his more liberal colleagues promote measures as varied as cutting off all war funding to initiating impeachment proceedings against Bush and Vice President Dick Cheney, Obama's oft-stated position is that America has an obligation to provide U.S. forces with the funds required to accomplish their mission and ensure their safety.

In the 2008 presidential campaign, Hillary Clinton got off on the wrong foot by refusing to apologize for her vote to authorize Bush to commit the U.S. to a military invasion of Iraq. This was in sharp contrast to John Edwards' frank apologies for his similar vote and exhaustive explanation for why he cast it. Calling the war a "mistake" was as far as Hillary Clinton would go, before retreating into a barely credible argument that she believed her vote was not authorizing war but merely the possibility of it if Iraq weapons inspections and other measures short of war failed. As it happened, Clinton senatorial colleague Carl Levin (D-Mich.) had introduced a safeguard amendment on that very question, and Clinton had chosen not to support it. Since everyone in Washington knew the vote was really about giving Bush the green light to invade Iraq, observers were left to conclude that Clinton was either naive about how Bush would use the Congressional authority just conferred upon him or striking a hardline pose in advance of a presidential bid.

U.S. SENATE

Heralded as a political rock star by the national media, Barack Obama frequently pointed out that he ranked 99th in seniority in the U.S. Senate and would have ranked lower, save that Illinois outranked Colorado, another state to send a new member to the Senate in 2004. Obama respectfully avoided the media spotlight in his first year or so, but he did quickly assemble a crack team of domestic- and foreign-policy advisers. His legislative focus in the 109th and 110th U.S. Congresses was international weapons control, nuclear terrorism, climate change, U.S. energy independence, phased U.S. withdrawal of combat troops from Iraq, campaign-finance reform, greater care for U.S. military personnel returned from missions abroad, and increased transparency on how public funds are spent. Obama also sharpened his skills at bipartisanship. His respect and not infrequent affection for Republican leaders was evident in the few but telling kind words that he had for President George W. Bush in *The Audacity of Hope* (2006), Obama's personal commentary on U.S. politics.

Given his rookie status and that he served only a third of his Senate term before launching his presidential bid, the volume and variety of legislation Obama spearheaded and the frequency of his official foreign visits was unusual. He would be thwarted, however, along with fellow Democrats in both the Senate and House of Representatives, in efforts to reverse course in Iraq — even after Democrats regained a one-vote Senate majority in 2006. Indeed, by 2008, a Congress viewed as ineffectual in ending the war would score lower in popular-approval polls than Bush, who was setting new records for presidential unpopularity in modern-era polling with a job-approval rating below 30 percent.

Obama travels widely in Illinois during 2004 to become better acquainted with white and rural voters. He is easily elected to the U.S. Senate from Illinois, where he continues to serve, against a field of weak candidates in a stunning 70 percent landslide. It is his first state-wide race. He wins majorities in mostly white and rural counties, in addition to carrying Chicago. He becomes the fifth African-American to serve in the U.S. Senate, only the third to be elected (two additional senators were appointees), and currently is the Senate's sole black member.

Obama's candidacy is boosted by an uplifting keynote address at the 2004 Democratic National Convention (DNC) in Boston. At a time of sharp ideological divisions in the country, he calls for a new era of unity and bipartisanship. He presents his story — the child of a biracial couple raised in modest circumstances yet now poised to win a seat in the U.S. Senate — as an example of opportunity for advancement that is unique to America. (The theme of Obama's address — "There's not a liberal America and a conservative America — there's the United States of America" — would also be the theme of his later presidential bid.) In his community-organizer days in Chicago,

Obama gave some colleagues the impression he ultimately sought a career as a writer. While professional speechwriters have been pressed into service in Obama's presidential run, Obama wrote his DNC address himself.

During his U.S. Senate campaign, Obama is criticized both by rival pro-choice candidates for the Democratic nomination and his pro-life GOP adversary in the general election for the large number of "present" votes he has cast on abortion-related measures — an issue that would resurface in his presidential campaign. Obama defenders point out that a peculiarity of the Illinois Senate is the privilege to vote "present," rather than "aye" or "nay," in order not to duck controversial issues — although the practice is sometimes used for that purpose — but show partial support or opposition to a bill, pending amendments that would make the proposed legislation more palatable.

Obama campaigns extensively during the 2006 off-year (non-presidential) general election for Democratic House and Senate candidates. He gains contacts nationwide, collects political IOUs, and familiarizes himself with local and regional issues far beyond Illinois in an election that sees the Democrats regain control of both the Senate and the House of Representatives.

Obama's second book, *The Audacity of Hope: Thoughts on Reclaiming the American Dream* (2006), is a blockbuster immediately upon publication and is one of the best-selling books of its type in U.S. history. The book is a personal commentary on U.S. politics, and its popularity enables Obama and his wife to finally pay off their student loans. In contrast to *Dreams from My Father* — a candid, poignant triumph of lyrical nonfiction — *Audacity* is a more prosaic compilation of policy prescriptions, hardly different from the pre-campaign tomes that candidates for high office are expected to put out. Yet *Audacity* sells in the millions on the strength of Obama's celebrity. (Two years after its hardcover publication, the paperback edition is still ranked fourth on the *New York Times* best-seller list in the spring of 2008.) *Audacity*, which takes its name from the title of a sermon by long-time Obama pastor Jeremiah Wright Jr., himself inspired by a passage of Martin Luther King's, generates enormous media coverage, which inevitably fans interest in, and speculation about, an Obama presidential bid. The fall 2006 author tour across America, along with Obama's campaigning for fellow Democrats, sets him up nicely for the announcement of his presidential candidacy in **February 2007**.

BIPARTISANSHIP

Obama was an unusually active rookie U.S. senator in a chamber controlled by the opposing party, and he tried with some success to practice the bipartisanship he had identified as essential to U.S. renewal in his DNC speech.

Working with Senate Republicans, Obama cosponsors Arizona senator John McCain's immigration-reform bill, the Secure America and Orderly Immigration Reform Act. With Indiana senator Richard Lugar, Obama gains passage of the Lugar-Obama initiative to expand the Nunn-Lugar cooperative-threat-reduction scheme to include land mines and shoulder-fired missiles. Obama and Lugar also introduce the American Fuels Act, designed to spur the commercialization of biofuels. With Oklahoma senator Tom Coburn, Obama secures passage of the Coburn-Obama Transparency Act, which creates USAspending.gov, an Internet search engine enabling citizens to more easily track government expenditures. Partnering again with John McCain, Obama cosponsors a global-warming bill to cut greenhouse-gas emissions by two-thirds by 2050. (Environmentalists are less impressed with an Obama initiative forcing power utilities to inform state and local authorities of wastewater contamination, concluding its provisions are diluted because of Obama's campaign-finance support from Exelon, America's largest operator of nuclear power plants.) With Nebraska senator Chuck Hagel, Obama cosponsors legislation to reduce threats of nuclear terrorism; a provision of their bill gains Senate passage in 2007 as an appropriations-bill amendment.

In **2005**, Obama passes an amendment, along with Senators Chuck Hagel (R-Neb.), Patrick Leahy (D-Vt.), and Judd Gregg (R-N.H.) to provide thirteen million dollars for the Special Court for Sierra Leone. This funding allows the court to try former Liberian president Charles Taylor, accused of war crimes in Sierra Leone's civil war. With then-senator Jim Talent (R-Mo.), Obama passes legislation to provide gasoline stations a tax credit for installing E85 ethanol refueling pumps. (E85 fuel is an 85 percent ethanol/15 percent gasoline blend.)

In **December 2006**, Obama joins Kansas senator Sam Brownback at the Global Summit on AIDS and the Church, sponsored by prominent evangelicals Kay and Rick Warren. The senators publicly take an HIV test in an effort to help de-stigmatize the disease and promote the responsible behavior required to curb its spread.

Also with Senator Brownback, Obama cosponsors the Democratic Republic of Congo Relief, Security, and Democracy Promotion Act, which gains bipartisan support and is signed into law by President George W. Bush in December 2006.

Obama cosponsors the McCain-Lieberman cap-and-trade climate change bill in **2008**, which also contains billions of dollars in subsidies for the nuclear power industry. In May, with the Obama-versus-McCain battle for the presidency already underway, McCain asks that he be included as an original cosponsor with Obama and Coburn on a bill that would open federal government contracts to public scrutiny, and Obama readily assents. On the campaign trail at the time, McCain is assailing Obama as naive on foreign policy and lacking legislative achievements, the record to the contrary notwithstanding.

DEMOCRATIC MAJORITY

Obama and Wisconsin Democrat Russ Feingold win passage of the Honest Leadership and Open Government Act in 2007, which prohibits legislators from accepting gifts of travel on corporate aircraft from lobbyists. It also mandates disclosure of "bundled" campaign contributions, which are large corporate donations in the guise of smaller individual contributions by corporate employees.

Obama sponsors the Iran Sanctions Enabling Act, which encourages divestment by state pension funds of investments in Iran's oil and gas industry. An Obama-sponsored amendment to the State Children's Health Insurance Program (SCHIP), to provide a year of job protection for family members caring for military personnel with combat-related injuries, gains both Senate and House passage but fails to become law as part of Bush's wider October 2007 thwarting of SCHIP reform. Obama is successful with an initiative to end the Department of Veterans' Affairs practice of charging Armed Forces members hospitalized at the Walter Reed Medical Center for their meals.

Obama serves on the following Senate committees: foreign relations, environment, public works, veterans' affairs, health, labor and pensions, and homeland security and government affairs. He also chairs the Senate Subcommittee on European Affairs. (During the 2008 presidential campaign, Obama is criticized by Hillary Clinton for convening just one meeting of that subcommittee.)

FOREIGN MISSIONS

As a Committee on Foreign Relations member, Obama makes three official foreign visits: to Eastern Europe, the Middle East, and Africa. The mission of Obama's **August 2005** trip to Russia, Ukraine, and Azerbaijan is to gain better control of nuclear, biological, and conventional weapons, with a focus on missing nuclear warheads, or "loose nukes," that could fall into the hands of terrorist groups. (Of the three major presidential candidates remaining in the race by May 2008 — Obama, John McCain, and Hillary Clinton — Obama alone emphasizes unsecured and unaccounted-for nuclear materials as a threat on par with global warming and the energy crisis.)

During a tour of Kuwait, Iraq, Jordan, Israel, and the Palestinian territories in **January 2006**, Obama accurately warns Palestinians, two weeks before Hamas wins control of the territorial legislature, that the U.S. will not recognize a Hamas government unless it renounces its stated mission to eradicate Israel.

In **August 2006**, Obama travels to South Africa, Kenya, Djibouti, Ethiopia, and Chad. His focus in Ethiopia is the renewed tension between Ethiopia and neighboring Eritrea and the rampant warlord violence in Ethiopia's southeastern neighbor Somalia. In Chad the issue is the humanitarian disaster in the Darfur region of neighboring Sudan, with Chad struggling to cope with Sudanese refugees. In his father's homeland of Kenya, Obama succeeds in thwarting efforts of rival tribal leaders to be seen as aligned with the famous American visitor. Obama sparks controversy with a University of Nairobi speech in which he attributes the economic and cultural slide of Kenya in recent decades to widespread political corruption and praises local journalists who brought it to light.

PRESIDENTIAL CAMPAIGN

A total of twenty-one candidates sought the 2008 presidential nominations of the Democratic and Republican parties (ten Democrats and eleven Republicans), a reflection of the heightened public awareness of the consequences of good and bad governance as evident in the Iraq conflict, the bungled response to the devastation wreaked by Hurricane Katrina, and the worsening U.S. economic conditions in 2007–08. Also, 2008 would be a rare "open" contest in which there would be no incumbent president seeking reelection, no incumbent vice president seeking to replace his boss, and no opposition-party stand-bearer who had been defeated in the previous election attempting victory with an encore effort. The election campaign was unusual, too, in that the three major candidates still in the race by spring 2008 — Obama, Hillary Clinton (D-N.Y.), and John McCain (R-Ariz.) — were U.S. Senators, and voters hadn't elected a president directly from the Senate since John F. Kennedy's narrow win in 1960. The campaigning also featured the first viable woman and African-American candidates. More important was that the campaign unfolded against the backdrop of an unpopular foreign war and a domestic economic slowdown highlighted by hundreds of thousands of home foreclosures and a sense of diminished wealth among a far greater number of American homeowners, whose properties had plummeted in value between 30 and 50 percent, depriving them of home refinancing as a source of income for buying cars and other big-ticket items. In 1968, incumbent Vice President Hubert Humphrey narrowly lost a presidential bid when the country was torn over an unpopular war in Vietnam, but the economy was booming; in 1992, Bill Clinton won an upset presidential victory in a peacetime America because of an economic slump about which incumbent George H.W. Bush seemed indifferent. The 2008 contest was the first in modern times in which one party, the Republicans, was on the defensive about both a disastrous war and a slumping economy.

On **February 10, 2007**, Obama announces his U.S. presidential candidacy in the Illinois capital of Springfield, chosen for its association with Abraham Lincoln, who also served in the Illinois legislature. He lays out what he expects to be the three top priorities of his campaign: ending U.S. military involvement in the Iraqi conflict, providing universal health care, and securing energy independence. These priorities will change as the campaign gets underway.

Iraq fades as the leading concern of Americans as the surge of additional U.S. troops ordered by President Bush, primarily to Baghdad, appears to quell Iraqi violence. Meanwhile, the U.S. is sliding into an economic downturn with the collapse of a national housing "bubble" and plummeting house values that result in massive write-offs at America's major banks and brokerages and tens of thousands of home foreclosures. The latter prompts a decline in consumer spending growth. Main Street's obsession with the faltering economy sharpens further with a 70 percent hike in gasoline prices in the second half of the year; by the spring of 2008, pump prices are heading toward four dollars a gallon.

Clinton is seen as having more depth on domestic policy issues, including health care and the economy, which had boomed during her husband's presidency. Even if her 1993 to 1994 effort at health-care reform while first lady had failed to win Congressional support, Clinton can credibly claim that knowledge of her earlier mistakes makes her the Democratic hopeful best equipped to make health-care reform a reality for the forty-seven million Americans lacking health-care insurance and the millions more struggling with rising insurance premiums, co-payments, and deductibles.

In the summer and fall, the novelty factor in Obama's favor is fading. In national polling of Democrats, the junior Illinois senator significantly trails Clinton, regarded as the prohibitive favorite to win her party's presidential nomination due to her national recognition after eight years as first lady in the 1990s; the fundraising prowess of Clinton and her husband, former President Bill Clinton; and the anticipated popularity of Bill Clinton, who left office in 2001 with higher approval ratings than Ronald Reagan, on the campaign trail.

It also appears that Obama is getting off to a late start. Rival John Edwards (D-N.C.), the party's vice presidential candidate in 2004 and a former U.S. senator, had launched his second presidential bid weeks earlier in New Orleans' impoverished 9th Ward, which had not recovered from the devastation of 2005's Hurricane Katrina and is symbolic of perceived Bush administration incompetence. Edwards is the first major candidate of either party to unveil a universal health-care plan, and it is more innovative than those later offered by Obama and Clinton. Only Edwards embraces the single-payer, government-run health-care coverage long ago adopted by all of America's industrialized peers, as one of three options in his plan from which Americans could choose.

Clinton and Edwards have their own liabilities, however. Clinton, long a polarizing figure, enters the campaign with the highest negative polling numbers of any presidential candidate in modern history. In the course of the primary and caucus contests in the first few months of 2008, polling also shows that she is deemed least trustworthy of the leading Democratic contenders. Many Democrats had a dim view of the Clintons' legacy. The debacle of Hillary Clinton's failed health-care reform set back that cause for fourteen years and helped the Democrats lose control of both houses of Congress in 1994, just two years into Bill Clinton's presidency. Bill Clinton later became only the second president in history to be impeached, in the Lewinsky scandal. The latter so disgusted Vice President Al Gore that he chose not to run on Clinton's undeniable economic success, a blunder that cost the Democrats the White House for eight years.

There was also, among media pundits and elements of the public, a backlash against "dynastic" politics. For twenty years, beginning in 1988, when Bush's father, George

Herbert Walker Bush, was elected president, the White House has been occupied by someone named Bush or Clinton. Was America so starved of presidential talent that this record might extend to twenty-eight years?

Edwards had been a dud as John Kerry's running mate four years earlier, letting Bush's running mate Dick Cheney put him on the defensive with a string of falsehoods Edwards didn't have the gumption to challenge in their one nationally televised debate. In the 2004 general election, Edwards had failed to carry either his home state of South Carolina or adopted state of North Carolina for the Democratic ticket. (Victories in both would have put Kerry in the White House.)

Having a previous 2004 presidential bid under his belt, Edwards had an advantage in navigating the peculiarities of the nomination process and knew the pacing required to endure the two-year process of seeking the White House. But while he is the most policy rich of the 2008 candidates, he also suffers an image of slickness, not helped by a media obsession early in the primary season with revelations about his four-hundred-dollar haircuts. For the media pundits, that doesn't jibe with Edwards' populist message, and neither did the "monster home" Edwards and his wife had just built for themselves. Oddly, the mainstream media fail to cover widely rumored problems in the Edwards' marriage, which surface in the blogosphere in July 2008, long after Edwards has quit the race and endorsed Obama.

If the national media were weary of Clinton and cynical about Edwards, they rediscover their ardor for Obama when he wins an upset victory in the first nomination contest, in the Iowa caucuses on **January 3, 2008**. So do African-American voters, for whom Bill Clinton had been a favorite president and who believed that America still wasn't ready to elect an African-American president. All that changed with Iowa — a white, rural state won by an impressive margin by an urban black candidate. From that point on, African-Americans give 90 percent or more of their primary and caucus votes to Obama. And Clinton's third-place Iowa showing finally raises doubts about her "prohibitive favorite" status.

The Obama campaign is electrifying for a media always hungry for a new face and rooting for the underdog. It's also historic, not so much because an African-American is suddenly viable as a presidential candidate, but due to the state-of-the-art nature of the Obama campaign. Exploiting the Internet as no major candidate had done before, Obama, the former community organizer, has more storefront organizing offices than his rivals, has recruited more donors (more than 1.5 million) and volunteers, and is the only candidate running a fifty-five-state-and-territory campaign in search of every nominating delegate available. He also raises more campaign funds than any presidential candidate in history. (Former Vermont governor Howard Dean, now head of the Democratic National Committee, and his campaign manager, Joe Trippi, pioneered online fundraising and get-out-the-vote efforts in the political realm in Dean's 2004 U.S. presidential bid. Dean flamed out early, however, and John Kerry, like McCain four years later, made a deathbed recovery to capture the nomination.) The Clinton strategy, by contrast, was to use its vaunted fundraising contacts to generate just enough monetary contributions from wealthy donors to carry that campaign through to "Super Tuesday," February 5, when about two dozen states and territories vote, including the delegate-rich states of New York, New Jersey, and California, the biggest single prize.

But after Iowa, Obama is packing seventeen-thousand-seat arenas with exuberant supporters, and an Obama-friendly media reports exhaustively on the many fans turned away at Obama events and the joyous reception he is getting from Alaska to South Carolina with his message of hope, change, and optimism, which contrasts sharply with seven years of American economic and foreign-policy failures. Obama — at forty-seven the youngest of the hopefuls, with the fluid movements of the basketball player he still is — signals change not by his skin color but with his eloquent oratory of a type not heard since Jack Kennedy in 1960. Americans younger than forty-eight were hearing in Obama the most impressive public speaker in their lifetimes.

Inexperience is the Achilles' heel that Obama's rivals kept pounding on. Yet of the three candidates still standing by May 2008 — Obama, Clinton, and the presumptive Republican nominee McCain — Obama alone has run a superb campaign. McCain's hired help ran his then-fledgling campaign into the ground in the summer of 2007, emptying the McCain treasury with a poll standing in the single digits to show for it. Clinton also runs out of money, with embarrassing reports of unpaid caterers and other creditors becoming routine by February 2008. She has to lend her campaign money, a total of $13.2 million from her personal funds by July 2008.

Obama, meanwhile, is able to tap his grassroots small-money Internet donors indefinitely; their repeated twenty-five-dollar and one-hundred-dollar contributions are well short of federally mandated donation ceilings. Clinton's elite donors had made their legal-maximum $2,500 donations the previous year. If the campaign had gone according to plan, it wouldn't have mattered. Clinton raised an astonishing two hundred million or so dollars before the primary season began; that sum was sufficient only if Clinton wrapped up the nomination by Super Tuesday (**February 5**), when 52 percent of all pledged Democratic delegates were at stake. In the four pre–Super Tuesday contests, Obama wins Iowa, only narrowly losing New Hampshire and Nevada, and wins a landslide victory in South Carolina. And instead of crushing Obama on Super Tuesday, Clinton merely ties him. After Super Tuesday, Clinton is trailing in delegates and will have to fight on, after all, but has run out of money.

Obama goes on to win the next eleven consecutive contests. While many of these victories are small, the unbroken streak creates within the media the sense of an inevitable Obama nomination, justified by the narrow but insurmountable delegate lead he has accumulated. The Obama campaign had been faithful to his initial directive to avoid infighting. The unflappable, confident demeanor of campaign strategist David Axelrod, a veteran of Obama's success in his 2004 U.S. Senate contest, and of campaign manager David Plouffe kept the Obama staff at ease and unified in purpose. All three major candidates were U.S. Senators and had never run anything larger than a U.S. Senate staff or, in Clinton's case, her East Wing staff when first lady. To the question of inexperience, Obama responds that he has built and is successfully running an organization of seven hundred paid staff and an unprecedented 1.5 million volunteers.

Obama's only major setback happens in **February 2008** with the Internet distribution of rants by his Chicago pastor, Reverend Jeremiah Wright Jr. of Trinity United Church of Christ. Wright was held in such high esteem that he was one of a half-dozen clerics President Clinton invited to the White House to minister to him during the Lewinsky scandal. But in selected video clips that become ubiquitous on the Internet, Wright is shown blaming the September 11, 2001, terrorist attacks on misguided U.S. foreign policy just weeks after that tragedy, inveighing against continued racial inequality ("They say God bless America, I say God *damn* America"), and repeating the conspiracy theory that Washington imported the AIDS virus from Africa to eradicate the African-American population. (That canard had been floating around African-American churches since the 1980s, but until now it had traveled under the media radar.)

Obama already had denounced the more fiery rhetoric of the pastor who had led him to Christ, married him, and baptized his children. But the media storm doesn't dissipate. On **March 18**, Obama gives a formal address on the perfectibility of America — a concept he says Reverend Wright and many of his generation refused to grasp because of their decades-ago experience with official segregation and other forms of racial injustice. The address eclipses Obama's DNC speech four years earlier and is regarded as one of the greatest in the history of American political oratory. Obama dissociates himself from Wright's preaching, but not the pastor himself. Wright's subsequent, and bizarre, recitation of his more absurd claims at an appearance at the National Press Club in Washington forces Obama to make a clean break with the pastor.

Obama wins the North Carolina primary on **May 6** and holds Clinton to a virtual tie in Indiana. The media declares the contest over, although Obama has not yet officially secured a majority of delegates. The *Washington Post* editorializes that "Against a formidable, indeed, supposedly unstoppable, opponent, Mr. Obama ran a campaign that would have been impressive for a veteran; it was amazing for a relative newcomer."

In June, the Obamas quit Trinity United church after a white guest pastor does a pantomime mocking Hillary Clinton.

Obama officially secures a majority of delegates on **June 3**, becoming the de facto Democratic presidential candidate.

At the Democratic National Convention in Denver (**August 25–28**), Obama becomes the first African-American presidential candidate of either of the two dominant U.S. political parties in the republic's 232-year history.

PERSONAL LIFE

As described in his memoir, *Dreams from My Father* (1995), Obama made friends easily in his youth and was seldom not in a romantic relationship from high school to his community-organizing days in Chicago. Prior to his studies at Columbia University, Obama was an indifferent student, focusing on basketball, surfing, and other athletic activities in Hawaii and California rather than academic pursuits.

Drug use

Obama acknowledged in *Dreams from My Father* occasional recreational drug use, a topic he has addressed when asked about his marijuana use and infrequent experiments with cocaine in news-media and talk-show interviews. Obama briefly described his teenage use of mood-altering substances in *Dreams from My Father*: "Pot had helped, and booze; maybe a little blow when you could afford it. Not smack, though."

Invariably, Obama counsels against illicit drug use, describing it as a dead end or trap. Again in *Dreams*, Obama sensed his dismal prospects if his drug use continued: "Junkie. Pothead. That's where I'd been headed. The final, fatal role of the young would-be black man." Obama says that drugs accompanied his youthful struggles with religious faith, his black identity, what role was expected of African-Americans in U.S. society, and indecision about career choices. But perhaps mostly — and tied up with the above — it accompanied his attempts to reconcile the stories his mother, aunts, and uncles had told him about his absent father's illustrious career as an economist and influential public official in Kenya and the reality, which Obama later discovered, of the philandering, alcoholism, and lack of personal responsibility that reduced Barack Hussein Obama Sr. to a penniless outcast in a homeland where he had once enjoyed renown. Obama saw his father just once after Obama Sr.

deserted him at age two, during a brief return visit Obama Sr. made to Hawaii when his son was ten.

For all that, college and career contemporaries of Obama interviewed for a 2008 *New York Times* investigation reported that Obama's drug use was in fact minimal, and many close friends were surprised to hear of it, insisting Obama's only addiction was to tobacco.

Allegations of impropriety

In his Illinois state Senate and U.S. Senate races, Obama accepted donations from Antoin (Tony) Rezko, a ubiquitous Chicago developer who first offered him a job after his graduation from Harvard Law School. (Obama declined the offer.) Rezko held a fundraiser for Obama in his home, and would raise a total of $250,000 for Obama's campaigns. The developer was a great cultivator of political contacts and donated to every major Democratic politician in Chicago, a town dominated by Democrats. In 2003, Rezko also helped raise $3.5 million for U.S. President George W. Bush's reelection bid by cosponsoring a fundraiser for the president. Obama says that in twenty years of knowing Rezko, the developer "never asked me for anything. I've never done any favors for him."

In scouting for a new Chicago home in 2005, Obama sought Rezko's advice, since he knew the Kenwood neighborhood where Obama wanted to relocate. Rezko bought the lot next door to the one bought by the Obamas — the two transactions, with the same seller, closed the same day — and then sold a ten-foot strip of his lot to Obama at what the local press alleged was a below-market price. Rezko's later sale of his lot, at a considerable profit, showed Obama had paid fair market value for his share of the Rezko lot.

Still, Obama would later concede: "I am the first one to acknowledge that it was a boneheaded move for me to purchase this ten-foot strip from Rezko, given that he was already under a cloud of concern. I will also acknowledge that from his perspective, he no doubt believed that by buying the piece of property next to me that he would, if not be doing me a favor, it would help strengthen our relationship."

In 1998, state senator Obama wrote a letter in support of a publicly financed affordable housing project codeveloped by Rezko. Rezko's lawyer later reported that Rezko had not asked Obama to do so. Obama was among three local elected officials to endorse the project, not surprising given it commanded strong support among Obama's low-income constituents. In June 2008, Rezko was convicted by a federal jury on sixteen counts, including fraud, money laundering, and bribery. Obama was not implicated in any wrongdoing.

Soon after becoming a U.S. senator from Illinois, Obama provoked a controversy over his use of corporate aircraft at subsidized rates, including two trips on private jets owned by Archer Daniels Midland Co. (ADM), a huge agribusiness firm based in Decatur, Illinois, and an aggressive proponent of ethanol use as transportation fuel. ADM is the U.S.'s largest producer of ethanol, a product heavily subsidized by federal funds. Most U.S. ethanol is made from corn, of which Illinois is the second-largest American producer.

In March 2007, a *New York Times* report raised questions about Obama's investments totalling one hundred thousand dollars in two risky stocks, Skyterra and AVI BioPharma, the latter a firm developing a treatment for avian flu. In March 2005, soon after making a five-thousand-dollar investment in AVI, Obama began to lead a legislative effort to increase federal funding for avian-flu research. (The five thousand dollars, however, was a trifling sum against the $1.9 million contract Obama had just signed to write three books.) The stocks, as it happened, were in a blind trust set up by Obama's friend, its contents unknown to Obama until one of the companies accidentally mailed him shareholder information. At that point, Obama asked his friend to sell the stocks, on which he suffered a thirteen-thousand-dollar loss.

PRESIDENTIAL VICTORY

On November 4, 2008, Barack Obama and vice-presidential running mate Joseph Biden defeat the rival G.O.P. ticket of John McCain and Sarah Palin. The Democrats achieve a resounding mandate to govern, winning the White House by a wide margin and adding to their majorities in the U.S. Senate and the House of Representatives. The Obama–Biden ticket wins states in every region, including the traditionally "red" states of Virginia, North Carolina and Indiana; and secure more than 50 percent of the popular vote, a goal that eluded Bill Clinton in his two successful presidential contests.

A uniter in victory, as he had repeatedly described himself in the recent campaign, Obama selects as his secretary of state his chief rival for the Democratic nomination, Hillary Rodham Clinton, and as his defence secretary the incumbent Robert Gates, a Republican and Bush appointee. Obama's policy team immediately plugs itself into the Bush Administration with daily conference calls, a process the outgoing president graciously encourages. Obama promptly meets with both the Republican and Democratic leadership on Capitol Hill. In addition to meetings with George W. Bush, Obama shares a tête-à-tête with McCain to seek the Arizona senator's input on cabinet selections and legislative strategy.

The traditional "first 100 days" for U.S. presidents begins after their inauguration. Given the crises of the moment — the worst economic downturn in memory at home, and American forces waging two wars abroad — Obama's first 100 days begins with his election victory. In record time, Obama announces his cabinet and most of his agency-head selections. While repeatedly stating that "America has only one president at a time," Obama appreciates that it's he and not his lame-duck predecessor that the world financial community and fellow heads of state are looking to for signs of America's new policy on a range of issues. Obama is thus involved in everything from Bush initiatives to stabilize the banking system to bailouts sought by the Detroit Three automakers long before he takes the oath of office.

In his one speech before his formal inauguration, Obama makes a compelling argument for rapid Congressional passage of a massive stimulus package to revive the economy. Obama had earlier deferred to Congress, insisting that it, not he, author the most sweeping legislation in modern times, likely amounting to more than $1 trillion in middle class tax cuts and spending on infrastructure, alternative energy development, and investment in education and healthcare, among other initiatives.

Given the urgency of the hour, relatively few observers notice that Obama is attempting to use the mood of emergency to piggyback on the economic stimulus package at least some elements of most of his campaign agenda. The result will be one of the most complex pieces of legislation in history. If it works, said early Obama promoter David Brooks of the *New York Times* in early January 2009, Obama's audacious legislative strategy would make him a great president in a year's time, or a "broken" one if the unprecedented attempt to confront so many problems at once failed.

INTERNET RESOURCES

The following Internet sites are useful in tracking the activities of the Obama administration and of the U.S. Congress.

Andrew Sullivan *andrewsullivan.theatlantic.com* (conservative and liberal)
Commentary on policy and news developments from a conservative essayist with a liberal view on certain, mostly social, issues.

The Conscience of a Liberal *krugman.blogs.nytimes.com* (liberal)
New York Times columnist and economist Paul Krugman critiques GOP and Democratic policy and strategy.

The Huffington Post *huffingtonpost.com* (liberal)
Commentary and breaking news, with a mixture of political and celebrity coverage. Unique in hosting "posts" by contributors as varied as Mia Farrow (on Darfur), Donald Sutherland, Barbara Ehrenreich, and, on one occasion, Barack Obama.

Instapundit *instapundit.com* (conservative)
Copious links to political and other breaking news by conservative Internet veteran Glenn Reynolds.

National Review Online *nationalreview.com* (conservative)
NRO is a leading platform for conservative policies and views.

Robert Reich's Blog *robertreich.blogspot.com* (liberal)
Former Clinton administration labor secretary, and economist and potential Obama administration official analyzes Democratic policy and strategy.

Slate *slate.com* (neutral)
General-interest online magazine with superb political coverage.

Talking Points Memo *talkingpointsmemo.com* (liberal)
TPM is a stable of political Web sites, rare for having a paid staff of reporters; source for breaking news and sage analysis.

Town Hall *townhall.com* (conservative)
Burgeoning roster of conservative pundits, including George Will, Charles Krauthammer, Bill O'Reilly, Robert Novak, Tony Blankley, and Ann Coulter.

BIBLIOGRAPHY AND SELECTED READING

BOOKS

Bernstein, Carl. *A Woman in Charge: The Life of Hillary Rodham Clinton*. New York: Alfred A. Knopf, 2007.

Cooke, Alistair. *Letter from America: Essays 1946–2004*. London: Penguin Books, 2004.

Cramer, Richard Ben. *What It Takes: The Way to the White House*. New York: Random House, 1992.

Donald, David Herbert. *Lincoln*. New York: Simon & Schuster, 1995.

Harrison, Maureen, and Steve Gilbert, eds. *Barack Obama: Speeches 2002–2006*. Carlsbad, California: Excellent Books, 2007.

Ivins, Molly, and Lou Dubose. *Shrub: The Short but Happy Political Life of George W. Bush*. New York: Vintage, 2000.

Mendell, David. *Obama: From Promise to Power*. New York: HarperCollins, 2007.

Obama, Barack. *Dreams from My Father: A Story of Race and Inheritance*. New York: Random House, 1995.

———. *The Audacity of Hope: Thoughts on Reclaiming the American Dream*. New York: Crown Publishers, 2006.

Steele, Shelby. *A Bound Man: Why We Are Excited About Obama and Why He Can't Win.* New York: Free Press, 2007.

Wilson, John K. *Barack Obama: This Improbable Quest.* Boulder, Colorado: Paradigm Press, 2008.

PERIODICALS AND PROFILES

Becker, Jo, and Christopher Drew. "The Long Run: Pragmatic Politics, Forged on the South Side," *New York Times,* May 11, 2008.

Belkin, Douglas. "For Obama, Advice Straight Up: Valerie Jarrett Is Essential Member of Inner Set," *Wall Street Journal,* May 12, 2008.

Boss-Bicak, Shira. "Barack Obama: Is He the New Face of the Democratic Party?" *Columbia College Today* vol. 31, no. 3 (January 2005).

Collins, Lauren. "The Other Obama," *New Yorker,* March 10, 2008.

Dorning, Mike, and Christi Parsons. "Carefully Crafting the Obama 'Brand,'" *Chicago Tribune,* June 12, 2007.

Ehrenstein, David. "Obama the 'Magic Negro,'" *Los Angeles Times,* March 19, 2007.

Finnegan, William. "The Candidate: How the Son of a Kenyan Economist Became an Illinois Everyman," *New Yorker,* May 31, 2004.

Fornek, Scott. "Michelle Obama: 'He Swept Me Off My Feet,'" *Chicago Sun-Times*, October 3, 2007.

Graff, Garrett M. "The Legend of Barack Obama," *Washingtonian*, November 1, 2006.

Helman, Scott. "Early Defeat Launched a Rapid Political Climb," *Boston Globe*, October 12, 2007.

Jackson, David, and Ray Long. "Showing His Bare Knuckles," *Chicago Tribune,* April 4, 2007.

Jackson, David, and John McCormick. "Building Obama's Money Machine," *Chicago Tribune,* April 13, 2007.

Jones, Tim. "Obama's Mom: Not Just a Simple Girl from Kansas," *Chicago Tribune,* March 27, 2007.

Kaufman, Jonathan. "For Obama, Chicago Days Honed Tactics," *Wall Street Journal*, April 21, 2008.

Kovaleski, Serge F. "Old Friends Say Drugs Played Bit Part in Obama's Young Life," *New York Times,* February 9, 2008.

Langley, Monica. "Michelle Obama Solidifies Her Role in the Election," *Wall Street Journal,* February 11, 2008.

Leeder, Jessica, and Rod Mickleburgh. "He Told Us He Was an African Prince. We Believed Him," *Toronto (Ont.) Globe and Mail,* January 14, 2008.

Lizza, Ryan. "The Agitator: Barack Obama's Unlikely Political Education," *New Republic,* March 19, 2007.

———. "Above The Fray," *GQ,* September 2007.

———. "The Relaunch: Can Barack Obama Catch Hillary Clinton?" *New Yorker,* November 26, 2007.

———. "Making It: How Chicago Shaped Obama," *New Yorker*, July 28, 2008.

MacFarquhar, Larissa. "The Conciliator," *New Yorker,* May 7, 2007.

McClelland, Edward. "How Obama Learned to Be a Natural," *Salon,* February 12, 2007, salon.com/news/feature/2007/02/12/obama_natural/.

Mundy, Liza. "A Series of Fortunate Events," *Washington Post Magazine,* August 12, 2007.

Olive, David. "Blank Screen: David Olive on a man who would be U.S. president," *Toronto Star,* February 11, 2007.

———. "Does Obama Talk the Talk," *Toronto Star,* February 9, 2008.

———. "The inconvenient candidate: What Obama really stands for," *Toronto Star,* April 13, 2008.

Packer, George. "The Choice: The Clinton-Obama Battle Reveals Two Very Different Ideas of the Presidency," *New Yorker,* January 28, 2008.

Pallasch, Abdon M. "Professor Obama Was a Listener, Students Say," *Chicago Sun-Times,* February 12, 2007.

Parsons, Christi, Bruce Japsen, and Bob Secter. "Barack's Rock: Obama Calls His Wife Michelle 'An Unbelievable Professional, and Partner, and Mother, and Wife' — and Integral to His Campaign," *Chicago Tribune,* April 22, 2007.

Payne, Les. "In One Country, a Dual Audience," *Newsday,* August 19, 2007.

Pearson, Rick, and Ray Long. "Careful Steps, Looking Ahead: After Arriving in Springfield, Barack Obama Proved Cautious, But It Was Clear to Many He Had Ambitions Beyond the State Senate," *Chicago Tribune,* May 3, 2007.

Pierce, Charles P. "The Cynic and Senator Obama," *Esquire,* June 2008.

Pinckney, Darryl. "Dreams from Obama," *New York Review of Books,* March 6, 2008.

Powell, Michael, and Jodi Kantor. "After Attacks, Michelle Obama Looks for a New Introduction," *New York Times,* June 18, 2008.

Ripley, Amanda. "A Mother's Story: Barack Obama's Greatest Influence Was a Woman Most People Know Nothing About. How Her Uncommon Life Shaped His Views of the World," *Time,* April 21, 2008.

Saulny, Susan. "Michelle Obama Thrives in Campaign Trenches," *New York Times,* February 14, 2008.

Scharnberg, Kirsten, and Kim Barker. "The Not-So-Simple Story of Barack Obama's Youth," *Chicago Tribune,* March 25, 2007.

Scott, Janny. "A Mother's Influence: Free-Spirited Wanderer Who Set Obama's Path," *New York Times,* March 14, 2008.

———. "At The State Level, Obama Proved to Be Pragmatic and Shrewd," *New York Times,* July 30, 2007.

Secter, Bob, and John McCormick. "Portrait of a Pragmatist," *Chicago Tribune,* March 30, 2007.

Senior, Jennifer. "Dreaming of Obama," *New York,* October 2, 2006.

Sirota, David. "Mr. Obama Goes to Washington," *Nation,* June 7, 2006.

Slevin, Peter. "Obama Forged Political Mettle in Illinois Capitol," *Washington Post,* February 9, 2007.

Sullivan, Andrew. "Goodbye to All That," *Atlantic,* December 2007.

Tammerlin, Drummond. "Barack Obama's Law: Harvard Law Review's First Black President Plans a Life of Public Service," *Los Angeles Times,* March 12, 1990.

Tomasky, Michael. "The Phenomenon," *New York Review of Books,* November 30, 2006.

Traub, James. "Is His Biography Our Destiny?" *New York Times Magazine,* November 4, 2007.

Wallace-Wells, Benjamin. "The Great Black Hope: What's Riding on Barack Obama?" *Washington Monthly,* November 2004.

———. "Destiny's Child," *Rolling Stone,* February 7, 2007.

Weisberg, Jacob. "The Path To Power: Barack Obama Lays Down a Grand Challenge to His Own Party — And It May Get Him Elected President One Day," *Men's Vogue,* September–October 2006.

Weisskopf, Michael. "How He Learned to Win," *Time,* May 19, 2008.

Wieseltier, Leon. "Miracle Man," *New Republic,* January 30, 2008.

———. "Forever Young," *New Republic,* February 12, 2008.

Wolffe, Richard, and Daren Briscoe. "Across the Divide," *Newsweek,* July 16, 2007.

Zernike, Kate, and Jeff Zeleny. "Obama in Senate: Star Power, Minor Role," *New York Times,* March 9, 2008.

Zorn, Eric. "Disparagement of Obama Crime Votes Doesn't Hold Up," *Chicago Tribune,* March 9, 2004.

COMMENTARY

Ackerman, Spencer. "The Obama Doctrine," *The American Prospect,* March 24, 2008.

Alter, Jonathan. "The Politics of Talking to Dictators," *Newsweek,* July 27, 2007.

BBC News. "Obama Warns Pakistan on al Qaeda," August 1, 2007, news.bbc.co.uk/2/hi/americas/6926663.stm.

Baldwin, Tom. "Stay-At-Home Obama Comes under Fire for a Lack of Foreign Experience," *Sunday Times* (London), December 21, 2007.

Bartiromo, Maria. "Barack Obama on Taxes and Why He Is the Best Manager," *Business Week,* April 14, 2008.

Brody, David. "Obama to CBN News: We're No Longer Just a Christian Nation," Christian Broadcasting Network, July 30, 2007, cbn.com/CBNnews/204016.aspx.

Brookhiser, Richard. "What's a Resume Got to Do with It," *Time,* January 29, 2007.

Brooks, David. "How Obama Fell to Earth," *New York Times,* April 18, 2008.

Brownstein, Ronald. "The First 21st-Century Campaign," *National Journal,* April 19, 2008.

Crook, Clive. "The Hawk Versus The Pragmatist," *Financial Times* (London), February 25, 2008.

Crouch, Stanley. "What Obama Isn't: Black Like Me," *New York Daily News,* November 2, 2006.

Dionne, E.J. "Score One for Change-Agent Obama," *Seattle Times,* July 29, 2007.

Dowd, Maureen. "Brush It Off," *New York Times,* April 20, 2008.

Editorial board. "Democrats Must Pick Obama," *Financial Times* (USA), April 21, 2008.

Franklin, Ben A. "The Fifth Black Senator in U.S. History Makes F.D.R. His Icon," *Washington Spectator,* June 1, 2005.

Gapper, John. "Obama Still Has Lessons for Business," *Financial Times,* January 10, 2008.

Goldberg, Jeffrey. "The Starting Gate: Foreign Policy Divides the Democrats," *New Yorker,* January 15, 2007.

Harris, Paul. "The Obama Revolution," *Guardian* (Manchester), February 4, 2007.

Hart, Gary. "American Idol," *New York Times,* December 24, 2006.

Hayes, Stephen F. "Obama and the Power of Words," *Wall Street Journal,* February 26, 2008.

Hunter, Jennifer. "From Beans to Basketball, Obama Knows What He Wants," *Toronto Star,* May 3, 2008.

Javers, Eamon. "Business, Obama-style: His Proposals and Advisors Don't Always Fit Neatly into the Left-Leaning Democrat Mold," *Business Week,* February 25, 2008.

King Jr., Neil. "Obama Tones Foreign-Policy Muscle," *Wall Street Journal,* September 5, 2007.

Kirchgaessner, Stephanie, and Christopher Grimes. "Reaching Out: Can Obama Avoid Being the 'Black Candidate'?" *Financial Times* (London), February 5, 2008.

Klein, Joe. "The Fresh Face," *Time,* October 23, 2006.

———. "Petraeus Meets His Match: The General Has Made Real Progress in Iraq. But He Doesn't Have an Answer for Barack Obama," *Time,* April 21, 2008.

Krauthammer, Charles. "The Audacity of Hype: Just What Else Has Obama Wrought?" *Boston Herald,* February 15, 2008.

Kristof, Nicholas D. "Obama: Man of the World," *New York Times,* March 6, 2007.

Leibovich, Mark. "The Upside of Being Knocked Around," *New York Times,* May 11, 2008.

Lerner, Michael. "U.S. Senator Barack Obama Critiques Democrats' Religiophobia," *Tikkun*, July 3, 2006.

Maddox, Bronwen. "Why the World According to Obama Is a Cause for Concern," *Times* (London), August 24, 2007.

Milloy, Courtland. "Invited to Wrestle in a Racial Mud Pit, Obama Soars Above It," *Washington Post,* March 19, 2008.

Moracha, Vincent, and Mangoa Mosota. "Leaders Support Obama on Graft Claims," *Standard* (Nairobi), September 4, 2006.

Noonan, Peggy. "The Man from Nowhere," *Wall Street Journal,* December 15, 2006.

———. "Out With the Old, In With the New," *Wall Street Journal,* January 4, 2008.

Norman, Matthew. "The Audacity of Treating Voters Like Adults," *Independent* (London), March 21, 2008.

Page, Clarence. "Is Barack Obama Black Enough? Now That's a Silly Question," *Houston Chronicle,* February 25, 2007.

Pickler, Nedra. "Obama Calls for Universal Health Care within Six Years," *San Diego Union-Tribune,* January 25, 2007.

Price, Melanie T. "What Obama Means," *Hartford Courant*, March 16, 2008.

Raban, Jonathan. "I'm for Obama," *London Review of Books,* March 20, 2008.

Rachman, Gideon. "America's Optimism Can Benefit All," *Financial Times* (London), February 5, 2008.

Rich, Frank. "Party Like It's 2008," *New York Times,* May 11, 2008.

Rundle, Guy. "War of the Worlds," *Melbourne Age,* May 11, 2008.

Sheehan, Paul. "Stupidity Foils the Black Prince," *Sydney Morning Herald,* May 5, 2008.

Tumulty, Karen. "The Candor Candidate: Why Obama Tells People What They Don't Want to Hear," *Time,* June 11, 2007.

Turow, Scott. "The New Face of the Democratic Party — And America," *Salon,* March 30, 2004, archive.salon.com/news/feature/2004/03/30/obama/.

Wenner, Jann S. "A New Hope," *Rolling Stone,* March 20, 2008.

Wills, Gary. "Two Speeches on Race," *New York Review of Books,* May 1, 2008.

Younge, Gary. "Obama: Black Like Me," *Nation,* November 13, 2006.

SELECTED OBAMA WRITINGS AND SPEECHES

Key Obama essays and speeches in addition to those appearing verbatim in this book and in Obama's two books, Dreams from My Father *and* The Audacity of Hope.

Murray, Mark. "Obama Denounces Wright," MSNBC, April 29, 2008, firstread.msnbc.msn.com/archive/2008/04/29/957771.aspx
— Reverend Jeremiah Wright Jr., Obama's pastor, was among the few viewers of Obama's landmark, nuanced March 18, 2008, speech on race in America who didn't seem to grasp Obama's pained effort to calm the waters while candidly acknowledging the continuing race issue in America. Soon to retire from his decades-long pastorship, and feeling himself to be unfairly demonized by video clips of his more inflammatory remarks, Wright addressed the National Press Club in Washington and unleashed the same hurtful and bizarre commentary that first ignited the controversy. Obama put this fire out immediately. Having said in his March 18th address that he could not bring himself to disown the pastor who first brought him to Christ, Obama then did so in unequivocal terms, finding Wright's divisive comments to be destructive to the unity for which his candidacy stood.

Obama, Barack. AIPAC Policy Forum Remarks. AIPAC Policy Forum, Chicago, Illinois, March 2, 2007.
— Outlines Obama's hard line against Iran and lauds Israel's central role as America's chief ally in the Middle East. (The American Israel Public Affairs Committee [AIPAC] is an influential advocacy group describing itself as "America's Pro-Israel Lobby.")

———. "Barack Obama Video," Democratic National Committee Winter 2007 Meeting, Washington, DC, February 2, 2007, video, democrats.org/a/2007/01/barack_obama.php
— Obama, early in his presidential candidacy, calls for a policy- and solutions-driven campaign, warning fellow Democrats that American voters won't tolerate the usual negative campaigning given Iraq, the health-care crisis, and other serious issues at stake.

Eight of Obama's original ten Democrat rivals embraced this above-the-fray approach, but the Clinton campaign abandoned it early in the 2008 primary season, reverting to traditional negative tactics once it fell behind in the delegate count. Obama's campaign responded in kind, until Obama called a halt, reminding top staffers he had set down as one of his two conditions for running that the times called for a "high-road" campaign, which would be key to distinguishing himself from competitors in the Democratic and Republican fields. (The other condition was that there be none of the usual infighting among campaign staff.) In a powerful signal to his own staff, Obama went public in April 2008 with an apology to voters, explaining that in the heat of battle his campaign had sometimes engaged in negative tactics but that this would end.

———. "Remarks of Senator Barack Obama: Apostolic Church of God," Chicago, Illinois, June 15, 2008, barackobama.com/2008/06/15/remarks_of_senator_barack_obam_78.php
— Ostensibly an occasion for celebrating parenthood, Obama lectures his largely African-American audience on the corrosive impact of negligent parenting, citing the poor example set by his own father and, to a much lesser extent himself. He describes the burden of single parenthood as experienced by his own mother, the grievous social consequences of absent fathers, and the imperative of personal responsibility, for which government intervention is no substitute.

———. "Renewing American Leadership," *Foreign Affairs,* July–August 2007.
— Details a new post–Cold War, post-Iraq U.S. foreign policy in an Obama administration, including a holistic renewal of military, diplomatic, and moral leadership in which "we can neither retreat from the world nor try to bully it into submission," and that America must "lead the world, by deed and by example."

Obama, Barack, and Sam Brownback. "Policy Adrift on Darfur," *Washington Post,* December 27, 2005.

Obama, Barack, and Richard G. Lugar. "Junkyard Dogs of War," *Washington Post,* December 3, 2005.

"Obama, Schiff Provision to Create Nuclear Threat Reduction Plan Approved," U.S. Senate Office of Barack Obama, December 20, 2007, obama.senate.gov/press/071220-obama_schiff_pr/
— Describes the Obama-Schiff initiative to track down missing and stolen nuclear materials, particularly in Russia and Central Europe, before they can be acquired by terrorist groups.